Nonprofit Leadership:
Life Lessons from an
Enterprising Practitioner

Nonprofit Leadership: Life Lessons from an Enterprising Practitioner

Robert P. Giloth

iUniverse, Inc.
New York Lincoln Shanghai

Nonprofit Leadership: Life Lessons from an Enterprising Practitioner

Copyright © 2007 by Robert P. Giloth

All rights reserved. No part of this book may be used or reproduced by any means, graphic, electronic, or mechanical, including photocopying, recording, taping or by any information storage retrieval system without the written permission of the publisher except in the case of brief quotations embodied in critical articles and reviews.

iUniverse books may be ordered through booksellers or by contacting:

iUniverse
2021 Pine Lake Road, Suite 100
Lincoln, NE 68512
www.iuniverse.com
1-800-Authors (1-800-288-4677)

Because of the dynamic nature of the Internet, any Web addresses or links contained in this book may have changed since publication and may no longer be valid.

The views expressed in this work are solely those of the author and do not necessarily reflect the views of the publisher, and the publisher hereby disclaims any responsibility for them.

Photo Credit for Thom Clark for two photos

ISBN: 978-0-595-45411-2 (pbk)
ISBN: 978-0-595-89724-7 (ebk)

Printed in the United States of America

*To my parents, Paul and Frances Giloth,
and sisters, Barbara, Copper, and Sandy*

Sometimes I make lists of things to do in years ahead ... These lists get lost. Opening an old notebook, I find that I had already planned something accomplished a decade later ... But also, I notice a forgotten project that interests me again: In the old notebook I make new notes.

>Donald Hall, *Life Work*, 1993

When it's over, I don't want to wonder
if I have made of my life something particular, and real.
I don't want to find myself sighing or frightened
or full of argument.

>Mary Oliver, *New and Selected Poems, Volume 1*, 1992

Contents

Acknowledgments..xi
Preface xiii
CHAPTER 1   Adventures in Community Economic Development (CED).. 1
CHAPTER 2   Thinking about Leadership 17
CHAPTER 3   Values Matter: Unpeeling the Onion.......... 35
CHAPTER 4   Investing Yourself: The Risks and Rewards..... 48
CHAPTER 5   Building on Personal Assets (Deficits) 63
CHAPTER 6   Time: Obstacle, Friend, Tool, and Teacher..... 77
CHAPTER 7   Managing Messiness 92
CHAPTER 8   Mistakes Are Your Résumé 109
CHAPTER 9   Unusual Partners and Allies................. 122
CHAPTER 10   Mentored and Mentoring 139
CHAPTER 11   Tell Your Own Story (Or Someone Else Will).. 154
CHAPTER 12   And Now What? The Adventure Continues ... 170
Appendix 181
Bibliography 183
Index... 199
About the Author 205

Acknowledgments

Writing books while holding down a job and having a family requires the right combination of masochism, selfishness, and the good will and help of others. What started as an assignment for career planning turned into a two-year writing project that disrupted (and enriched) many aspects of my life. At some point, this book took over my personal calendar and turned into that joyful but painful obsessiveness that characterizes writing.

So I have a lot of debts, first to Kari, Emma, Lian, and Jack, who allowed me the space after dinner and during early weekend mornings to make some progress on this book. As usual, my wife, Kari, read and commented on all of the chapters, heard me play out incoherently a variety of ideas, and kept saying that this was important to do. We share a common interest in planning and policy ideas, social change, and the strategies and tactics of getting things done in organizations.

This book has been an extra-curricular endeavor pursued on trains and planes and after hours, yet it couldn't have happened without my deep connection to the Annie E. Casey Foundation and bosses and colleagues like Ralph Smith and Doug Nelson. They encourage reflection and doing your homework, and have shaped an organization that is not afraid of trying new things and facing new mistakes. Their support has come in many different ways, and I'm deeply appreciative that I've had the opportunity to be a part of this unique philanthropic enterprise.

Richard Yocum of Argosy International worked with me for several years as an executive coach and prodded me into writing this book. He's read and commented on all the chapters and, as a coach, has helped me be more explicit about particular ideas, stories, and chapters. His gentle but sometimes pointed encouragement has been a model for me of the coach's skills.

In the middle of writing the book, I asked for feedback from friends and colleagues to get a better sense of whether I was on the right track in producing useful insights and lessons. I shared my adventure in community economic development with a number of these folks. I was greatly pleased to receive lots of good comments and advice about what worked and what didn't work in the book—and how I could improve the manuscript. I want to thank the following for taking the time and care to read parts of the book: Michael Bennett, Jean Bernard, Bob Brehm, Paul Brophy, David Casey, Susan Gewirtz, Gary Gillespie, Ed Hatcher, Christopher Hillbrunner, Richard Kordesh, Kirsten Moy, Ken O'Hare, Peter Plastrik, Michael Puisis, Tom Rhodenbaugh, Jerry Rubin, Bill Schweke, Marie Anne Sliwinski, Helina Teklehaimanot, Nik Theodore, Tom Waldron, Bob Weissbourd, Wim Wiewel, Peter Wissoker, and Albert Woodward.

Many others have shared my nonprofit adventures. *Pilsen*: Terry Medina, Maria Gallegos, Pat Wright, Ray Santos, Mario Cruz, Ed Martinez, Ramiro Borja, Chris Burgess, Jim Bautista, Lionel Bottari, Dick DeVries, Soyla Villicana, Jacinto Alvarado, and Bob Stark; *Chicago Rehab Network*: Thom Clark, Doug Gills, Barb Beck; *University of Illinois at Chicago*: Juan Betancur and Joel Werth; *Cornell University*: Pierre Clavel and Ken Reardon; *City of Chicago*: Steve Alexander, Greg Longhini, Donna DuCharme, Judy Waitz, Margie Gonwa, Roz Paaswell, Hal Baron, Josh Lerner, Susan Rosenblum, Diana Robinson, and Howard Stanback; *Southeast Baltimore*: Cinder Hypki, Jo Fisher, Sister Bobbie English, John Papagni, Barbara Ruland, Linda Cox, Janet Byers, Anne Blumenberg, and Carolyn Boitnott. *Jobs Initiative*: Anne Keeney, Mary Jean Ryan, Marie Kurose, Rhonda Simmons, Bob Watrus, Joel Rogers, Laura Dresser, Steve Holt, Linetta Gilbert, Tom Dewar, Scott Hebert, Judy Taylor, Marlene Selzer, Carolyn Seward, John Colburn, Margaret Berger-Bradley, and Fred Dedrick; *Making Connections*: Theresa Fujiwara, Mai Nguyen, Gail Hayes, Eloisa Gomez, Linda Usdin, Carol Bebelle, Juanita Gallion, Frank Farrow, and Bill Shepardson; *FES Projects*: Brandon Roberts; *AECF*: Irene Skricki, Robin Cheswick, Bonnie Howard, Patrice Cromwell, Gwen Robinson, Amanda Fernandez, Sheryl Lewis, Mia Hendricks, Latecha Fennel, Irene Lee, Sandra Jibrell, John Padilla, Miriam Shark, Georgianna Skarlatos, and Mark McDaniel.

And I would also like to acknowledge a number of colleagues who are no longer with us but whose influence lives with me today: Darryl Burrows, Laura Duenes, Ben Harrison, Barclay Gibbs Jones, Judy Kauffman, Winston Mecurius, Robert Mier, Cindy Marano, and Eric Parker.

While I've received lots of help and advice along the way, this book ultimately represents my thoughts, opinions, and judgments. I take full responsibility for its mistakes and folly and for getting it wrong (and right).

Preface

> Am I leading the life that my soul,
> Mortal or not, wants me to lead is a question
> That seems at least as meaningful as the question
> Am I leading the life I want to live
>
> —*Carl Dennis*

Nonprofits knit together communities, help those in need, and invent solutions to vexing social problems. Nonprofits are an important component of the American social fabric. But, like all fields, the nonprofit world needs attention and advice. In particular, I believe that we must encourage new nonprofit leadership and increase the capacity of nonprofits if we are to ensure the sector's long-term contribution.

After spending many years in the nonprofit field, I have some insights, short cuts, stories, and reminders to share with current and emerging leaders. My nonprofit career has coincided with the explosive growth and evolution of the nonprofit sector during the past thirty years. There has been a 115 percent growth in nonprofit organizations that employ more than eleven million workers—more than 7 percent of our overall labor force.[1] Nonprofits have become the main delivery system for social welfare and community development in the United States and have contributed to creating and restoring the social fabric and glue needed for improving social cohesion, solving longstanding social ills, and bridging the public and private sectors.

One can pick almost any aspect of life—birth, housing, arts, or education—and find nonprofits playing important roles. Although charitable giving, volunteerism, and civic associations have historically been a mainstay of American values and culture, we have witnessed an unprecedented growth, diversifica-

---

1. Lester M. Salamon. The resilient sector: The state of nonprofit America. *The Nonprofit Quarterly*, Winter 2002: 32-38.

tion, and impact of the civic, nonprofit sector in recent decades. Yet, in spite of this growth, the nonprofit sector is in trouble. Paul Light, in *Sustaining Nonprofit Performance,* reports on a 2003 survey in which "70 percent said nonprofits had the right programs but were simply inefficient."

Nonprofit growth will continue during the twenty-first century. There will be an estimated $10 trillion transfer in intergenerational wealth in the next fifty years, in part to the field of philanthropy.[2] New dimensions of the nonprofit sector are emerging each year like faith-based and immigrant and refugee organizations or responses to natural disasters. Foundations based upon so-called new wealth are a different breed; they like to stay engaged, achieve short-term results, and go their own way, not bound by the strictures of traditional philanthropy.

Our expectations of the nonprofit sector are placing more emphasis on results, civic and social entrepreneurs, venture philanthropy, high performance, social replication, new financing tools, and mergers and turnarounds. Nonprofits are being asked to take on additional roles, achieve larger impacts, and be more cost effective at the same time that Congress and the public have witnessed scandals in nonprofit operations and fundraising that rival corporate transgressions, if not in scale, at least in disregard of ethics and the law. Robert Egger, in *Begging for Change*, concludes that you know a nonprofit executive is on the wrong track "when the person begins to believe in his or her own entitlement." At the same time, the public does not understand the nonprofit sector. Paul Light quotes nonprofit expert Lester Salamon that "the public remains largely in the dark about how nonprofit organizations actually operate in contemporary America."[3]

My nonprofit career touches on many of these issues. I'm still working in the nonprofit field today and probably will put in another twenty years. Yet, I represent a new challenge for the nonprofit sector, and this challenge is a primary reason for writing this book. Nonprofit leaders are aging, and the sector faces the overarching problem of a transition of leadership, a problem that all stakeholders in the nonprofit sector should be concerned about because it threatens the ability of the sector to survive and thrive.

This problem is not new in itself; what is new is the size of the transition in the decades ahead, an increase of 15 percent or more in turnover of executives above current rates in the next five to seven years. A recent survey of twenty-two

---

2. Philanthropic Initiative, Inc. *Lessons from Wingspread: The Ten Trillion Dollar Intergenerational Transfer of Wealth: A Philanthropic Game Plan.* Boston: MA: Author, 1994.
3. Paul C. Light. *Sustaining Nonprofit Performance: The Case for Capacity Building and the Evidence to Support It.* Washington, DC: The Brookings Institution, p. 35.

hundred nonprofits by the Annie E. Casey Foundation found that 65 percent of the respondents expected leadership transitions by 2009.[4] Other studies project a 75 percent turnover of nonprofit executives in the next five years. Addressing this problem requires more than identifying and cultivating a new group of leaders; it requires rethinking some of the basics of nonprofit organizations, such as compensation, fragmentation, and financing.[5]

I've experienced and observed the impacts of two failed nonprofit leadership transitions in organizations that I formerly led, one of which had already been languishing after a prior failed leadership transition. And I've witnessed multiple nonprofit meltdowns of different types. A lot of social investment, competence, capacity, and efficiency are lost in these failed transitions; it is remarkable that investors in the nonprofit sector have allowed these failures to happen so regularly. With the impending transition of so many founding directors in the near future, it is imperative that we pay explicit attention to the next generation of leaders.

Nonprofits also face a world that keeps changing and is full of "inevitable surprises," in the words of Peter Schwartz. Long-term deficits, globalization, political disorder, technological change, demographic changes, and quality of life changes are but a few of the predictable factors that will keep on producing surprises for the nonprofit, for-profit, and public sectors. In the United States, thirty-seven million people live in poverty, five million kids drop out of school each year, and we rank tenth among advanced economies in literacy levels. Having the ability to respond and adapt effectively to these challenges will be the long-term test of the effectiveness of the nonprofit field.

Listening at the dinner table as a boy awakened my earliest awareness of management and leadership challenges. My father was my earliest leadership coach. He probably didn't know I thought of him in that way, and, in fact, I didn't realize I valued his coaching until midlife. My father was fond of saying that he had never gotten out of bed in the morning and not wanted to go to work. Never! That was a hard act to follow. Who could possibly make a statement like that after twenty, thirty, forty years of working in the same firm? Of course, my mother stood behind this exemplary behavior.

---

4. Frances Kunreather. *UpNext: Generational Change and the Leadership of Nonprofit Organizations.* Baltimore, MD: Annie E. Casey Foundation, 2005; Denice Rothman Hinden and Paige Hull. Executive leadership transition: What we know. *The Nonprofit Quarterly*, Winter 2002: 24-29.
5. See, for example: William P. Ryan. *Nonprofit Capital: A Review of Problems and Strategies.* New York: The Rockefeller Foundation, 2001.

Work, for my father, was an adventure that engaged him fully as a designer, problem solver, manager, and person. As an engineer with the Bell Labs, now Lucent, he knew, in some fashion, that his adventure was a part of a bigger story about telephones, technology, economic growth, and globalization. He treated his good luck and hard work as the way things were or ought to be. His only regret was that he hadn't started with the company at a younger age, so he could have worked more and advanced more quickly, but he was busy working himself through college and learning about radar in the Signal Corps during World War II.

My father managed, among other things, the installation and debugging of big (4ESS) electronic switching systems. We grew up in Bell Labs' enclaves around the country in the 1950s and 1960s, went to schools with other Bell Labs' kids, played in Bell Labs' dumps, and heard lots of Bell Labs' stories, tales of corporate life and the knowledge worker.

These stories introduced me to management and leadership, although I didn't realize the value of this treasure trove for years. In my earlier years, I frequently, and sometimes unkindly, wrote my father off as being a full-fledged member of the corporate technology elite. What knowledge and insight could he possibly have to share with someone like me, dedicated to social change—as evidenced by my few years and months in the trenches working for fledgling community development corporations in inner-city neighborhoods? I was fortunate that my father had a long life and was forgiving, and that I became a bit more humble and certainly smarter about what he had to offer and what I needed to learn.

A first lesson was about teamwork. Every so often—while I'm waiting to board an airplane—I observe a cluster of men and women talking together in low voices. You can usually guess who are the leaders, not by any obvious deference to them, but because they command attention in a non-directive manner. If I'm close enough, I usually am able to infer that they are all engineers and that they have traveled together to solve some nagging problem in the field. They are continuing their problem-solving discussion as they wait for the plane; the unresolved problem or some other challenge has caught their attention. They don't all look the same, no doubt have different types of expertise, and participate in the group in different ways. But they are quite obviously a team.

Effective teams are made up of people with different skills and experiences—inventors, mechanics, planners, installers, and problem-solvers. An important skill of effective leaders is the ability to assemble the diverse skills needed by teams to achieve specific results.

A second lesson may be derived from a cautionary group of tales about Bell Labs' mistakes, both constructive and non-constructive mistakes. Sometimes these mistakes even embroiled our neighbors, families that we knew—families that lived down the block and worked for the Labs. I remember stories about bosses who promoted technical wizards with lots of degrees and patents—much like themselves—but who had few management skills and fewer good instincts about how to implement projects. Inevitably, as if in a fairy tale, the big projects failed and the boss and his or her clones were demoted and sent away to submarine duty—a lab that had dead-end projects on the way to retirement.

The lesson, of course, is to find the best person to do the job, hopefully with management experience or with management potential commensurate with the job at hand. At the same time, it's important to reward the technical wizards with money, resources, praise, and perks to keep them happy and to convey the message that management is not the only road to success.

A third lesson, also a cautionary tale for all times and places, was that telling the truth frequently lands you in trouble and makes you not well-liked by the powers-that-be. Of course, one has to be sensitive as well as savvy about how to tell the truth, not setting up your bosses, and owning your own piece of the problem. But still, even when exercising the utmost finesse in telling the truth about poor design, cost overruns, delays, and mistakes, telling the truth can bring the roof down on your head. My father had that happen to him several times; in one case, he lost a major promotion because he aggravated his new boss with too much truth. My father was a person of integrity, spoke the truth, took his lumps, and gained the admiration of his colleagues. And he still liked going to work every day.

My father was an optimist at heart and believed solutions existed for most problems. He had his blind spots, of course, and overcame some of them, but not all of them. He wasn't perfect. When he finally had to move into a senior housing complex after being a homeowner for fifty years, one of his biggest complaints at eighty-five was that there were no more problems to chew on and solve—no more leaky garbage disposals or out-of-whack cabinet or closet doors. He spent time with his retirement buddies contemplating the fall of Lucent, how Lucent had missed the next cycle of innovation in the 1980s.

Always full of surprises, my father told me that *faith* was difficult for him, even though he was a believer, regularly attended church, and was a loyal member of a Bible study group. His job for many years involved detecting and debugging millions of errors in mega-electronic switching systems. Faith wouldn't get the job done. The job required critical skepticism as one worked through mistakes to make things work. Yet my father was not just a *bug detector*; he was able to switch gears and make faith a mainstay of his life.

By the end of his career, my father had developed a list of commandments and cardinal sins for his colleagues. These nuggets of advice don't break any new ground and sometimes read as platitudes, but they show a manager and leader at work and have resonated with my nonprofit career. (See Appendix, which also includes some of my reactions to his management principles.)

I've worked in small- and medium-sized nonprofit organizations and have played a variety of roles, including executive director. My primary skill has been the design and implementation of new products and services, whether job training programs for low-income young adults, aging-in-place housing for seniors, preservation of industrial districts, or orchestrating community plans. I've gained my experience primarily in one domain of the nonprofit sector—the field of *community economic development* (CED), the goal of which has been to increase economic opportunities for low-income families and communities. I've not only worked in the field, I have also studied and written about CED.

My major qualification for writing this book is my many years of successes and failures. Lots of things have worked out as expected, even better than expected in some instances. My successes, however, have a distinctive look and feel that only a sports metaphor adequately communicates. Singles and doubles have defined my CED career, not home runs. I have a good batting average as far as results go, am consistent and dependable, but I'm not the long-ball hitter who brings the crowd to its feet.

I have to admit, though, that I've learned the most from my mistakes, not my good batting average. My successes sometimes have had the feel of mystery, as if they were predestined or it just was a matter of great timing. Mistakes, however, are complicated, full of substance, and emotionally trying, like a failed nonprofit business venture, no one showing up at an important meeting, the unforeseen negative consequences of a good project, or cost overruns from a supposedly cost-effective investment.

I invested in nonprofits and CED when I worked for local government and now do similar work with a national foundation. In the latter capacity, I have invested in long-term initiatives that sought to improve employment and family well-being in low-income communities. The *Jobs Initiative* (JI) was our eight-year effort to create better connections between low-income communities and regional economies and to advocate for improved workforce systems. We worked in six cities and attempted to improve the long-run job retention of low-income, low-skilled workers and job seekers. *Making Connections* has been Casey's ten-year community-building initiative to strengthen family economic success, social connections and supports, and children's success in school in tough neighborhoods, including White Center, Seattle. We ultimately worked in low-income neighborhoods in ten cities while advocating for broader policy changes that would support children, families, and communities.

These initiatives illustrate a nonprofit field that is dynamic and rich. Yet, this field has not produced a management and leadership literature grounded in the experiences of nonprofit leaders. There are crossovers from the world of business, like Peter Drucker, but few others of note.

At the same time, few good role models exist for those of us who want to stay in the nonprofit field. I'm transitioning, gradually, from being a project guy to coaching nonprofit and community-building leaders. Coaching is tough work if done well. Coaching means that one has to dig deep into one's own experience to pull out, synthesize, and make explicit the *know-how* knowledge that one has developed over a lifetime. That kind of reflection produces explicit knowledge that can be shared while re-energizing the values that led one into the CED world in the first place.

So, my aspiration for this book of reflections is to provide useful advice and counsel to colleagues in the nonprofit sector so that they are better equipped to take on more expansive roles in years to come, attract and retain new staff, create better conditions for the growth and development of high-performing nonprofit organizations, and address the big issues of the twenty-first century. I focus on some bedrock elements of leadership as well as on a number of paradoxes, and unresolved tensions that I have confronted, and still confront, in my nonprofit work. The best way to read this book is by asking yourself questions about your career as you read. I provide some guiding questions to prompt your thinking.

To be honest, I have another reason for writing this book. Maybe, if I'm lucky, it will turn into my version of my father's list of cardinal sins and commandments about nonprofit leadership. Although I suspect he would accuse me of being longwinded, I hope my father would still find that my list of lessons and tensions rings true with his experience.

But I have one more reason—an especially important, personal reason. I'm writing this book in order to get a third wind, or maybe it's a fourth wind, for my own nonprofit career. I hopefully have a few decades left to devote to the nonprofit sector and community economic development in some capacity. Just as organizations occasionally need to reinvent themselves to meet new challenges, so do nonprofit leaders.

I hope these reflections help each of you catch your next wind. As Myles Horton, the great community organizer at Highlander Center, said, it's a "long haul." He cautioned that we must keep the fire alive by "burning like embers" for this long haul. Burning out in one fantastic big blaze may provide some personal satisfaction, but almost always leads to exiting the field.

As a final prefatory note, authors often provide advice about how to read their books, inspired, I think, by a suspicion that they will attract different types of readers with different objectives. Hence I feel compelled to offer some navigation advice. Chapters 1, 2, and 12 address directly the theories and practices of community economic development (CED), although the world of CED infuses the entire book. These chapters often adopt a style of reporting and teaching. Chapters 3, 4, and 5 are highly autobiographical and show how one practitioner has tried to come to grips with values, experiences, decisions, skills, and flaws. Chapters 6, 7, and 8 address perplexing problems and new skill requirements for civic leaders and CED. Chapters 9, 10, and 11 argue that civic leaders must develop an array of effective relationships. The unifying threads in all the chapters are my concrete CED experiences, my reflections about them, and my attempt to distill lessons for CED and nonprofit colleagues.

1

Adventures in Community Economic Development (CED)

○ ○
The vitality of thought is in adventure.
Ideas won't keep. Something must be
done about them.

—*Alfred North Whitehead*

There's a memorable scene in the film *Chinatown* in which Jack Nicholson tears through a title-recordation book in a rural California courthouse, searching for bad guys.[6] His goal? To confirm that powerful interests related to the Los Angeles Municipal Waterworks were buying up vast amounts of property in Owens Valley for the construction of an aqueduct from Owens Valley to Los Angeles. Ostensibly the buyers were looking to supply much-needed water. In reality, these quasi-public interests were seeking to spur the growth of land values in nearby San Fernando Valley—much of which they also owned. This growth would be achieved at the cost of substantial public funding, the dumping of surplus water, and the destruction of farm communities.

I'm no Jack Nicholson, but, like his character, I learned early on the value of researching property ownership. Indeed, my adventure in CED began in Chicago, working with community organizations to use property research to fight urban greed. I also learned that there is always a relationship between land and local government. Jack Nicholson could have been in Chicago's City Hall uncov-

---

6. This chapter draws on many of my writings about CED over the years. Many of these publications are identified in the Bibliography.

ering Alderman Tom Keane's zoning scam, Charlie Swibel's profitable real estate on Skid Row, or a hundred other creative Chicago real estate deals.

My burrowing into the Recorder of Deeds office in the 1970s was part of a long process of fighting disinvestment in urban neighborhoods by public and private institutions, whether from mortgage redlining, racial steering, arson, blockbusting, or contract buying. I learned title and tax searching from Calvin Bradford and his colleagues, who were also working to establish the South Shore Bank, support Gail Cincotta's National Peoples Action's campaign to pass the Community Reinvestment Act (CRA), and fight Federal Housing Administration (FHA) discriminatory foreclosure practices. My title searching was part of a movement to win back neighborhoods and community investment. Unfortunately, this fight continues today, now against predatory lenders and gentrification.

During thirty years in the field, I have come to appreciate that CED involves a host of efforts to improve economic opportunities for low- and moderate-income residents. While I have worked in urban neighborhoods in the U.S., the same challenges and many of the same solutions apply to rural communities and developing countries.

After two introductory chapters, this book begins with three chapters that recount the essential facets of my CED career, as a manager and leader. The second section of three chapters delves into several challenges facing the CED field and other civic endeavors that require social innovation and problem solving—time, complexity, and mistakes. The third set of chapters discusses cultivating relationships and building alliances with other civic stakeholders to get the work done and to ensure that it continues. In the final chapter, I ask, "What's next?"

As you read this chapter, ask yourself the following questions to stimulate your thinking about community economic development:

- What is your CED adventure?
- What conceptual and strategic frameworks are you using to guide your work?
- Is your work making a difference? How do you know?
- What is your next CED challenge?

My CED Adventure Continues

My CED career has involved testing assumptions about CED and the strategies that are appropriate for different situations. No better method exists for testing assumptions than going somewhere new. In 1992 I led a contingent of Baltimore colleagues on a study tour of Hungary and Romania with the Village Development Association (VDA), a coalition of village organizers and associations. We had provided an internship for the lead organizer of VDA for the previous year as he studied at Johns Hopkins University. He asked us to be part of this learning exchange in those first years after the fall of Communism.

In the village of Redelesalja, we spoke with the mayor about an herb-collecting cooperative that their folk high school had initiated. It provided work for unemployed villagers. People collected herbs in nearby open fields, dried them, and sold them at regional markets. In Pilisszentlelek, we visited with village and church leaders who had set up a small business that sold religious artwork. The proceeds of the business were used, in part, to support a community center that contained a library, museum, and performance space for dance and theatre. In Perkupa, we rode with a village caretaker while he delivered hot meals to senior citizens who could not get out. He also provided transportation for school children and in general functioned as the problem-solver who knitted the village together. In Cluj-Napoca, on the eastern border of Transylvania, police chased us throughout empty streets after a meeting with Hungarian community activists.

Our Hungarian counterparts formed citizen associations in order to reinvent civil society and democratic governance. While the grassroots leaders of Hungary reinvigorated our sense of democracy, we offered them insights and experiences about designing and managing grassroots organizations and coalitions. As in the U.S., the basic work of democracy in Hungary is a local affair that begins around kitchen tables and in church halls. It is an ongoing process of dialogue and debate.

Many other episodes of my CED journey are recounted throughout this book. Each has stretched my thinking in different ways. I've found myself in a beat-up Volkswagen bus at the crack of dawn in the middle of a Chicago winter, picking up bags of recycling as a part of a community-based pilot program. I attended a trade association conference for burial monuments to obtain information about the business so that we could intervene in the threatened plant closing of Trinity Bronze, a manufacturer of specialty burial plaques, possibly by initiating a worker buyout. While working for the City of Chicago, I researched the use (or misuse) of public incentives for neighborhood job creation that showed that more jobs were being lost than gained. In Baltimore, we had the gumption to organize a brainstorming design meeting about the abandoned American Can plant along the southeast waterfront because the owner and the city had reached a stalemate about redevelopment. Our purpose was to generate creative ideas about how to reconfigure the site into parcels and finance the project in phases. I've supported an exhibition of family photos taken by a famous African American photographer in New Orleans to illustrate the multiple meanings of family strengthening. And I've helped build hundreds of units of affordable housing and retain and create thousands of jobs over the years.

Today, my CED adventure continues in supporting watchdog groups monitor the jobs and contracts in the post-Katrina Gulf Coast rebuilding and providing legal counsel to low- and moderate-income homeowners. We're supporting new institutional mechanisms to access union-based health benefits for childcare and homecare workers, and we're investing in the startup of a nonprofit checkcasher to provide affordable financial services. Over the next few years, I know I will become more embroiled in understanding the predatory nature of used-car loans and how credit scores may represent a new form of community *redlining*. If I were starting over in CED today, I would focus my work on labor rights and organizing, environmental sustainability, and global poverty.

What Is Community Economic Development?

The journalist Stuart Chase, a member of urbanist Lewis Mumford's Regional Plan Association in the 1920s, wrote *The Tyranny of Word* about abstract nouns—like democracy, community, or the multitude of *isms*—that have too few or too many concrete referents in reality. Although *tree* and *house* are abstract generalizations about trees and houses in all their diversity, we do have an immediate, common sense understanding of these words. This is not so for the big words of life. Three consequences flow from this problem: 1) defining and redefining the big words is ongoing; 2) establishing consensus meanings for these words is contentious and inconclusive; and 3) good and bad interests capture and manipulate the meanings of abstract nouns for good and bad reasons.

I have tried for decades to make sense of the abstract nouns *neighborhood* and *community*. Neighborhood immediately suggests boundaries and place, but also includes neighbors, organizations, participation, and collective action. Community suggests shared interests, regardless of proximity, related to shared ethnicity, gender, political affiliations, workplaces, networks, or hobbies. No matter how hard I try, I inevitably end up using these words interchangeably.

Douglas Smith, in *On Value and Values*, even argues that a continued focus on *place* may be misleading. He provocatively states, "Seeking to breathe new life into place-based community and place-based citizenship is a stillborn proposition." His is yet another, and certainly not the last, declaration that community is dead in America, no matter what we exactly mean by it. He offers, instead, that "organizations are our new towns—they are the social formations in and through which we make a difference today." And yet *organization* is another abstract noun in search of content.

CED is best illustrated by some examples that capture the breadth of the field. CED is about:

- Constructing affordable homes and developing preparatory pipelines to home ownership that include financial education, credit repair, matched savings, home-ownership training, and a variety of public and private incentives and loans;

- Revitalizing neighborhood shopping districts by organizing businesses into associations, cleaning up streets, improving façade treatments, establishing special taxing districts to support revitalization; providing marketing, business attraction, and business assistance; assembling land for targeted redevelopment; and promoting housing reuse for the upper floors of old commercial buildings;

- Negotiating with financial institutions to commit mortgage lending to low- and moderate-income neighborhoods, make available new account and savings products and services, join Earned Income Tax Credit (EITC) asset-building campaigns, and fund local homeownership counseling;

- Establishing social enterprises that take advantage of local assets like partnerships with major companies, underutilized land, and park and city maintenance/landscaping opportunities and that provide jobs and training for the formerly incarcerated;

- Setting up community development financial institutions (CDFIs) to assemble low-cost capital from private, religious, public, and philanthropic sources to invest in charter schools, low-income housing, job-creating companies, and energy conservation;

- Organizing partnerships of employers, community-based organizations, community colleges, unions, and religious institutions to provide access to good-paying jobs and the training and support that are needed to make this a success for both workers and businesses;

- Fighting for living wage and inclusionary zoning laws, and against predatory lending. Developing coalitions with innovative unions like the Service Employees International Union (SEIU);
- Working with neighborhood associations and local businesses to establish a community development corporations (CDCs) that focus the entrepreneurial energy and assets of neighborhoods to design, find partners, and finance and implement CED projects on an ongoing basis;
- Monitoring how public and private investments are benefiting, ignoring, or hurting low- and moderate-income neighborhoods in terms of jobs, business opportunities, and affordable development. Negotiating community benefit agreements (CBAs) to promote accountable development; and
- Partnering with local health institutions to provide jobs, career advancement, and business opportunities to residents in the surrounding neighborhoods.

CED defies simple definitions. A few years ago, in an article co-written with urban planning professors Michael Teitz and Wim Wiewel, we concluded that a compelling, overall CED theory was impossible because of its multiple dimensions: job creation or commercial district marketing, neighborhood-focused development or regional partnerships, or planning and organizing rather than development. I remember attending an annual meeting of the Center for Urban Economic Development (CUED) at the University of Illinois at Chicago in the 1980s at which African American activists launched a spirited debate about the definition of CED. A retired steelworker who had fought against the closing of Wisconsin Steel on Chicago's southeast side argued for public-sector-led local and national steel authorities' reinvestment in basic manufacturing in our cities, thereby creating and retaining livable-wage jobs. A younger activist, from Chicago's devastated Englewood neighborhood, had a different perspective. He advocated entrepreneurship for inner-city communities of color as a way to generate income, wealth, and independence.

A sometimes rancorous debate breaks out about defining CED. Reverse commuting strategies, for example, which connect people to suburban jobs, have been denounced as urban apartheid. Sectoral or industry workforce practitioners have critiqued place-based or neighborhood efforts, such as those of CDCs. A chorus of criticisms aimed at CDCs has focused on their inability to stimulate economic development, alleviate poverty, or connect to regions. The traditional antagonism between community organizing and development has been reignited in debates about living-wage ordinances or corporate welfare. In a broader sense, some progressive analysts critique CED as another form of *localism*, which has minimal capacity (i.e., power) to ameliorate or even confront the effects of the global economy.

More agreement exists about why CED is needed than about the best form of CED. CED is a response to market and public sector failures that have produced and reinforced uneven development across populations, communities, and regions. Because private actors do not pay the full costs of their actions—unemployment, environmental pollution, and human suffering—society bears these costs. In the pursuit of profit, investors may also overlook or disinvest in viable market opportunities, such as inner-city supermarkets or branch plant manufacturing plans, which do not appear to measure up to other investment opportunities or locations. How pervasive or intractable these market failures are influences whether CED is a corrective or an alternative to the market.

CED responds to the inability of government to act effectively on behalf of those affected by market failure. That public failure has several attributes. The first is government's only modest commitments to social welfare and full employment policies, a not surprising outcome given the lack of political power of low- and moderate-income communities. The second is that government has difficulty acting in the focused, flexible, coordinating, and entrepreneurial manner necessary to develop innovative responses to market failures that affect local communities. Government bureaucracies are conservative and typically more responsive to business or other political interests. A third failure that CED addresses is cognitive failure: public and private institutions' lack of knowledge about solutions to poverty and neighborhood revitalization. CED is a process-oriented and experimental response that generates development innovations and frequently builds community-wide consensus about priority investments.

A starting point for understanding CED is to acknowledge simultaneously its compelling rationale and lack of an overall unifying theory. The diversity of CED practices relates to competing strategies, constituencies, starting points, and even outcomes. Some might argue that CED is unfocused or too eclectic, or perhaps too marginal. I believe that the diversity of CED approaches does not represent a failure, but rather indicates a field of inquiry and action whose performance requires different intellectual, organizing, planning, and investment tools.

Improving economic opportunity involves *people and place* as well as *micro and macro* strategies. The *people-versus-place* dilemma poses the question whether public and private investments should focus on enhancing the individual skills, assets, and mobility of low-income people, or whether, instead, investments should emphasize the revitalization of neighborhoods where low-income people reside. The dilemma is that if investment focuses on people, people who start doing well may make the rational decision to move out of their neighborhoods in order to optimize quality-of-life opportunities for their families. They do better, but the neighborhood suffers because it loses income and families moving up. If investment focuses on place, in contrast, neighborhood revitalization sometimes does not benefit the families who currently live there. In some cases, if neighborhoods improve, existing residents, especially renters, may be forced to relocate.

The *micro-versus-macro* distinction acknowledges that individual and business decision-making, as well as aggregate or economic structural factors, shapes uneven development and poverty. For labor markets, structural and technical changes in the economy influence the quality and quantity of jobs and the demand for specific job skills. Globalization, for example, has increased pressures to lower the social wage in advanced economies. Tight labor markets produce undisputed and widespread benefits, yet many low-income individuals lack the skills, certifications, and experience to navigate the new economy and workplace. For urban development, while economic growth in most regions has encouraged new commercial and residential development, many inner-city neighborhoods and inner-ring suburbs lack the access, location, and infrastructure to take advantage of these market opportunities. Urban sprawl exacerbates this problem. Shrinking cities face a particular problem because housing abandonment is diffused rather than concentrated, leaving in its wake disinvested neighborhoods in which land assembly is a nightmare. Alternatively, in other cities, neighborhood revitalization may make neighborhoods unaffordable for people with low incomes.

These distinctions and dilemmas mean that CED comprises workforce, enterprise, human service, community-organizing, and public policy practices. These practices influence the generation of wealth, the distribution of wealth, and key institutions related to wealth creation. Successful CED practices are market-oriented, community-sensitive, flexible and integrative, customized, entrepreneurial, and results-oriented. At their best, these practices adapt to the changing constraints and opportunities in the marketplace and in relation to the populations and places they serve.

Mapping CED

I've created four strategy maps of CED during my nonprofit career. My goal in making these maps has been to describe CED innovations, make them more intelligible (to myself, first of all), elucidate their theories of change, whether development, policy, or community organizing, and suggest that the diversity of strategies is a strength rather than a weakness. My purpose has not been to create a comprehensive atlas of all CED practices. In addition to CED, I've named these strategy maps *targeted economic development, job-centered economic development,* and *family economic success.* Each phrase addresses slightly different outcomes, constituents, and strategies. (See box.)

FIGURE 1
CED STRATEGY MAPS

MAP 1	*LINKAGE*	*CAPITAL*	*ENTERPRISE*	*NEW MARKETS*	
MAP 2	*JOB BROKERING*	*SECTORS*	*SPATIAL MOBILITY*	*HUMAN SERVICE RESOURCES*	*BUSINESS/ CAPITAL*
MAP 3	*JOBS*	*WEALTH*	*PLACE*		
MAP 4	*EARN IT!*	*KEEP IT!*	*SAVE IT (GROW IT)!*		

Map 1. My first CED strategy map, developed in the 1980s, derived from a close reading of two popular CED publications: *The Neighborhood Works* (TNW) of Chicago and *City Limits* of New York. In the context of tough economic times for many cities, the focus was on business development and linking large-scale public investments to jobs, housing, and neighborhood improvements.

Map 2. My second strategy map—*targeted job-centered economic development*—recognized the sustained economic growth and federal policy changes of the 1990s. This approach advocated creating better labor market connections with economic development, new business generation, and human service expenditures like child care. Its point of departure was family-supporting jobs for the disadvantaged in the short run, not as long-term outcomes from investment in business creation, technology, and infrastructure.

Map 3. My third CED strategy map evolved in the mid-1990s as I became more involved in designing and implementing community-building initiatives. Place-based, neighborhood investments came back on the table as the persistence of concentrated poverty affected more and more people and neighborhoods. At the same time, the CED field expanded beyond neighborhoods and increasing income to embrace a range of strategies that came under the rubric of asset building.

Map 4. The fourth CED strategy map, called *family economic success* (FES), built upon these other maps in the new century. It sought to overcome the fragmentation of CED efforts to achieve greater impact. Focusing on families and neighborhoods, FES seeks to integrate jobs, work supports, asset-building, and community investment strategies and investments. Its slogan is *Earn It! Keep It! Save It!*

I'm sure that other CED practitioners and strategists might draw different strategy maps of CED. Christopher Gunn, for example, in *Third-Sector Development*, maps the array of institutions that make up what he calls the *third sector*—nonprofits, co-ops, pension funds, credit unions, and CDCs. These institutions have a democratic and social equity-oriented approach for accumulating and distributing capital. Nonprofits represent more than 10 percent of Gross National Product (GNP); ten thousand credit unions serve seventy-five million members; and there are fifty thousand co-ops serving 120 million members. Gunn's criteria for third-sector activity are "creating and retaining social surplus; providing jobs at a living wage; operating in environmentally sustainable ways; creating dynamic linkages, multipliers, and spin-offs; and meeting basic needs."

My CED strategy maps will keep evolving. Having a CED framework is important so that we can communicate with each other about the concrete benefits and costs of different approaches. CED should stay focused on improving outcomes for families and neighborhoods. That's the objective, not the strategies themselves.

Metaphors and CED

A fundamental challenge is how to apply the multiplicity of CED approaches to different situations and places. Traditional strategic planning is only modestly helpful in charting a path for CED investment. Other tools are required to guide CED thinking, tools that build upon available information and local knowledge and that focus on the levers of CED change like market access. Improved CED strategizing is important because CED fashion cycles and copycat behavior have created a proliferation of small, disconnected projects. One helpful approach for identifying CED opportunities is to use metaphors to explore varying community and economic contexts. Metaphors are multivalent images that call attention to salient and unexpected relationships, contrasts, analogies, underlying structures, levers of change, and unrecognized opportunities. Gareth Morgan, in

Images of Organization, for example, uses metaphors like *brain* or *machine* to explore the information processing and functioning of organizations. Robert Mier and Richard Bingham have applied the metaphors of *problem solving* and *incubator* to understand city economies, relevant policies, and development actors. Anthropologist Robert Redfield, in *The Little Community*, states, "Metaphor and analogy offer different and parallel images for understanding the whole, as does the parable." Metaphors open windows on the critical parts of abstract nouns like neighborhood, organization, and CED.

FIGURE 2:
CED METAPHORS

1. *PLUGGING THE LEAKS*—INCOME, SAVINGS, ENERGY
   What resources drain from families and neighborhoods?

2. *BROKERING CONNECTIONS*—GEOGRAPHY, SOCIAL NETWORKS, DECISION-MAKING
   How are neighborhoods unplugged from the mainstream?

3. *ASSET MANAGEMENT*—LOCAL SKILLS, RESOURCES (i.e., LAND), AND ASSET PRESERVATION
   What are unrecognized community assets?

4. *LADDERS AND WEBS*—CAREERS, MUTUAL SUPPORT, INDUSTRIES, AND CLUSTERS
   What steps are missing for families to move up?

5. *ENHANCING MARKETS*—SOCIAL ECONOMY, EXPORTS, COMPETITIVE ADVANTAGE
   What voluntary exchanges are occurring to build markets?

6. *CREATING LEVEL PLAYING FIELDS*—POWER, VOICE, RESOURCES
   What are the imbalances that disadvantage families and neighborhoods?

Six metaphors provide tools for a more comprehensive reading of the potential situations and places in which CED can be applied: plugging the leaks, brokering connections, managing assets, building ladders and webs, creating a level playing field, and enhancing markets. No doubt there are other metaphors that we could add to the list, such as *families as businesses,* which would further enrich our design and implementation. The basic idea is to walk around a neighborhood or family economy, trying on each metaphor as a way to reveal opportunities, barriers, and resources. Figure 2 summarizes these metaphors and the questions they provoke.

CED is multifaceted and evolving, reflecting the complexity of neighborhoods and economies. Competition surely thrives because of different approaches, whether defined by a focus on jobs, wealth, or place. Our purpose should not be to reduce the complexity through oversimplification or special interest advocacy, but to help community actors creatively engage the complexity and design better interventions that improve economic impacts for families and neighborhoods.

CED Impacts and Future

Has CED made a difference for families and neighborhoods? Are they better off than they would have been without these investments? Has the CED field helped to change public and private investment patterns and policies? What should the next generation of CED strategies and institutions look like based upon these impacts? Answering these questions, or at least knowing what we don't know, is critical for imagining the future of the CED field.

While there hasn't been one comprehensive evaluation of CED, more focused evaluations of specific CED elements suggest cautious optimism. At the macro level, for example, the CED field of CDCs, financial intermediaries, and advocates has provided important leadership and models for reinvesting in urban neighborhoods. We now more often rebuild than tear down or disinvest in low- and moderate-income communities of color. Of course, some critics, like journalist Nicholas Lemann, have lambasted CDCs for not solving the problem of concentrated poverty. He is right in the global sense, but to argue that this social problem was the sole responsibility of CDCs reveals a shocking naiveté. Several thousand CDCs have emerged and become key producers of affordable housing and neighborhood commercial development.

The research and advocacy that produced the Community Reinvestment Act (CRA) and Home Mortgage Disclosure Act (HMDA) in the mid-1970s moved financial services institutions to reinvest in cities and neighborhoods. This shift of capital and underwriting would not have happened without the CRA. And today a good measure of the success of this advocacy is that many banks say they reinvest because it is good business, not because of regulatory pressure. The CRA movement also spurred the growth of hundreds of community development financial institutions (CDFIs), which have assembled multiple sources of capital to invest in CED. While there are questions about the scale and sustainability of CDFIs for the future, these financial institutions have become key players in financing charter schools, child-care facilities, job creation, and affordable housing.

Many specific CED strategies have undergone evaluations that have shown positive results. These studies have focused on microenterprise, CDFIs, Individual Development Accounts (IDAs), and social enterprises. On the other hand, evaluation studies have revealed mixed success for workforce development programs, showing modest increases in family income. In contrast, longer-term workforce programs like Project QUEST in San Antonio have demonstrated significant income and job retention results.

Two CED elements remain controversial—community organizing and place-based development. These approaches present unique challenges for evaluation studies in terms of methodology, and the evaluation findings about them raise some big questions about traditional CED assumptions. The basic argument for community organizing is that sustainable, accountable change will not occur without ongoing investment in community leadership and the coalitions that express and support their aspirations. This statement probably overstates the role of community organizing for all circumstances, but it is true that our progress is fragile, and community voices are essential to maintain and expand CED gains. And institutional changes frequently require a good push. Unfortunately, community organizing is not as prevalent and well-supported as it should be in all parts of the U.S., even though it is spearheading important work related to living wages, regional equity, and affordable housing.

I can't count the number of times someone has asked me to give them a short list of the low-income neighborhoods where all the CED pieces have been put together to raise family incomes and revitalize neighborhoods. What people are actually asking for, or perhaps questioning, is whether there really are any real-life models. I grow uncomfortable as I scramble for answers and then begin a recitation of the usual suspects, the South Bronx, New Community Corporation in Newark, South Shore Bank in Chicago, Dudley Street in Boston, Harlem, and so on. Soon my answer trails off into saying how tough it is and how some neighborhoods or cities do some things well and some things not so well.

Why is this question so difficult to answer after all these years and investments? A part of the problem is related to inadequate resources and the lack of capacity and willingness of public and private investors to target their resources to particular neighborhoods. We have not had a comprehensive neighborhood-rebuilding program since the 1960s, and few of those investments were surefire successes. In today's environment of diminished resources, it's difficult for city councils and mayors to target resources to one or two low-income neighborhoods, although there are examples of such leadership in cities like San Francisco, Baltimore, and Washington, D.C. Another part of the problem is that it's difficult to work in multiple neighborhoods and initiate innovative programs at the same time. CDCs are fragile organizations that have to be built over time, that have to connect to other players inside and outside neighborhoods, and that are opportunistic. Moreover, CDCs are, for the most part, only as good as the broader community-wide support infrastructure of which they are a part. They can't go it alone. Still another problem is that the success of CDCs and of revitalizing neighborhoods also rests on the opportunities outside of the neighborhood—job creation, economic development, public policies, and regional connections. That is, success in a particular place relates to broader community success.

The final problem returns us to the people-versus-place dilemma discussed earlier in this chapter. An empirical regularity in the U.S., barring persistent and widespread discrimination, is that when people move up economically, they move out of their current neighborhood. That is, people with more money buy more house, land, and education—a possibility given the way our metro areas have evolved. Unless low-income neighborhoods offer good choices for families in terms of housing, crime, and education, sensible consumers will look elsewhere to obtain the best quality of life for their families. That's what everybody does, but the consequence is that poor neighborhoods are constantly losing the asset-building families who are moving ahead and potentially have the most leadership resources to offer.

Even if adequate investments are made in neighborhoods to make them attractive, there is no guarantee that benefits will accrue to the lowest income or to those most in need. Families move not only in order to move up, but also because limited incomes make them vulnerable to eviction and extremely poor and unstable housing conditions. Moreover, if neighborhoods remain home for the concentrated poor, markets and housing values will likely stagnate and fail to attract other investments. On the other hand, investment in stronger market neighborhoods may tip the balance toward gentrification, leading to the relocation or displacement of those renters with the fewest resources.

What do these evaluation studies and family and neighborhood impacts mean for the future of CED? I have two answers, but will return to this question in Chapter 12.

In 1992, I worked with a team of scholars and practitioners at the University of Illinois at Chicago to review the state of health of CDCs in Chicago. We published our research, observations, and recommendations as *Choices Ahead: CDCs and Real Estate Production in Chicago*. Although we were narrowly focused on CDCs and real estate development in that study, in contrast to this chapter's broader discussion of CED, I believe that aspects of this report are helpful for thinking about the future of CED. At the time, we sketched three future scenarios for CDCs: creation of a full-fledged *Social Sector* for CED, *No Change and Drift*, and *Strategic Improvement*.

The *Social Sector* scenario called for a ramping up of piecemeal efforts in Chicago to support the building of several dozen high-performing CDCs and a handful of CDCs operating at a larger scale. Creating this sector would require a more explicit, better financed, and comprehensive support infrastructure for CDCs. The *No Change and Drift* scenario portrayed little change from the status quo for CDCs, piecemeal efforts, less focus on economic development, smaller scale, and a mix of high and under performance. The danger, of course, was that CDCs and CED would not receive the strategic attention they require to move ahead. The *Strategic Improvement* scenario involved targeted interventions that moved CDCs and CED forward without facing the difficult and perhaps impossible challenge of building a robust nonprofit sector. This scenario involved a better and smarter use of existing resources and improved messaging that CDCs and CED are an important civic asset worthy of support.

These scenarios are the reflections of CDC advocates and researchers from the early 1990s looking forward as the CDC movement reached the height of its success. From today's vantage point, much value remains in these scenarios as options, but we must acknowledge several strategic assumptions about CED that have changed. Broader recognition now exists that CED must relate to regional economies and diverse metropolitan communities; and that mixed-income housing contributes to breaking up concentrated poverty and creating sustainable communities. No longer can CDCs or CED be narrowly focused on single neighborhoods without attention to the bigger, regional picture. Moreover, many new immigrants are bypassing cities for the inner-ring suburbs because of cost factors and better amenities. At the same time, gentrification is pushing demographic change as well as making housing development more difficult for CDCs, which now must compete with private developers.

CED is still alive and well but must continue to evolve.

- Avoid the temptation of buying into one narrow CED theory or investment approach. Develop search tools—like metaphors—for exploring multiple CED opportunities.

- CED organizations need to develop the capacity to learn, innovate, and advocate at the same time that they are effective *nuts-and-bolts* implementers.

- CED also falls into the trap of multiple silos—jobs, assets, and place, for example. Keeping a focus on families and communities pushes CED practitioners to create holistic solutions.

- The future of the CED field is not just an extension or expansion of the past. CED leaders need to be in the forefront of confronting future challenges of geography, demography, markets, technology, and policy.

2

Thinking about Leadership

○ ○

The more I see of human lives, the more I believe the business of growing up is much longer drawn out than we pretend. If we achieve it in our forties or even fifties we're doing well.

—*John W. Gardner*

Forty years ago, the field of community economic development had a handful of community development corporations (CDCs), nonprofit organizations that promoted and implemented CED strategies. Today there are a few thousand CDCs, and together they are now the largest producer of affordable housing. Among the national financial intermediaries supporting CDCs is the Local Initiatives Support Corporation (LISC), which has scores of local offices and recently celebrated its twenty-fifth anniversary. Meanwhile, *Living Cities*, the largest philanthropic, private, and public funding collaborative for community development, has committed another $150 million for CED.

The mission of CED has also broadened. It began with a primary focus on economic development and affordable housing, but now has expanded its strategic repertoire to include matched savings called individual development accounts (IDAs), micro-lending for small business, industry-focused workforce development, anti-predatory lending, community development financial institutions, transit-based development, regional equity strategies, community land trusts, and a host of public policy campaigns. Most public and private investors now recognize, and have frequently adopted, the basic tenets of CED—investing in low-income communities and working hand-in-hand with residents and community institutions.

The CED field has not been centrally planned or even imagined as a unified endeavor. Its essential entrepreneurial energy has been local in nature. Disagreement, tension, and competition continue as a part of the evolving CED world as it adjusts to new realities and opportunities like mixed-income housing, reviving inner-city markets, regionalism, lackluster federal policies, and even the future of CDCs. Nevertheless, CED suffers the same fragmentation into silos as other parts of the social policy world, making holistic and coordinated action difficult. Yet, scores of leaders and organizations of every stripe work every day to invent and knit together the field in new ways.

Take my friend and colleague David Casey. This Methodist minister and community developer is the lead organizer for Baltimore Regional Initiative Developing Genuine Equity (BRIDGE), an affiliate of the Gamaliel Foundation congregation-based community-organizing network, recently launched in the Baltimore area. Dave was pastor of a small church in southeast Baltimore for many years and became president of the South East Community Organization (SECO), which hired me as the director in the late 1980s. After working as a low-income housing developer and a U.S. Department of Housing and Urban Development (HUD) community builder, Dave took the leap into community organizing, a mid-career change full of risks and new challenges. BRIDGE's agenda is to create mixed-income, affordable housing opportunities in the suburbs through inclusionary zoning legislation at the county level and new "housing equity" financing tools to make it happen. That's a tall order, but it's an approach that spreads CED to the suburbs and links the best of community organizing and development.

Take my friend and colleague Carol Bebelle, co-director of Ashé Cultural Center in New Orleans, located on historic O.C. Haley Boulevard in the Central City neighborhood. Carol is a poet, impresario, and social entrepreneur who has worked in public health, education, and community development. She brings people together to collaborate and learn from one another, whether competing nonprofits in the community, resident leaders who are becoming conscious of their own skills, or schools and parents. Carol is an organizer and developer. At Ashé, she uses the talents of multiple artists to uncover and illuminate the cultural ties that bind communities together, whether family photos, poetry, music, or dance. Ashé is a special communal gathering space that celebrates cultural assets as it supports new community building efforts. It is a center. Ashé and Carol Bebelle now face the incredible challenge of helping to rebuild Central City and New Orleans after the Katrina hurricane tragedy in 2005.

Take my friend and colleague Jesus Garcia. I met Jesus in the late 1970s and tried to hire him to work at the CDC I directed in Chicago's Pilsen neighborhood (i.e., the Eighteenth Street Development Corporation). Within a few years, Jesus became a state representative for his district and an ally of Harold Washington, Chicago's first African American mayor and a supporter of neighborhood-based development. After losing his seat in the early 1990s, Jesus didn't abandon the community he came out of and cash in on his political standing; rather, he helped start the Little Village Community Development Corporation. After surviving a few tough years of start-up, Jesus and the CDC have pursued neighborhood development with explicit attention to community organizing. The CDC led an organizing effort with resident and parent leaders to do something about the poor schools in Little Village. The community won, and a new school has been built.

If Chapter 1 defined the playing field for my career—CED, its strategies and challenges—Chapter 2 is about the leadership roles that I have played during my CED career—as practitioner, manager, and social entrepreneur. I can't claim that I've been as effective as David, Carol, and Jesus, but I've tried to make a difference for families and neighborhoods. In this book, I use leadership and management interchangeably because the old distinctions no longer hold; the same folks have to do things right as well as do the right things. Of course, these roles can never be adequately understood without also paying attention to economic conditions, organizational dynamics, and public policy.

This chapter reflects on the meaning and practice of CED leadership. The main point is that ongoing, critical reflection on life and CED practice is a prerequisite for improving leadership performance of CED practitioners. This seems so obvious that it no longer needs to be said. But the reflection I'm talking about is a kind of personal, continuous improvement and self-discovery in which we explicitly learn as we go. We seldom make this commitment.

The chapter begins by taking stock of the leadership and management literature. It then detours through ancient philosophy to suggest spiritual exercises for leaders who embrace reflection as an integral part of everyday life. The chapter compares and contrasts reflective, deliberative, and enterprising practitioners—three models from the world of planning and organizational change that are relevant for CED. I explore the contemporary role of social investor as leader and conclude the chapter by offering an organizing framework for the subsequent chapters.

As you read this chapter, reflect on your roles as leader and manager.

- What organizational roles have you played that required leadership and management skills?
- What leadership training has been useful for you? Who, if any, are your leadership gurus?
- How do you go about reflecting and learning as a way to improve your skills and self-awareness?
- How have you combined roles as leader, practitioner, and investor?

CED and Leadership

A robust literature on leadership has not emerged from the CED movement, even though there are important lessons to be learned from this entrepreneurial experience for civic, private, and public sector leaders. This is not to say that there isn't any recognized literature about CED. On the contrary, multiple volumes have been published on its history, theoretical underpinnings, strategies and tactics, local manifestations, evaluation outcomes, industry development, best practices, public policies, and prospects for the future. A small academic sub-discipline tracks the CED phenomena.

What is lacking, in my estimation, is a more popular literature on CED leaders—biographies, autobiographies, reflections, and *tell it like it is* leadership manifestos. A few exceptions exist. This type of writing exists for the community-organizing dimension of CED, including Saul Alinsky and Myles Horton as two of its premier practitioners. At the core of community organizing theory is the commitment to identify and develop a power base of grassroots leaders connected to associations or congregations who, together, can make change. A recent volume, *A Guide to Careers in Community Development* by Paul Brophy and Alice Shabecoff, includes a cameo portrait of my CED journey. The book provides a comprehensive picture of the array of career options and choices in the CED field, and hence, as a byproduct, addresses the CED leadership challenge. Several recent books by major field-building entrepreneurs like Michael Sviridoff, in *Inventing Community Renewal*, and Paul Grogan, in *Comeback Cities*, underscore the history, strategies, and successes of CED; but these important leaders were not, for the most part, in the trenches building the movement from the ground up. *Hum Bows, Not Hot Dogs!* by Bob Santos signals the emergence of more on-the-ground musings by a CED leader.

An exception to this paucity of leadership musings has blossomed under the rubric of social entrepreneurship. Social entrepreneurship represents a larger field of endeavor than CED and includes the nonprofit sector, non-governmental organizations (NGOs), and citizen organizations throughout the world. Social entrepreneurship acknowledges the unrecognized entrepreneurial skills and behaviors of the nonprofit world that create social innovations, dynamic and adaptive organizations, and social enterprises—those double bottom-line activities that generate revenue as well as social benefits. David Bornstein starts *How to Change the World: Social Entrepreneurship and the Power of New Ideas* by saying, "This is a book about people who solve social problems on a larger scale. Most of its characters are not famous." Books, articles, case studies and manifestos, and biographies like *Revolution of the Heart* by Bill Shore proliferate on CED bookshelves. Leadership training programs like the Denali Initiative have sought to cultivate, nurture, and reward social entrepreneurs.

A related notion of leadership is civic entrepreneurship, as coined by Douglas Henton, John Melville, and Kimberly Walesh in *Grassroots Leaders for a New Economy*. Civic entrepreneurship is the explicit effort of leaders to build regional collaborations that link economy and community to enhance global competitiveness. What is striking about these leaders is that they cluster in cities and regions, and grow their membership over time, recognizing that a division of labor among the many is needed to motivate, incubate, implement, and sustain collaborative initiatives.

The nonprofit sector has developed its own perspectives and literature on leadership against a backdrop of negative publicity surrounding the fundraising scams and mismanagement of several well-known charities. Notwithstanding the nonprofit sector's image, capacity, and performance problems, no lesser light than Peter Drucker has written about nonprofit leadership in *Managing the Nonprofit Organization* and has celebrated the talents and achievements of leaders like Frances Hesselbein, who headed the Girl Scouts and the Peter Drucker Foundation for many years. At the heart of the nonprofit leadership challenge is managing organizations defined by social mission (always fraught with definitional ambiguity), while developing a knowledgeable and durable group of civic stakeholders who steward nonprofit resources into the future. Nonprofit capacity building and leadership requires, as it has in the private and public sectors, establishing high-performing learning organizations. Becoming high-performing is no small challenge for nonprofit organizations, however, because they do not, for the most part, have the flexible resources needed to support full-fledged and ongoing infrastructure development and organizational learning. To make matters worse, the nonprofit sector faces the difficult challenge of large-scale executive succession in the coming decades.

Enterprising leaders are the lifeblood of nonprofit and civic associations. It is striking how we have ignored what these leaders have to teach and how we might support them in more effective ways.

Lessons from the Management/Leadership Literature

Nurturing leaders is essential for CED and the nonprofit arenas in which I have worked. Yet, I'm skeptical about leadership training and the plethora of management books, training manuals and courses, and pep rally leadership speeches given by civic luminaries. Something doesn't ring true for me about this jumble of words. Important things are not being said or are being glossed over. My uneasy feelings about most leadership discussions, whether about social entrepreneurs or corporate leaders, are signals I've learned to ignore at my own risk.

Nonetheless, my recent splurge of reading about leadership uncovered many relevant ideas for nonprofit leaders and CED. I discuss these ideas using a three-part framework that also organizes the chapters in the rest of the book: *Personal Attributes for Leadership, New Skills for Leadership,* and *Relationship Building for Results.* But first I address several overarching themes.

Several common leadership ideas are identified in the collection of articles, *The Leader of the Future,* prepared by the Peter Drucker Foundation. The first common idea is almost a truism: all organizations—public, private, and nonprofit—are confronting environments characterized by dynamic change, constant innovation, and globalization. No organization can stand still or feel safe. It is no surprise that leadership analysts in this book have invented a variety of new roles for leaders to help navigate this new terrain: "animators, designers, teachers, entrepreneurs, internal networkers, community builders, integrators, pathfinders, stewards and agitators." Moreover, the notions of *followership* and *servant leadership* suggest that effective leaders are anything but top-down figures.

The second idea is that we must identify and nurture leaders at every organizational level, not just at the top, not just in the middle, and not just in one organization. The need for leaders is pervasive in our communities and must be addressed if we are to make progress as a society. The change we need cannot succeed if led only from the top. James Kouzes and Barry Posner conclude, "When we liberate the leader in everyone, extraordinary things happen."

The third common idea is that many factors, in addition to management and measurement, contribute to the achievement of business and civic results—the most important perhaps being the elusive but salient role of organizational culture, the composite of everyday organizational values, habits, and ways of thinking and acting.

Leading organizational culture theorist Edgar Schein states, "[L]eaders of the future will be persons who can lead and follow, be central and marginal, be hierarchically above and below, be individualistic and a team player and, above all, be a perpetual learner."

While many leadership books recognize these common ideas, they tend to focus on specific skills, pitfalls, and frameworks that they think are most important. Yet, these common ideas represent the most powerful levers for change externally and internally, for all organizations. Almost all other leadership advice is built upon these ideas of dynamic environments, organization-wide leadership, and organizational culture.

Personal Attributes of Leaders. Resonance is the fundamental concept of the emotional intelligence literature on leadership and is a *way of being* available to leaders at all organizational levels and in almost all situations. Daniel Coleman, Richard Boyatzis, and Annie McKee, the authors of *Primal Leadership*, assert, "When leaders drive emotions positively ... they bring out everyone's best. We call this effect resonance." The simple fact, so frequently ignored, is that our emotional presence affects everyone around us, no matter our intent, no matter the situation. While there are multiple applications of emotionally intelligent leadership, such as visioning or coaching, all styles eschew the old "command and control" top-down approach, and all embody personal skills and attributes in the domains of self-awareness, self-management, social awareness, and relationship management.

The practical importance of emotional intelligence is demonstrated by Roger Fisher and Daniel Shapiro in *Beyond Reason: Using Emotions as You Negotiate*. They argue that relationships build solution options through recognizing the emotional consequences of "appreciation, affiliation, autonomy, status, and role." The more negotiators connect, the more likely they are to reach agreement.

At the heart of emotional intelligence are authentic connections to others in our families, workplaces, and communities. *Leadership and Self Deception*, by the Arbinger Institute, argues that we're "out of the box," or on the way to effective leadership, when "I see myself and others more or less as we are—People." We're "in the box" when we treat others as objects, treating them as the source of problems or as obstacles to success while we fail to take the risks and time to recognize them, and us, struggling to make a go of things as human beings. We blame them instead of acknowledging them. The Arbinger Institute, in a prequel, *The Anatomy of Peace: Resolving the Heart of Conflict*, shows how being "out of the box" is important for avoiding war and promoting peace in marriages, families, and workplaces.

Dissonant leadership and being "in the box" produces "evil" in organizations in which people are turned into "phrogs," in the words of Jerry Harvey in *The Abilene Paradox and Other Meditations on Management*. People are forced, and force others, to do bad things to fellow workers. Harvey offers an unusual and no doubt tongue-in-cheek suggestion that we should encourage cheating on tests from an early age in school in order to nurture teamwork, the group problem-solving that healthy, ethical organizations require.

Leaders must be able to make tough decisions. Joseph Badaracco, in *Defining Moments*, identifies a subset of those decisions as having to decide between "right and right." There is no one correct answer, but one answer is needed to move forward.

New Skills for Leadership. Jim Collins, in *Good to Great*, extrapolates from Isaiah Berlin's famous philosophical parable of *The Hedgehog and the Fox*. The hedgehog in this story knows one big thing, while the wily fox knows many things—he's a bit of a gadfly. In Collins's interpretation of this story, in which he underappreciates the fox, knowing one big thing trumps multiple smarts. Hedgehog skills define high-performing companies. A good example is how Kimberly-Clark gave up the paper production business to concentrate its investments in consumer paper products like diapers and paper towels. Another example is how Walgreen's got out of the prepared food business to concentrate on convenient, high-profit-per-customer drugstores. These companies read the marketplace and their core competencies in entirely novel ways. Paradoxically for me, CED is by nature a fox.

Innovation is at the heart of CED, and business competitiveness and creativity is the lifeblood of innovation and of cities, according to Richard Florida, author of the *Rise of the Creative Class*. Cities are now classified by whether they have the requisite diversity and urbanity to attract and retain the creative class. Occupations and industries are being dissected to reveal their implicit and explicit creativity requirements. Soon schools will take up the goal of cultivating habits of creativity in their students. As Daniel Pink argues in *A Whole New Mind*, the Masters of Fine Arts (MFA) is becoming the new Masters of Business Administration (MBA).

In *The Medici Effect*, Frans Johansson demonstrates that the source of creativity is living and thinking at the *Intersection*, where diverse cultures, disciplines, and ways of thinking cross-fertilize each other, whether types of cuisine, architecture, and the study of ants, or rock and classical music. Creative entrepreneurs have low associational barriers and generate a constant flow of ideas, practical applications, and creative breakthroughs. They cultivate Daniel Pink's "six senses": design, story, symphony, empathy, play, and meaning.

New ideas have to be put into action to make a difference. Many companies and nonprofits prefer to innovate rather than to embrace the rocky road of long-term and sustained implementation, full of old-fashioned management and new-fashioned organizational learning and redesign. In *Managing the Unexpected*, Karl Weick and Kathleen Sutcliffe argue that an overriding sensitivity to operations distinguishes mindful organizations that can't afford to make big mistakes, such as nuclear reactors or aircraft carriers. These sensitivities are embodied in intuition, "the ways we translate experience into action," according to Gary Klein in *The Power of Intuition*. Jim Collins, in *Good to Great*, refers to this focus as the culture of discipline, or the sustained attention to execution. Simply, you've got to deliver the goods, over and over.

Relationship Building for Results. Creativity, teams, and business partnerships across industries and nations require that leaders be relationship builders. Marcus Buckingham and Curt Coffman, in *First, Break All the Rules*, argue that talent—strength-focused leadership—unleashes personal and organizational productivity by turning on its head conventional wisdom about leaders' keeping their distance from employees or fitting people to jobs. Figuring out how to use and grow talent is a business necessity.

Developing talent requires coaching and teaching. Eric Liu, in *Guiding Lights*, showcases inspiring teachers who, knowing how to listen as a first step of teaching, help students overcome inner obstacles to expression, creatively reframe subject matter, draw sustenance and guidance from cultural resources, and learn through becoming teachers themselves. He portrays informal and formal teachers who teach acting, clowning, jazz, and baseball pitching; their lessons are relevant for many careers and fields.

Some years ago, my close friend and collaborator Robert Mier and I coined the phrase "cooperative leadership" in *Social Justice and Local Economic Development* to describe a new form of coalition that brought together unusual partners. We witnessed extraordinary civic leaders in Chicago during the 1980s who combined the personal attributes of integrity with organizing skills in brokering, negotiating, collaborating, and assembling path-breaking coalitions that found common ground among industries, workers, community residents, city dwellers, and suburbanites, and across the divides of race, ethnicity, and gender. Rosabeth Moss Kanter suggests, "Leaders must become cosmopolitans who are comfortable operating across boundaries and who can forge links between organizations." Further, Douglas Henton, John Melville, and Kimberly Walesh, in *Grassroots*

Leaders for the New Economy, argue, "The new model is regional and collaborative, and it depends upon a new kind of leader."

Who has put together multiple pieces of advice into a coherent and compelling agenda for leaders? In my estimation, Jim Collins, in *Good to Great,* and Jim Collins and Jerry Porras, in *Built to Last,* capture the dual objectives of organizational excellence and sustainability, a real-life pragmatic feel of what it takes compared to achieving partial triumphs in limited situations. Their top companies synthesize the best advice and translate it into sustainable leadership action for long-term results. In fact, Jim Collins, in the recent *Good To Great and the Social Sectors*, argues that his framework works for all sectors as long as attention is paid to key differences in leadership, resources, and success measurement.

Leadership and Spiritual Practice

The fundamental advice of this book is to embrace experience and reflect upon that experience as a regular part of life and as a primary source of leadership strength. This perspective is missing in much of the leadership literature and defies simple formulas. It acknowledges that our lives hold many answers. Peter Han, in *Nobodies to Somebodies*, suggests that what distinguished the one hundred leaders he talked with "was their deep self knowledge and the resulting openness to change and improvement." John Gardner observes that creative leaders have an "exceptional openness to their own inner life."

Reflection on one's experience seems simple, but in reality it's an adventure. Reflection begins with self-consciousness—the acute awareness that our actions, behaviors, and ideas are not simply givens in our lives, nature, or history; they represent choices, large and small, in the here and now. Philosophy provides a language and discipline to guide us in this awareness of self and in recognizing its limitations. Many of us recall, for example, the foundational maxim of Western humanism, "Know thyself," from the pre-Socratic philosopher, Thales. And I recall being intimidated, at an early age, by Plato's belief that maturity began at age thirty, the recognition that self-knowledge required more time than graduating from college. Thirty now seems young from my vantage point. Self-knowledge is unfolding and never fully achieved.

The French historian of philosophy, Pierre Hadot, in *What Is Ancient Philosophy?* restores balance to our understanding of the origins and purposes of philosophy. Without going into too much detail, his argument is that ancient and even some contemporary philosophy have two independent but related purposes: to offer a rational explanation of the world and advice about how we can know it; and to aid everyone, especially the young, in "personal transformation"—pursuing excellence of character in individual, family, and community action. Personal transformation occurs not through one-time revelatory insight, but through repeated "[spiritual exercises] in the acquisition of self consciousness." Such exercises were a mainstay of ancient and Hellenistic philosophers and their philosophical practices and schools. Philosophy was seen as a "way of life."

Hadot discusses two exercises for increasing self-consciousness, "concentration of the self ... and the expansion of self." In addition to various techniques for purging the self of unnecessary "desires and appetites," a distinctly New Age preoccupation, the first type of spiritual exercise focuses on enabling the separation of self from everything else going on in one's life. This is an act of engaging with and being in the present. In the words of the Roman senator and philosopher Cicero, "The life of a fool is hard and worrisome. It is wholly devoured by the future."

The separation from self supports the critical self-examination of one's moral life—"mistakes, weaknesses," and all else. This self-examination exercises the conscience, the "inner court" in which we sort out our progress or lack thereof on a daily basis, even as encountered in our dreams. Many philosophers of the time required the daily practice of self-examination from their students enrolled in their philosophical schools. Spiritual exercise represents "training in death" because of the distancing of self from action and because of the simple question one must ask regularly, What if this were the last moment of my life?

While the first spiritual exercise leads to a sharper self-consciousness and engagement in daily life, the second exercise requires that we extend or stretch ourselves into the "immensity" of the universe. Hadot writes, "The 'I' thus experiences a twofold feeling: that of its puniness and that of its greatness." Hadot further concludes, "We must not only perceive and live each moment of time as if it were the last; we must also perceive it as if it were the first, in all the stupefying strangeness of its emergence." If this sounds strangely like a hybrid of Eastern and Western philosophy, it's no surprise, because I discovered Pierre Hadot when reading *An End to Suffering: The Buddha in the World*, by Pankaj Mishra. The heart of Buddhist teaching is revealed in the Four Noble Truths—that life is suffering (Duhkha), and that suffering arises from craving, the attachment to the phenomenal world, a life of change, the unstable self—in short, impermanence. But suffering can be overcome by following the Eightfold Path of right thinking and living. In the words of Seneca, quoted by Pierre Hadot, "In every good person, there lives a god. Which god? We cannot be sure—but it is a god."

Why has the spirit of practical philosophy, with its emphasis on self-consciousness, become submerged and secondary within the history of philosophy—philosophy as a way of life losing out to philosophy as theory? Practical philosophy reemerged briefly in the sixteenth century during the Renaissance in writers like Montaigne and with pragmatist philosophers like John Dewey and Richard Rorty in the twentieth century. The preoccupations with *belief* and *certainty*, rather than critical and ongoing self-examination, became a standard feature of monotheism, whether Christianity or Islam, and in modern philosophy starting with Descartes. The world and how to behave in it were revealed once and for all, and the scientific method gained hegemony as the only path to knowledge. Stephen Toulmin, in *Cosmopolis* concludes,

> Thus, from 1630 on, the focus of philosophical inquiries has ignored the particular, concrete, timely and local details of everyday human affairs: instead, it has shifted to a higher stratospheric plane, on which nature and ethics conform to abstract, timeless, general, and universal theories.

After the disruptions of the Thirty Years' War and the crumbling of Renaissance society, thinkers emphasized certainty at the expense of self-consciousness in everyday life.

Are these spiritual exercises helpful for today's nonprofit leadership? Aren't these exercises essentially the same self-help advice offered in popular leadership books wrapped up in the philosophical language of ancient sages? I don't believe so. In my mind, these spiritual exercises recommend and cultivate critical self-examination, daily practice, recognition of "immensity," and interdependence. These exercises nurture the values of humility, deliberativeness, skepticism, integrity, and awe—all important personal traits for today's leadership. Adopting these values or behaviors can only be done through hard work and over time.

Reflective, Deliberative, and Enterprising Practitioners

Another form of practical knowledge traceable to the Greeks is called *metis*, or "cunning intelligence." It is knowledge of local conditions that combines "know-how, common sense, and a knack" as described by James Scott in *Seeing Like a State*. This is not theory-driven, abstract, and generalizable knowledge, but "rules of thumb … largely acquired through practice (often in formal apprenticeships) and a developed feel or knack for strategy." Practical knowledge, or *metis*, is essential for everyday problem solving in the home, workplace, and community, and is often thought of as "indigenous," or local, knowledge. As with spiritual exercises, *metis* came under attack with the rise of modern philosophy, science, and the nation state, each of which preferred systematic inquiry and certainty to local, diverse, and particular knowledge.

Metis is important for leaders who function as members of professions. The so-called "minor" professions, such as architecture, city planning, and social work, are distinguished from the major professions like medicine because they operate without a high level of certainty about the predictable relationships among problem definition, interventions, and outcomes. That is, there is no hard body of theory and evidence about how to solve poverty or lift up poor neighborhoods. As a consequence, these professions navigate ambiguous environments, trying to make sense of problems, bringing the right folks together for the right conversations, testing assumptions and design ideas, reworking designs, and ultimately creating the belief that concerted action is possible and likely to solve problems. Not surprisingly, these professionals develop quite a bit of implicit, intuitive, rule-of-thumb local knowledge about how to make a difference. For this reason, it makes sense to call these leaders practitioners of *metis*.

Practitioner Leadership. In the past several decades, the planning profession has developed several models of practitioner leadership—the reflective practitioner and the deliberative practitioner. A third model is the enterprising practitioner. These practitioner models are not mutually exclusive; each calls attention to different leadership norms, skills, and behaviors, and each is relevant for different situations.

The Reflective Practitioner: How Professionals Think in Action, by Donald Schön, was published in 1983 and continues to be path-breaking and inspiring for many practitioners in the CED field and beyond. The book does three things. First, Schön articulates the underlying methodology that city planners and architects, at their best, actually use in practice, even though it is rarely spoken of as such. This description affirms what practitioners know on the ground: design is not the one-time application of tried and true knowledge and principles. It's messy. Second, in making explicit the methodology of designers in the minor professions, Schön addresses the credibility gap that these professions suffer under the broader public because of the misplaced assumptions about how good designs are constructed. In a 1984 review of Schön's book in *The Neighborhood Works*, I stated, "These professionals don't have cookbook problems or solutions. Instead, they 'converse' with situations and listen to their 'backtalk' by trying out models, simulating solutions, and testing hypotheses." The reflective practitioner is an experimenter, learner, and risk taker who engages in an iterative process of problem-setting, design, and redesign. And third, Schön argues for the reform of how these professions conduct training and education.

Reflective practitioners appear misunderstood, heroic professionals, whether acting alone or as part of an elite team. The design process is still essentially about them, even as they frame problems and reflect-in-action. The deliberative practitioner, as portrayed in *The Deliberative Practitioner* by John Forester, facilitates "consensus building" among disparate, often conflictual, partners so that they can find common meaning and advance common solutions. Forester argues that planners "can promote effective processes of public learning, practical and innovative instances of public deliberation, even consensus building...." The deliberative practitioner model assumes that some solutions can be invented only by larger groups. Institutional procedures and norms are not always in place to ensure open and democratic decision-making. Practitioners, often at some peril to their own careers, must create spaces in which authentic communication and decision-making can occur. In helping to create these learning spaces for consensus-building, deliberative practitioners can foster hope, ethical action, and the building of community.

In the early 1990s, several planning scholars asked a group of us to write commentaries on a new book about city planning in the United Kingdom for a special issue of *Planning Theory*, a relatively obscure planning journal published in Italy. The most interesting part of this exercise was the cultural and political misunderstanding it revealed between U.K. and U.S. planning practitioners. The heart of the misunderstanding was that the U.S. practitioners perceived themselves as less institution-bound and more comfortable in roles in which they could invent problems, constituencies, campaigns, and policies. They were *enterprising practitioners* in part because they constantly had to fight within the institutional context and resource constraints of minimalist government and social welfare policy in the U.S.

If reflective practitioners are somewhat individualistic, and deliberative practitioners specialize in enabling voice and listening even in bad situations, enterprising practitioners invent situations and are akin to civic and social entrepreneurs. They work with colleagues to assemble new institutional frameworks, invent new strategies, and advocate for appropriate investments and policies. Enterprising practitioners are particularly relevant for the CED field because CED is in a state of perpetual invention and advocacy *vis-à-vis* mainstream economic development strategies. Enterprising practitioners are implementers and builders, not just designers or consensus builders. They thrive on results.

Are reflective, deliberative, and enterprising practitioners substantively different? Yes and no! It is quite possible for practitioners to combine the roles of designer, consensus-builder, and implementer on the same project, or over time, on different projects. At the same time, these practitioner roles and skill sets are quite different. Indeed, they embody contrasting definitions of design, decision-making, change strategies, and professional roles. They do share, however, a strong commitment to community problem-solving.

Social Investor as Leader

An unusual form of leadership occurs through the provision of financial capital, technical assistance, and governance accountability. In the private sector, venture capitalists bankroll new companies and products that promise big returns in exchange for financing big risks. Few companies qualify for their support. In the nonprofit world, social investors provide similar types of assistance—on different terms, of course—to stimulate social innovations and policy change. The selection process for these investments is less rigorous and more artful, except perhaps in the global search for social entrepreneurs by groups like *Ashoka*. At their best, both types of investors accelerate innovation and increase the likelihood that entrepreneurial initiatives are successful.

Thinking about social investors as leaders recognizes the important role they play in the CED field and the nonprofit sector. I brought my years of experience in the CED field to social investing, for example, when I joined the Annie E. Casey Foundation in 1993. More broadly, social investors are becoming part of a growing movement for high-engagement philanthropy, especially because the philanthropic sector is projected to grow in the coming decades. At the same time, a confluence of interests in social investing has occurred because of the double bottom-line aspirations of social enterprises that promise market and social returns, and the increased use of low-cost debt instruments by foundations to complement grant-making—what are called *Program-Related Investments (PRIs)*. As a consequence, foundations seek program officers with business and financial experience. And underwriting procedures for social investments have influenced grant-making to become more entrepreneurial and results-oriented.

A certain amount of ego inflation is inevitable with a phrase like social investor. Greg Dees of Duke University states, "we can define philanthropic entrepreneur (i.e., social investor) as the productive efforts that reform or revolutionize the patterns by which private resources and relationships are mobilized and deployed to effect social change." Yet foundations are partial fabrications of the tax code and are not as accountable as they should be. Few foundations have adopted the social investor mindset or made a serious commitment to measuring the results from their billions of dollars of investments. Moreover, the principles of high-engagement philanthropy (i.e., the mimicking of the world of venture capitalists) have always been present in the attitudes and behaviors of philanthropists like Andrew Carnegie, who was active in building libraries around the country at the turn of the century. Bill Gates and groups like Social Venture Partners haven't broken that much new ground, except with increased resources.

"Venture capital is a contact sport," according to Douglas Henton, John Melville, and Kimberly Walesh, in *Grassroots Leaders for the New Economy*. And social investing is no different; if taken seriously, it requires major changes in how foundations behave and organize their work. The first requirement is that foundations are clear and rigorous about their own results, theory of change, investment strategies, and measurement protocols. Reducing ambiguity and sticking with strategies where you add value helps everyone, but it means that discretionary, opportunistic behavior may be curtailed—the loss of a treasured perk of foundation life. A second requirement is that social investors are committed to helping grantees (i.e., customers) achieve success by making investments beyond one to three years and treating them as on the road to success rather than as only seekers of foundation lucre. Foundations can't walk away and hide behind their grant agreements, only coming out to declare victory or to pronounce failure after grant periods have ended. A third and related requirement is that social investors must have substantive content and development expertise; they must bring these years of experience to the table and be able and willing to provide their customers with wise, hardnosed, and sometimes painful counsel. A fourth requirement is that social investors know how to end unproductive relationships and weather the inevitable conflict that ensues when poor-performing investments are named and acted upon. This stance is especially painful because social investors may have to admit their own unworkable ideas, lack of oversight, poor quality of technical assistance, bad timing, or misplaced reading of the opportunity at hand. In other words, being a "contact sport" means that social investing may not be the appropriate and safe field of play for venture capitalist wannabes. They should look elsewhere.

Social investors have created tremendous value for CED. While many acknowledge Saul Alinsky as developing the modern practice of community organizing, fewer know that the personal, long-term involvement of Bishop Sheil and Marshall Field III bankrolled his community efforts. Moreover, the CDC field grew from the long-term investments of the Ford Foundation starting in the late 1950s. And in the 1990s, the Rockefeller Foundation joined the fray by advocating for the formation of the national funding collaborative, *Living Cities*—initially named the *National Community Development Initiative (NCDI)*. In each of these cases, specific foundation leaders and program officers led the way, and continued to influence the evolution of the CED field even after they left foundation life. We could point to the recent CED turn toward asset building or the evolution of sector-based workforce development and identify similar social investors whose strategic investments nurtured these new CED approaches. Many other examples stand out of social investors who have shaped the CED field—regionalism, social enterprises, or immigrant rights.

Social investors are leaders and practitioners of a distinctive kind because their investments provide the resources and credibility necessary to help new approaches get off the ground and eventually join mainstream practice and policy. Social investors keep their eyes on the big-picture horizons of getting to scale, building fields, making major mid-course corrections, and focusing on public policy adoption. These are difficult tasks for anyone focused on the day-to-day work in CED.

The Plan for the Book

The first two chapters have provided an interpretive overview of the subject matter and leadership terrain that have defined my CED adventure. Chapter 1 defined CED, examined variations of CED theory and practice and how the field has evolved, offered advice about how to think about CED strategies, and outlined the current framing of CED in my work—*family economic success*. Chapter 2 explored leadership in the CED field from many perspectives. In addition to identifying different types of leadership relevant to CED, the chapter emphasized that a daily commitment to self-examination, personal growth, and reflection about life and CED are essential for improving nonprofit leadership effectiveness.

A few other lessons about civic leadership and CED are:

- Nonprofit leaders are the backbone of CED and of the civic, nonprofit sector that has expanded over the past forty years. A focused and deliberate literature on developing this leadership is needed.

- Organizations require leaders at all levels with the ability to play multiple roles inside the organization and in outside environments in which change is a permanent feature.

- A three-part framing of leadership roles and skills includes personal attributes for leadership through values; new skills for leadership like navigating messes and building upon mistakes; and relationship building for results through unlikely partners and stories.

- Leadership development is a spiritual practice in which we are committed to examining our own beliefs and actions as a part of everyday life.

The book contains my reflections, doubts, advice, and speculations about a life and career as a nonprofit and CED leader. The following chapters do not represent my nine secrets for CED excellence. These are topics and challenges that have been important for me to grapple with, again and again, during my career, and I believe they are important for the entire CED field. The following chapters model how one can apply the good medicine of self-examination while providing practical advice and tips for CED practitioners.

This book of reflections is oriented toward the future, my future in CED, and the future of CED. I return in the final chapter to my dreams as an early CED practitioner about a robust community-based, social economy sector that could provide a plausible alternative to market and government initiatives. This utopian statement of hope and rededication is an appropriate way to chart new pathways for nonprofit leadership.

3

Values Matter: Unpeeling the Onion

o o o o o o o o o o o o o o o o o o o o o o o o o o o o o o
How can people know what the problem
is for more than a hundred years, put a man
on the moon, make planes fly, but not answer
the question of why certain classes of people
are left behind.

—*Kevin McDonalds, Milwaukee*[7]

In August 1968, my friend Cliff and I skipped shoveling sewage at our summer jobs with the DuPage County Department of Public Works to play hooky at the Democratic National Convention in Chicago, replete with Yippies, tear gas, Mayor Richard J. Daley, and the National Guard. Called to protest the Vietnam War, the week-long demonstration had already produced riots, and more disruption was likely as protesters gathered in Grant Park across the street from the flagship Hilton Hotel. We were naïve, political sympathizers, curious, but without much protest experience under our belts.

By the end of the day we were sunburned and exhausted. We saw and heard lots of things that day, but two impressions have stayed with me. As we walked among the protesters and would-be rioters, I felt a distinct sense of self-indulgence and misdirected personal anger arising among some of the people in the crowd as they readied themselves for the next round of rioting. As much as we

---

7. See Roberta Rehner Iversen and Annie Laurie Armstrong. *Jobs Aren't Enough: Toward a New Economic Mobility for Low-Income Families,* Philadelphia, PA: Temple University Press, 2006.

were sympathetic with the cause and horrified by the crackdown, I was dismayed by the lack of political authenticity exhibited by some in the crowd.

On the way home to our western suburb aboard a packed commuter train that evening, we overheard corporate office workers scornfully dismiss the protesters. Several men half-joked that the rioters should have been shot. We held our tongues. But their all-too-easy dismissals, calls for violence, and lack of critical thinking only fed our alienation.

Looking back, I realize that my reactions that day reflected some of my deepest values—the importance of political engagement, authenticity, and civility, coupled with a need to rise above polarizing rhetoric and action. I haven't always remained true to these values, but they remain bedrock beliefs, ones that began to crystallize on that hot day in Chicago.

In this chapter I discuss social and moral values that have informed my life's work. With all modesty, I hope other CED practitioners can embrace similar values. But, more importantly, CED leaders must explore and examine their own values through self-reflection—"unpeeling the onion" of experience. Doing this requires reflecting upon what one believes and how one has behaved over time, in difficult situations, as a leader, and in the community. Sometimes values become clear only retrospectively, by looking backward. That's what I do in this chapter.

Ask yourself the following questions about values:

- What values got you into your field of endeavor?
- What values stand out in retrospect as guiding your work?
- How do you integrate your values and work on a daily basis?
- What values keep you going?

Starting Out

The social and political struggles of the 1960s—anti-poverty, civil rights, and peace—ignited and expanded my moral imagination. I wanted to contribute to social change if I could figure out what that meant and how I could play a part. I didn't have money to travel the continents, nor did I have a reserve of carefree risk-taking to support my meandering around the world and living off the land and other people. So I needed to get a job and do something. For the next two years, I lived and worked in Chicago and Philadelphia as I tried to figure out the world of social change in the 1970s.

The mixing of 1960s values of democratic participation, decentralization, and grassroots action with the density, chaos, and sheer size of big cities led me to discover the fields of city planning and CED. Living in cities, riding crowded buses and trains, feeling lost and isolated, relishing diversity, and observing urban poverty and disinvestment first-hand transformed me into a committed urbanite, despite having grown up in the suburbs. Books paved the way for a synthesis of my social change values and city experiences—I devoured *Death and Life of Great American Cities* by Jane Jacobs, the *Culture of Cities* by Lewis Mumford, *Anarchy and Action* by Colin Ward, and *The Uses of Disorder*, by Richard Sennett. All of these books argued that the messy life of cities, mixed land uses, and diverse people not only made life interesting and surprising, but created a context of moral tolerance, civic virtue, and entrepreneurial economic growth, even in the midst of political machines, urban renewal, and social and racial conflict. I made another key formative decision. I applied to graduate school in city planning back in Chicago—my attempt to bring together a commitment to social change with a better job and maybe even a career.

One of my first courses at planning school in Chicago in 1974 led a fellow student and me into the neighborhood of Pilsen, ten blocks south of the University of Illinois at Chicago. Pilsen, I soon learned, was home; my family had passed through it and moved westward soon after World War I as German immigrants. Our school project examined the potential role of citizen zoning boards as a regulatory tool to help communities control unwanted growth and development, in this case a master plan developed by downtown business elites to revitalize Chicago's greater central business district. The project turned into a summer job building playgrounds on empty lots with school children, an internship researching property ownership as a part of a community plan, a major group project on local industry and employment, and then a job offer to help start a new nonprofit community development corporation (CDC). I stayed in the job for five years, eventually becoming executive director.

Early in my studies I realized that I was being paid to do what citizens should be able to do as a matter of course. That is, I wandered City Hall, went to City Council committee meetings, researched abandoned properties, interviewed key political and community leaders, and debated policy options. This epiphany led to more probing questions. Why should city policies and practices be so complicated? Why should only professionals have the opportunity to learn about the intricacies of city development? Wasn't citizenship a basic right for every American? This confrontation with my privilege reinforced my commitment to putting my knowledge and energy to good use.

Values and Getting a Job

As I ended my city planning coursework, I took a CED job in Pilsen that shaped the rest of my career. I took a job that wasn't high paying or high prestige, even within a profession devoted to public service. I obtained subsequent jobs over the years guided by the values of community service.

That first job allowed me to learn a lot about CED, even though all I had to offer in return were my commitment, research skills, and willingness to work hard. I traded prestige and pay for the opportunity to learn, get dirty with on-the-ground development and organization-building challenges, make mistakes, and rub shoulders in the tumultuous world of urban development. This jack-of-all-trades implementation experience honed my understanding of how to get things done.

The openness of the Pilsen community to hiring an outsider with energy but little proven knowledge created in me a deep sense of obligation to deliver results for Pilsen and other communities like Pilsen that I have worked in over the years. Residents showed faith in me and allowed their challenges to inform my learning. In turn, I owed them and still do.

In my first weeks on the job in Pilsen, I faced the unenviable challenge of having to obtain liability insurance for our construction training program that rehabilitated abandoned buildings while providing job training and work experience for ex-gang members. We had a City of Chicago job training contract with the local Model Cities agency that required liability and workmen's compensation insurance. I learned quickly how to write a news story about our plight, quoting myself, for the neighborhood newspaper, the *West Side Times*. I received two calls in response. The first call was from a politically connected insurance firm; they said that they would be glad to write a policy for us at an inflated price. We signed up; there was no other choice at the time. The second call was from an old lady on the southwest side who recognized my name and wanted to talk about relatives and our home village in Germany.

This start-up experience on the job underscored two questions about values that have stayed with me and that all CED practitioners need to grapple with—the role of government and the meaning of community. The first question involves my ambivalence about the capacity of government to do good. I came of age at the tail end of the Vietnam War and painfully observed the human costs of moral and intellectual failure on a grand scale.

My early CED experience during the last few years of the reign of Mayor Richard J. Daley in Chicago exacerbated my doubts about government. Political patronage, urban renewal and neighborhood destruction, and mega infrastructure projects for downtown expansion characterized his twenty-year reign.

As many social activists of the time, inequality and the need for a more sensible and ethical distribution of resources led me to question the limitations of capitalist economies and so-called liberal democracies. But I never fell captive to the allure of centralized planning and alternatives to Western capitalism that circulated among young progressives in the 1960s and 1970s. Reading Roy Medvedev's *Let History Judge* in 1971 made me understand, in excruciatingly bloody detail, the human costs of anti-liberalism—no matter the ideological wellsprings.

I'm still skeptical about government. At the outset of my nonprofit career, I misread the policy underpinnings of the *New Deal* and *Great Society* because of the bureaucracy and abuse I saw at ground level, even though the federal government had created a safety net that lifted many out of poverty and broadened citizen rights. I came of age at a time of the accelerating collapse of these policy frameworks and couldn't reconcile Hubert Humphrey, the advocate of the full employment legislation and civil rights, with Hubert Humphrey, the Vietnam War hawk.

Yet I served in the municipal administration of an outstanding urban reformer, Mayor Harold Washington, in the 1980s. We had some stirring successes, but I also saw first-hand the intransigence of bureaucracy, the power of economic elites to shape governance and political discourse, the navel-gazing and self-protection of those in power, and the limitations of local governments for reshaping economic environments. On the other hand, I participated in a number of initiatives in which government reformers worked with outside advocates to create better outcomes for all Chicagoans.

I have always preferred the independent sector of civic and nonprofit organizations. But I've come to realize that building this sector is not sufficient; we need responsive public policies and institutions that support families and neighborhoods. In the post-1989 era of rebuilding former Communist bloc countries and in the face of fragile and disintegrating states around the world, I better appreciate the building blocks and stability of the liberal state's protected rights and freedoms. But having stable liberal states imposes costs: governmental institutions sometimes make things worse and become vehicles for narrow interests. In the words of Garry Wills, government is a "necessary evil."

The value question about community arose as I faced the question about why I cared about community building for poor people but not for myself. Middle-class communities held little interest for me as an arena for civic participation and advancing social justice; they take care of themselves most of the time without my help. Wasn't this a contradiction?

Some community developers feel betrayed when community residents pick up stakes and move to another neighborhood to buy a home or enroll their kids in better schools. This is copping out of community commitment in the eyes of dedicated advocates. Meanwhile, community developers pick neighborhoods based upon the usual criteria: safety, amenities, and convenience, and prefer living among agglomerations of like-minded, middle-class professionals. A similar condemnation is sometimes made of school voucher programs and charter schools, as if doing the best thing possible for your kids could reasonably be construed as betrayal.

I lived in a ramshackle Pilsen storefront within a stone's throw of the elevated Dan Ryan Expressway, and then in the basement apartment of a brick tenement in a state of perpetual renovation. Being on call 24/7 was a part of the neighborhood immersion experience—hearing gunfire, walking the streets, and experiencing vicarious dislocation. I depended upon the limited services available within a couple of blocks—food stores, restaurants, and laundromats. After being shot at one day, I decided to leave, like many people who wanted a safer neighborhood.

Over the years I've favored urban density, diversity, and dynamism in the places I've called home. I like to nod hello to my neighbors and know they are informally keeping an eye on things happening on the streets and after hours. But, aside from raising children, I don't spend my limited free time community building in my own neighborhood. I'm happy to be a follower.

My Big Values

The possibility of improving overall social equity attracted me to the CED field in the first place and has kept me engaged over the years. Four additional values have shaped my work and career and still cause me to rethink assumptions, beliefs, and behaviors: race, democratic participation, ideas, and skepticism. Other values—efficiency, results, and artistry—have also been important guideposts.

Race matters. Race mattered, in the words of Cornel West, on the first day of my experience as a student in a largely immigrant, Latino community in Pilsen, and race continues to matter today as I work as a social investor in communities of color. Confronting race is complicated. There is a temptation for community developers to say, "I'm culturally sensitive; I've been on the picket line—now I want to build housing." Other advocates have so completely adopted the paradigm of institutional racism that they cease to lend critical eyes and ears to community struggles.

Race, ethnicity, gender, and power are deep-seated, permeate most institutions, and shape our fundamental ways of thinking and acting. Continuing racial disparities in education and economic well-being are important indicators of how much further we still have to travel as a nation, but these indicators fail to capture fully the lived experience of sustained powerlessness and discrimination.

The late Robert Mier, my professor and public sector boss, concluded that race shaped all local economic development decisions and investments. Race influenced what business deals received public and private financing, where the firms located, and who got the jobs. Race influenced business leaders to fight for control of Chicago's Economic Development Commission after Harold Washington, Chicago's first African American mayor, threatened to merge the offices of economic and workforce development. Race influenced who got city jobs and city contracts.

Mier challenged all his colleagues about race in more fundamental ways that were highly personal in nature. He handed each of us a copy of Thomas Cochran's *Black and White Styles in Conflict,* and asked us to invest in understanding how race, ethnicity, gender, and power became embedded in the very ways we interacted within city government and with community constituencies.

Consciousness about race, ethnicity, gender, and power requires a lifetime commitment. In the 1983 inaugural words of Mayor Harold Washington, "We are at the crossroads of America ... In our ethnic and racial diversity we are all brothers and sisters in a quest for greatness ..." Achieving this goal requires knocking down barriers but also finding each other. Kwame Anthony Appiah, in *Cosmopolitanism: Ethics in a World of Strangers,* concludes:

> Once we have found enough we share, there is the further possibility that we will be able to enjoy discovering things we do not yet share. [W]e can simply be intrigued by alternative ways of thinking, feeling, and acting.

Sometimes in light of the present, we lose hope that we can make real progress in achieving racial equity and understanding. In those moments of doubt, I try to remember the long haul and the children, families, and neighborhoods I care about.

Democratic participation matters. Citizen engagement is essential for successful projects and social change. "The people" should make the key decisions about important things that affect their lives and well-being, whether in their workplaces or where they live. Democratic participation is easier extolled than practiced by community developers: there's lots of rhetoric, plenty of pitfalls, and too few good examples.

There is a tendency to equate democratic participation with place—neighborhoods, cities, and the nation. Douglas Smith, in *Value and Values*, declares that the real terrain for community building lies within formal and informal organizations. This provocative thesis forces us to confront where we spend most of our time and where we debate big and small things of consequence to ourselves and our families. In the end, as most provocative arguments, Smith's idea overreaches, but it does support the notion that we should appreciate democracy in all aspects of life.

In my experience, community residents play multiple roles. Families, first of all, advocate for the health and welfare of themselves and their children in a variety of settings—in the workplace, the neighborhood, and the schools. The associational life of citizens and communities is the lifeblood of civil society and politics. Community associations set priorities about broader social investment and policy advocacy—jobs, safety, good schools, or affordable housing. Moreover, community leaders articulate the values, competencies, and behaviors for good, family-supporting service delivery based upon their experiences. That is, how should local nonprofit organizations and government agencies become more *family friendly*? In a larger sense, communities hold institutions accountable for making progress and achieving results that everyone has agreed to pursue. Finally, community aggregates power and influence that can make institutions behave differently in how they support or impede community building. Most institutions do not budge from their old ways of doing business without receiving regular doses of pressure.

These are the basics of local democracy. But too often I've seen democratic guidance confused with citizens doing everything. For example, communities don't have to be the implementers or operators of social programs or members of the governance boards of all implementing organizations. Nor do community roles necessarily cancel out the important, top-down roles of public, private, and nonprofit actors. In fact, when community participation is viewed as the only authentic approach, community building frequently goes nowhere.

Community participation is challenging if one is, like me, an advocacy planner, community organizer, or community developer for low- and moderate-income neighborhoods. All of these roles bring various mixes of technical knowledge, time, and social and political networks. Many advocates have been sent packing because they couldn't figure out how to be accountable in the communities they were trying to help. Unfortunately, many committed experts have also been sent packing because they irritated local gatekeepers for community participation. The best advice is to get a good sense of the community's values right up front before you take on the assignment.

Ideas matter. Ideas combat the notion that the way things are is the way things have to be. Ideas reveal what public choices and constraints can be changed and how CED strategies can be invented. Being a source of good ideas for advocacy, design, and community education is one of the key roles I've played as a CED practitioner.

My favorite ideas help me understand the world and identify opportunities for action. Distinguishing *routine* and *non-routine* decisions, for example, identifies problems that require innovation. Non-routine problems are characterized by *uncertainty* about cause/effect relationships and of value consensus. Some have called these *wicked* or *messy* problems. *Collective action* ideas identify the cognitive, economic, and institutional barriers, incentives, and preconditions for individuals and organizations to act together, an especially important bundle of ideas for partnership building. I have a soft spot for Herbert Simon's notion that we *satisfice* rather than struggling endlessly for optimal solutions. As one of my professors said, "We have small brains and big problems."

Other ideas describe patterns of behavior. The *garbage can* theory suggests that we have a can full of solutions in search of problems, a common pitfall in the world of CED. That is, we have the answers and will apply them willy-nilly whenever we can. The notion that *small steps* can lead to big changes, drawn from chaos theory, forces us to be more mindful of the steps we do take. After all, we may be on the path to a *tipping point,* although I've found that many of my small steps don't get me very far. *Continuous improvement* suggests that our practice can get better over time if we learn by doing, if only learning were as rewarding as we make it out to be. In broader terms, *democratic experimentalism* is one way of understanding the fundamental strengths of our liberal democracy and the nature of policy development.

An amalgam of ideas is what we call a mental model, a representation of how something works or doesn't work. We use models for all sorts of things, including testing hypotheses, prototyping strategies, analyzing patterns and behaviors, and predicting future outcomes. Understanding mental models helps us overcome a "learning dilemma" identified by Peter Senge in *The Fifth Discipline* that "we learn best from experience but we never directly experience the consequences of many of our most important decisions." Organizations, budgets, strategies, and programs all rely upon, and express, models of the world and how various actors behave. Sometimes they are right. Sometimes they are wrong. The great thing about models and ideas more generally is that they can be improved upon.

Bruce Katz's notion of *idea virus* captures the power of those practical, breakthrough ideas that spread through relationships and networks via a contagion effect.[8] Idea viruses tend to be discrete ideas like displaying artistic cows around the city, like in Chicago, starting tax credit campaigns for low-income families, or thinking about community assets rather than deficits. These ideas have traveling power because they are simple and powerful and connect to plausible action, such as advocacy campaigns to reduce the *high costs of being poor*.

Because ideas matter, it's important to cultivate one's idea fluency. Reading, listening, observing, and communicating are my tricks of the trade. Reading remains our most important repository of thinking and ideas. Reading widely, and asking what others are reading, guarantees that we will encounter surprises as we get outside of our own comfortable niches. That's why many of us scan the office bookshelves of colleagues or take careful note of what others are reading on trains and planes.

Writing, teaching, power-pointing, speechifying, or storytelling forces us to synthesize, get to the point, and communicate in a way that others can understand. Acts of simplifying often produce powerful ideas that have been hiding amid complicated jargon and background noise.

Last, but not least, *skepticism matters*. The challenge is how to tell the truth and ask tough questions while building organizations, addressing human needs, and advancing social justice. To adapt a common adage, how can one be skeptical about the present and optimistic about the future? This notion recalls my father's dilemma of reconciling faith and debugging mega computer systems. Whether one is a full-fledged skeptic, critic, iconoclast, curmudgeon, or not, CED practitioners are called upon to provide the *inside scoop* about what really works or doesn't work no matter the hype.

A predictable organizational soap opera pits the "believer" against the "skeptic." "Believers" (or lieutenants) have fully adopted the organizational mission, bond with the words of top leadership, and energetically carry out every assignment that comes their way, seemingly without thought. It seems as if their psyches have merged with the organizational gods. The skeptic sees through organizational puffery at every step of the way and always fingers the faulty assumptions and contradictory behaviors, lack of expertise, and disadvantageous

---

8. Bruce Katz is Director of the Center for Metropolitan Policy at The Brookings Institution.

environmental conditions. What usually happens is that the believer is embraced by the organization and the skeptic is cast out of the inner circle, brought back, if he or she is lucky, for special occasions of truth telling.

Healthy organizations need both believers and skeptics. But many organizations are unable to cultivate a culture that supports both commitment and skepticism. In the words of philosopher Bertrand Russell, "[P]eople hate skeptics far more than they hate the passionate advocates of opinions hostile to their own." Too often I have been labeled a cynic—even when my behavior was that of a skeptic—questioning common assumptions and beliefs or acting like a smartass. In fact, one strategy of believers is to label skeptics as cynics—transforming them into organizational obstacles afraid to join the believers on the train of progress. These stereotypes represent two important sides of organizational brains and personalities. Organizations need visions that motivate them to act with ambition to accomplish great and unexpected outcomes. At the same time, high-performing organizations need critical thinking, adaptive learning, the ability to learn from mistakes, and, yes, whistle-blowing in certain situations.

Losing the ability to be surprised, failing to recognize that things change, falling into cynicism, or being unwilling to recognize contradictions are some of the most common pitfalls for the professional skeptic. Novelist Ward Just, in *The Translator*, reminds us of "[T]he misanthrope's iron law: history never repeats itself except perversely." Yet, too many times I've observed that projects, organizations, ideas, and approaches that I've dismissed for good reasons in the past gain new life and possibility. If I just project past concerns and doubts into the future as a good skeptic, I may miss the boat. This is not to say that there is not a continuity of bad ideas; there is, but not always.

Have I ever had to manage a skeptic? It's surprising how few skeptics I've hired over the years, maybe because I'm one, and one is more than enough. I've certainly had to manage a few cynics. The best antidote for cynics is to surround them with hopeful people who are making real progress.

Sticking with Values

Values have mattered in big and small ways for my career and for the nonprofit sector. How do we keep motivated as we change jobs, have a family, or move closer to retirement? What are the values that keep us going for the "long haul"?

Some of the folks who seem to have the easiest time staying the course are motivated by religious beliefs and affiliations. Their faith is a renewable resource that nourishes their commitment to social justice year in and year out. But this kind of faith doesn't work for me. In the words of philosopher Isaiah Berlin, I am "tone deaf" to the metaphysical aspects of religion.

Staying the course is a challenge for community developers. Upward mobility moves one from the front lines and neighborhoods to foundations, the public and private sectors, intermediary organizations, or to consulting. This mobility has occurred in the context of increased professionalizing in the community development sector, which has led CDCs to more proficiency in housing finance and fewer grassroots connections. Although there shouldn't be a trade-off, moving out of front-line organizations only exacerbates the upward mobility problem. Values shift from social justice to a narrow focus on housing or jobs production numbers and dollars leveraged.

Another challenge is the cumulative impact of tough neighborhoods, non-supportive public policies, worsening social and economic trends, and the complexity of problems and solutions on the morale of community developers and advocates. The erosion of hope and optimism over time undermines our ability to promote change. Each community developer needs to find a wellspring of hope and modesty to serve as countervailing forces against seemingly marginal progress and against the common pitfall of conflating personal achievement with societal gain.

As I ponder a perplexing and sobering future, I am not as clear as I once was about what social forces and allies I should align myself with. Partisan politics sometimes seems like a game of marginal gains and losses. Yet some differences really matter—like war, safety nets, and civil rights! I find myself increasingly aligned with a rather inchoate group of non-aligned independents, most of whom work at the local and state levels. The civic, independent sector continues to offer this avenue of engagement as it has made real progress over the past decades.

For me, the wellspring that renews my sense of hope, optimism, and commitment is a focus on "kids." This wellspring became clearer to me when I began to have children and a family. When I joined the staff of a national children's foundation, I realized that creating better outcomes for kids was a compelling and concrete vision of social justice that never lost its imperative and urgency for me, even when I was confronted by bad public policy and heightening economic insecurity. It related to my own life and never ceased to create an emotional commitment when I saw kids with so much potential experiencing deprivation. Values matter when entering the nonprofit, civic world; values are equally important for keeping one on track for the long haul.

Keep values in the forefront:

- Do a regular check-in with yourself about what values matter in work and life. Examine your behaviors, decisions, and non-decisions for the implicit values that they represent.
- Nonprofit organizations should commit to a "values audit" that not only revisits the mission statement, but also examines the degree to which espoused values have been put into action.
- Even in small nonprofit organizations, "value conflicts" are likely to occur in which *right* is posed against *right*. Make sure that there is the personal and organizational space to acknowledge these difficult situations.
- Renewing values should be a regular feature of individual growth and organizational sustainability. This is a matter of refinement and evolving points of view rather than trading in old values for new values.

4

Investing Yourself: The Risks and Rewards

○ ○

Fill your bowl to the brim and it will spill.

—Lao Tzu

I learned white water canoeing on the Delaware River in the 1960s. The river had some natural rapids, but most of the white water was created by the shifting rocks of the lamprey eel dams that dotted the river. These nineteenth-century dams were built to catch adult-age eels making their way downstream to spawn in salt water. The dams consisted of V-shaped funnels through which the yard-long eels swam and were caught in baskets—a technology that a century ago harvested tens of thousands of eels a year. Each year the rocks of these eel weirs shifted and created new formations that frustrated canoeists, closing old chutes and opening new ones. Canoe teams had to quickly analyze water movement and spot dangerous rocks to make it through unscathed.

Over the years I also canoed in Wisconsin and Michigan rivers, which continued to present strategic questions about risks and rewards. When faced with a set of rapids, each canoe team had to decide whether to portage and walk around the danger carrying the canoe, empty their canoe of camping gear, and shoot the rapids or go for it and risk a catastrophic loss or soaking of clothes, sleeping bags, and food.

We were often overly aggressive and ended up spilling canoes, losing gear, bending canoes, and being momentarily trapped by raging rapids pushing us hard against rocks. Sometimes, our decisions were simply foolhardy, based on our youthful belief that we could get away with anything. But each time through the rapids, we also learned a lot about reading the river, working together in risky situations, recovering from disasters, and, of course, having fun.

This chapter recounts my immersion experience in three CED jobs. Like river canoeing, I learned about CED by doing it—diagnosing neighborhoods and organizations, navigating political differences, and understanding when to take risks and when to play it safe. That has been critical know-how gained as I paddled through these jobs.

Ponder the following questions as you read about my personal investments:

- Have you made unusual personal investments in jobs?
- Is the risk-taking and learning from these personal investments worth the costs?
- Are there better ways to learn the lessons?
- Do organizations gain or lose from these personal investments in the long run?

Neighborhood Immersion

Three stories from my nonprofit career illustrate the challenges of balancing personal investment, career advancement, and organizational development.

The Eighteenth Street Development Corporation (ESDC) in Pilsen was a start-up organization in the mid-1970s taking the fledgling Pilsen Rehab Project and transforming it into a separate community development corporation—a CDC. The ESDC grew out of the efforts of a local community-organizing group, Pilsen Neighbors Community Council; it rehabilitated abandoned buildings by working with former gang members, providing them jobs and training. ESDC also served as a vehicle for implementing the *Pilsen Neighborhood Plan,* a community plan developed in opposition to a big downtown plan—the *Chicago 21 Plan*—that threatened to redevelop Pilsen as a middle- and upper-income community.

I stayed with ESDC until 1980, becoming the *de facto* executive director only months after starting the job. ESDC grew from four staff to more than fifteen in just a few years, training up to forty to fifty young people a year in construction skills, and taking on development projects that ranged from housing rehabilitation to model blocks, homeownership counseling, solar-reliant greenhouses, and community organizing. ESDC rehabilitated abandoned, multi-family buildings during my tenure, providing low-cost, large rental units for families. We became the premier construction training program in Chicago by working with three building trades unions to secure apprenticeships for young men and women. Dramatic programmatic and organizational growth stretched staff skills, experience, time, cash flow and financial management resources, governance oversight, and effective project management. We constructed a hybrid form of community, tenant, and worker control that was a model of 1960s hopefulness about participatory democracy, but proved much harder to implement in reality.

The personal investment I made in ESDC had three parts. I started as a Comprehensive Employment and Training Act Public Service employee at $7,800 a year, and by the time I left in 1980, I was making $11,000, paid for from public and private funds, as the executive director. We created a salary structure that can only be understood, if at all, by looking through the lens of the 1970s, administrative personnel, including me, were all paid about the same amount, while the carpenters who ran the training programs were paid prevailing wages. We reversed the typical organizational wage structure for a few years, managers making less than workers.

My work at ESDC was a total life commitment. I had an insatiable appetite for work that I had never experienced before in my life, whether in school or in the variety of part- and full-time jobs that I had held. The new feeling and commitment grew out of a combination of being in charge, doing something I thought was important, having interesting work that challenged me, and being blessed with youthful energy. This new feeling about work was physical. I bought abandoned buildings and fixed them up with the help of architects and contractors as I managed staff and boards, fundraising, and program development. A fledgling love relationship with a fellow planning student paled in comparison to the allure of committed work. I was addicted. Commitment meant long hours that extended into weekends, vacations, and evenings meeting with other young people playing roles similar to mine in other Chicago neighborhoods. And then home to my digs in the neighborhood. It was an immersion experience.

Working conditions were unusual. Our first office was in the first floor apartment of a building that we had fixed up. Lingering problems persisted, like clogged sewer lines that resulted in a slight but pervasive sewer smell in our office as we put on our best for visiting funders. But that space wasn't the most daunting. We soon moved to the second floor of a building under renovation. Without heating during a frigid Chicago winter, we stuffed a potbelly stove with old wooden lathes from the ongoing demolition to keep ourselves warm. I typed with gloves covering my fingers. Luckily, most of us lived only a few blocks away, so we ran home to use the bathrooms and warm up.

A final part of my personal investment in ESDC was about risk and annoyance. The annoyance side of things involved low salaries, high commitments, and living in semi-horrific apartments. I adopted a version of Bohemian poverty as canonized by Michael Harrington in *The Other America*.

The risk side of my work life at ESDC involved safely navigating neighborhood violence. I don't mean to overemphasize the violence in Pilsen, nor that I was heroic by working in its midst. It was just the way things were. On my first day of work, I recall looking down 17th Street and seeing a young man firing a silver pistol. I ran for cover. Young men in our training programs were former or not-so-former gang members, some with drug and alcohol problems, most with authority problems. These guys erupted from time to time, and sometimes their outbursts were aimed at me or those around me.

The most frightening experience for me was when the soon-to-be ex-husband of our administrative assistant, who happened to live in the apartment above me, threatened to set fire to our office building. ESDC was her source of financial independence from him, and thus the enemy. One summer night, sitting on our brick front porch, his car screeched to a halt in front of our house, and he rushed in to renew his battle with his estranged wife. On his way out he attacked me. I pressed charges against this former gang member for my scratches and bruises, not so much because of what he did to me, but as a measure to keep him from doing something worse to his family. After many months, the court case was thrown out by a judge who concluded that a big guy like me had to be part of the problem. For weeks and months, as the trial dates were postponed, the ex-husband stalked me in his white van, watching and tracking my moves in the neighborhood. Things finally reached a breaking point for me when one morning I awoke to find a bullet hole in my front window and a slug buried in my bedroom wall only a few feet from my pillow on the bed. The good news was that all this prolonged attention led him to leave his wife alone and eventually to leave the neighborhood. The bad news was that I had to escape Pilsen for safer quarters.

The ESDC story raises the vexing problem of nonprofit leadership transition and succession. I burned out on ESDC after five years, the precipitating reason being a tough personnel decision about a carpenter trainer who was not pulling her weight. When my board second-guessed the decision, my emotions snapped, and I quit, refusing to reconsider my rather precipitous decision. I had still not learned one of the fundamental lessons of emotional intelligence and self-management—cooling down for a few days before making momentous, life-changing decisions.

The late Tom Gaudette, the legendary community organizer close to Saul Alinsky, once told me that leaving a community job was like ending a love affair. What a rude awakening after that intense immersion experience. It was like going cold turkey. I was young and eventually got over it. Unfortunately, I'm not sure ESDC did. Despite having a competent and active board, ESDC made a series of bad decisions about directors that led to the decline of the organization or, more charitably, to its failure to build upon early successes. But it made a few comebacks along the way, and maybe will again.

Maybe the decline of ESDC in the 1980s was inevitable, given its underlying business model. Most of its funding derived from training young people through fixing up buildings; this became increasingly difficult with new employment and training legislation in the 1980s and diminishing community development funds. Whatever the contributing weight of these other factors, the way I left ESDC did not balance what was good for me and what was good for the community.

Back in the Neighborhood

The second story takes place in Baltimore. South East Community Organization (SECO) and Southeast Development Inc. (SDI) served the ninety thousand residents of largely white ethnic southeast Baltimore. Started in 1971, after a prolonged and ultimately successful campaign to stop a highway from destroying the neighborhood and the waterfront, SECO/SDI represented the second generation of CDCs started in the 1970s and was a leader in the rediscovery of white ethnic, working-class neighborhoods. Luminaries such as Senator Barbara Mikulski were among its early leaders. SECO/SDI ended up as a national model for ethnic-based neighborhood revitalization.

When I became executive director of SECO/SDI in 1988, however, the days of big organizing and development victories were a decade or more old. The SECO and SDI boards were fighting; SECO/SDI had run up a financial deficit; the community perceived SECO as the harbinger of progressive ideas in a socially conservative community; and SDI had become a colonial developer in the largely African American neighborhood to the north.

So why would I take such a job? To be honest, I needed to make some money, and there weren't a lot of alternatives in Baltimore. I had quit my job with the City of Chicago after two plus years of commuting to Baltimore to preserve a young marriage. Taking the job with SECO/SDI meant a large cut in pay after my job with the City of Chicago and considerably fewer resources and prestige.

Yet my eight months of community development volunteering in Baltimore had reawakened my community values and interests.

I spent five and one-half years at SECO/SDI. I'm proud of the work I was a part of at SECO/SDI. But I do not have the indelible memories of learning about work, community development, and neighborhoods. Maybe that happens only once in a work life.

I made four unusual personal investments in SECO/SDI. Again, I took a risk on salary and benefits. In the case of SECO/SDI, however, this was a case of downward mobility in a big way from my previous job as deputy commissioner in the Department of Economic Development in the City of Chicago. If things weren't complicated enough, I reduced my salary out of obligation and strategy as I occasionally took consulting jobs or taught a course or two at local universities. The saved salary helped to get the books in balance and to invest in new projects. Unfortunately, this approach eventually got me into trouble with the IRS.

Taking a lower-level job in a new city required me to eat humble pie as I struggled to turn around SECO/SDI. On the one hand, my pride was an obstacle: how did I get beyond *been there, done that* when I walked into work everyday? On the other hand, my previous job was highly resourced even though a local government, in terms of quality and quantity of staff, the existence and stability of financial resources, and the agenda-setting capacity of local government.

Another painful aspect of this downward mobility and re-entry into CED was that many folks perceived me as representing the interests and politics of white ethnics, as opposed to African Americans and Latinos. The pain was acute because I got into the civic, nonprofit field to advance civil rights, not to protect insular, narrow-minded communities. All of this was quite paradoxical because SECO/SDI served more African Americans and Latinos than whites and because the traditional white ethnic community rejected SECO/SDI, since they worked with people of color and promoted progressive ideas. Maybe we were doing something right.

I had learned my lesson with ESDC and Pilsen, so I lived in a different part of town from southeast Baltimore. I commuted back and forth each day by car; thus, from the outset of the job, I kept a certain social and physical distance between myself and work. This gave me personal space, shielded me from after-hours neighborhood craziness, but also kept me from really getting into the rhythm and dynamics of the neighborhood.

The day-to-day working conditions at SECO/SDI, however, were not much better than in Pilsen. We occupied an old Catholic boys' school that was built in the late nineteenth century and over the years acquired numerous stairways and oddly shaped building additions. Not many improvements had been made over the years, except for dropped ceilings, a few window air conditioners, a single new bathroom for the entire building, plywood cubicles, and the installation of fluorescent lights. I found myself running up and down the three flights of stairs to use the decrepit boys' room in the dank basement, being called in the middle of the night by the security company to come, armed with a baseball bat, to check out whether the building had been broken into, and overseeing a piecemeal renovation process that never got up a head of steam.

The other aspect of these challenges with working conditions had to do with existing staff and the lack of resources to hire additional staff. Initially, I had to cut back on staff to get the budget in line. But even then, I had a staff of good people who had not been managed. By managed I don't mean keeping track of people or encouraging more compliance behavior; the management I'm talking about involved challenging staff to think about their areas of work and their own professional development in a creative and open-ended way.

For at least a decade, SECO had managed a youth diversion program—providing enriched, community-based alternative programs for young people who had minor tangles with the law. Unfortunately, the staff person who had designed the program was long gone; the current director had started a few years before as a case worker and youth advocate. When I asked her why youth diversion was a good thing and what the evaluation literature had to say about it, the response I received was prickly irritation and non-comprehension of the question. Quite frequently youth diversion staff argued that the state didn't allow them to change or innovate. A few years later SECO lost its youth diversion program as the state came up with a new approach of intensive *tough love* that showed more promise than youth diversion. Everyone in the program was laid off.

A similar problem occurred for SDI's housing programs. We had a staff person who excelled at assembling packages of five abandoned buildings, construction and permanent financing, contractors, and ultimately homeowners. When asked about our community development strategy or other potential development roles or projects for SDI, there was anxiety, deflection, and non-comprehension. In both of these cases, good programs became complacent, and there was a mismatch between staff skills and the constant need for reinvention.

Working at SECO/SDI also involved risk-taking, not in the sense of navigating community violence, but in terms of taking chances on unpopular policies and politics. I walked a fine line in balancing political risks with maintaining buy-in from my board members—particularly a small, influential group tied to the traditional, white ethnic political clubs of southeast Baltimore. Taking risks, in the long run, encouraged this clique of board members to usurp control of SECO/SDI after I departed, one of the ingredients in SECO/SDI's ultimate demise.

Originally known as "Cannery Row," the working waterfront of southeast Baltimore was renamed the Gold Coast in the 1980s as condos and upscale commercial developments replaced packing, printing, and can-making enterprises and buildings. This investment threatened the entire community in the eyes of historic preservationists and working-family advocates because it drove up taxes, a particular burden for older homeowners, made new housing less affordable, and blocked scenic "view corridors" that connected Baltimore's hills and the waterfront.

I helped instigate the formation of a small working group of organizations and leaders, called the Southeast Linkage Group. We developed an innovative study of the increase in property tax assessments in relation to proximity to the waterfront and crafted a piece of enabling legislation, called *Impact Zones*. The legislation called for establishing geographic zones in which development threatened surrounding communities; real estate developers would be required to contribute to an Impact Zone Fund to mitigate these problems by, for example, investing in affordable housing. The study and proposed City Council bill received some initial hoopla, but ultimately lost by a landslide. The president of the City Council did agree to co-sponsor community planning in southeast Baltimore that would explicitly take account of development pressures, including those pressures related to specific industrial re-use sites along the waterfront. No legislation resulted, but the community produced the *Southeast Community Plan* in 1993, which, in turn, leveraged millions of dollars in resources and became a model for other community-planning efforts in Baltimore.

These waterfront development fights led to a neighborhood, populist challenge against two City Council members who represented the southeast district. Both were old timers, tied to political clubs, waterfront developers, and patronage politics. I joined the kitchen cabinet of a flamboyant neighborhood activist, the former editor of the neighborhood newspaper, who was a key leader in the Waterfront Coalition, a loose gathering of southeast groups opposed to unplanned waterfront development. He gathered around him a curious blend of progressives, neighborhood advocates, preservationists, small businesses, and long-term residents of southeast Baltimore.

I certainly liked the guy and his grassroots campaign, but other things were at work in my life that got me involved. I was going through separation and divorce while having a young daughter and needed to reconnect with myself and the world. A grassroots political campaign was great therapeutic medicine; I spent months walking the streets of waterfront neighborhoods, knocking on doors, getting other folks involved, and organizing Election Day poll watching. SECO even got into the action in the campaign by holding nonpartisan candidate forums that gave visibility to opposition candidates as the incumbents stayed away.

We won both seats and defeated the machine. Unfortunately, some of my board members were a part of the defeated political clubs, and they were not happy. SECO/SDI was turning around, getting traction with its projects and investments, and its staff was making a difference. And thus we became, consciously or unconsciously, a target for control and containment.

My last year at SECO/SDI was challenging as I began to look for other opportunities, started a new relationship, and, in several instances, took my eyes off the "management" ball.

When I left in 1993, SECO and SDI were in pretty good shape. They had active boards, new programs that were getting neighborhood and citywide attention, finances in balance, and new investors. Looking back from the vantage of several years, these assets were not sufficient for SECO/SDI to stay the course. A protracted search for a new director and two disastrous executive choices over eight years sapped organizational morale and resources. SECO and SDI have now formally separated and are negotiating over alimony and assets, including a shrinking endowment. Good programs and projects still exist and produce results, but much of the organizational momentum rebuilt by the early 1990s has disappeared.

Three reasons for SECO/SDI's decline are relevant for understanding the connection between personal investment and nonprofit sustainability. I was fond of saying at the time that executive directors should not pick their successors. It was dangerous for someone so close to the action to micromanage an organization's legacy. But my hands-off approach was equally problematic because I assumed the boards knew more than they did about what made SECO and SDI tick. These were good aspirations on my part, but SECO/SDI needed help. I didn't offer much help and, because of this, was not a good steward of the organization's assets or of my own personal investment over the years.

To make matters worse, several board members had an axe to grind about the politics and success of SECO/SDI and wanted to control the organization. I realize now that I underinvested in board and staff education and development. We developed a fairly innovative role for the new SECO/SDI that required keeping expenses low and not falling into the trap of wanting to control all the moving parts as we built issue coalitions and partnerships. Both of these elements, I realize now, were countercultural for most of the staff and board. I should have done more to prepare the organization for transition.

Finally, and perhaps most importantly, SECO/SDI's business model was unsustainable. Surprisingly, I've reached this conclusion only in the last few years as I've watched SECO/SDI stumble in its recruiting and support of executive talent. In the past, I argued vigorously for keeping this complicated organizational stew of community organizing, human services, and community development together. The synergies among these parts generated new opportunities for innovation, integration, and collaboration. Nevertheless, I've come to realize that if an organization can only recruit two directors in thirty years who can make the stew, then something is wrong with the model and recipe.

Taking a Chance on Government

My third story about personal investment takes place back in Chicago, in between the Pilsen and southeast Baltimore sagas. I worked for close to four years in the R&D Division of the city's Department of Economic Development, heading up the division during my last two and one-half years.

Personal investment in this job had three dimensions that contrast with my other personal investments in CED. My return to Chicago occurred a few days after I completed my doctoral exams and a few months after Harold Washington became Chicago's first African American mayor. Washington promised to bring in new voices and constituencies, open up government information and resources, and pursue policies guided by a new and more expansive sense of fairness. His charisma was a function of his intelligence, his history of dissent and resistance from the Machine, personal warmth, a commitment to multi-racial, multi-class coalitions for social change, and a sense of the big picture.

For someone coming of age under the "Boss" (i.e., Mayor Richard J. Daley) and Chicago's political machine, the job offer was irresistible. Many of my friends had joined the Washington campaign and were now part of municipal government, and the CED ideas we nurtured in the 1970s seemed to be getting a foothold in government. In short, the Washington era was the culmination of my immersion experience in Chicago. But this didn't mean that I should join the movement blindfolded; community-organizing friends warned me of the pitfalls of serving in local government.

There were two tough questions. First, my wife taught at Cornell University and was devoted to the academic life. We negotiated a package of commuting and a leave for her, made easier because she hailed from Chicago. The second question involved my doctoral studies; I was going off to take an applied research job when I had been on the track for academic teaching and research.

My original intention was to stay for two years and then move on, completing my dissertation and getting on with my life. A number of factors conspired to keep me in Chicago for two more years, delaying my dissertation, and producing another round of family commuting to Baltimore. I was offered a job—Deputy Commissioner of R&D—that I just couldn't turn down. Needless to say, the perks of the jobs were counterbalanced by a lonely home life, tiresome commuting, and, ultimately, a failed marriage. Yet, as I've come to appreciate even more as years go by, working for a mayor like Harold Washington was a once-in-a-lifetime opportunity and experience.

Joining the municipal administration of Harold Washington was a partisan, political affair, and thus full of personal and professional risks. Chicago remains the kind of town that punishes political opponents, especially those opponents who happen to land government jobs. In the last fifty years, Harold Washington stands out as an independent-minded mayor who put his equity ideas and beliefs into action. In this context, it is no surprise that most Washington appointees were summarily fired after the caretaker administration of Eugene Sawyer was defeated in 1989. I left city government three months before the tragic and unexpected death of Harold Washington in November 1987, four months after his re-election to a second term. Although time heals many wounds and forgetfulness can be a blessing, my tour of duty with Harold Washington has marked me as an independent partisan.

Partisanship was not simply a matter of abstract ideas and political positions. Partisanship reared its ugly head every day in relation to staff management, project design, City Council oversight, and, within a year, the relentless re-election effort. Staff loyal to the Machine, or their aldermanic protectors, undermined projects in a myriad of ways, regularly reported information about what the department was doing and filed civil service suit after suit to protect their jobs, patronage perks, and benefits. Our office was swept for electronic bugs on a regular basis during the first days, months, and year of the new administration. At the same time, we were partisan as well—I organized the downtown precincts for Washington's re-election in 1987.

One of the riskiest and most exhilarating aspects of working for Harold Washington was learning how to play the inside/outside game; what I have called joint problem-solving. We had to figure out how to get the best out of both the grassroots, electoral coalition that elected Harold Washington and the evolving governing coalition that brought new partners, constraints, and pressures into policy-making.

The key feature of the inside/outside game or joint problem-solving is deploying simultaneously the strengths of mainstream institutions like government or business and grassroots and neighborhood constituencies. Community advocates are good at taking on unpopular issues, mobilizing constituencies, and offering unconventional solutions and alternatives. Their weakness is that this process takes time, they frequently don't have the power to make changes, and they have a fragile resource base. It's difficult and expensive to break through the wall of complacency. Mainstream institutions, in contrast, are able to establish public agendas, have multiple resources at hand, and can mobilize opinion and investment on a larger scale. Their weakness, on the other hand, is that they are gun-shy and reluctant to act with dispatch, are frequently constrained unduly by members of their governing coalition, and are fragmented and unable to focus.

Two examples of joint problem-solving give a sense of what can be achieved, as well as the risks. In 1985, we worked with community and labor advocates to oppose the plant closing of the Playskool toy company, a company that had received low-interest, tax-exempt loans to expand and create jobs. They did the opposite, laying off workers and ultimately moving the company to Massachusetts. Sustained community organizing, coordinated with inside advocacy, led to the city's filing suit against the company and, in the end, negotiating for a better benefit and facility re-use package. Likewise, in the late 1980s, the city worked with business and neighborhood industrial councils to protect viable industrial properties from upscale real estate developers of housing and commercial development. Many in the development community, including city officials, believed that manufacturing was dead and that what developers wanted should drive the zoning process, no matter the costs and benefits.

The inside/outside game depends upon *boundary spanning* people in community and mainstream institutions who recognize each other's strengths and how to get their organizations to work together without giving up the game. This is the role I played in the above examples and in many others during this period. This was risky business, and lots of folks got burned as they found out that they were "flying without a net." What allowed me to play this role and survive was a set of ideas and goals, endorsed by the mayor, that permeated city government with our economic development strategy of fairness; a commissioner who was a mentor and gave me some free rein; and community partners who were a part of the Harold Washington coalition. But each time I played the inside/outside game, I knew it was a high-stakes game of risk and reward.

Government reform is always limited by the short-term nature of political administrations and the change of focus that inevitably comes with newly elected officials. It has an inherent sustainability problem. Without a run of at least eight years, it's fairly difficult to get long-term traction for reforms that are not institutionalized through legislation or court order. With only four years to generate innovation, cultivate a new operating culture of municipal government, and institutionalize reform, the administration of Harold Washington was unable to sustain many of its key initiatives. While local government was never the same after Harold Washington, the open and engaged manner of conducting local government business was lost.

The other problem with sustainability in this story is that most of the R&D Division left city government or transferred to other departments after Washington's re-election. A number of folks were simply promoted up and away. This high level of turnover in a city department was highly unusual, but not really surprising, given the talent, entrepreneurialism, and creativity of the R&D planners and advocates. They were not government long-timers or typical bureaucrats. Working for government, even a progressive administration, still involved bureaucracy, hierarchy, separation from the community, complacency, navel-gazing, self-righteousness, and arrogance. The Washington administration was not immune from these maladies, and this fact of life chafed against the skepticism and community commitments of many R&D folks. A simple truth, though, is that enough people have to stick around to pass on the innovations and the culture.

A Way of Life

These career stories illustrate the ups and downs of personal investments in jobs and nonprofit organizations. They suggest lessons for others working in the civic, nonprofit world. Take jobs that allow and support risk-taking and entrepreneurship. Choose jobs that are highly aligned with your values and skills in organizations that have a culture of risk-taking and boundary spanning and that mentor employees about how to be effective risk-takers, playing the inside/outside game while surviving. Turn down jobs that look interesting just on the surface.

Were my CED adventures worth the personal and family stress over the years? My CED investments produced lots of stress, but they were not the source of my broken marriage. That's another topic for reflection. In the long run, my CED investments have produced a level of security and flexibility that has made my family life possible. But this is a question people must answer for themselves.

My stories suggest that serious personal investment may support organizational growth and innovation, but may create unsustainable business conditions if organizations come to rely upon the overinvestment of key individuals. This is a quandary for nonprofits because their success depends upon individual leadership; yet the loss of this same leadership is so frequently associated with the demise of nonprofit organizations.

Leaving your organization in the right manner is as important as picking the right job. The long-term health and vitality of your organization is a key part of your legacy that you should care about. You must help facilitate effective leadership transitions, no matter how uncomfortable the process becomes for you as you suffer through all the problems of being a lame duck. Indeed, it might be a good idea to negotiate your role in facilitating transition as a part of your initial employment contract.

Understanding the business models underlying your job and organization is critical for strategic planning as well as for planning your career, and many times will require facing some hard truths. Starting a discussion about long-run financial viability can be a real gift to your organization, even though it may take a while to produce an action plan. But raising the flag of financial sustainability requires external as well as internal champions and a set of viable next steps if it is to stay on the radar screen.

Finally, the institutionalization and education process of staff, board, and stakeholders about underlying business models and social innovations must begin as early as possible—even as the results from these innovations are still emerging. This point of view may seem to be overly optimistic about advocating and teaching based upon hopes rather than results, but I believe there is no viable alternative given the unpredictable and inevitable nature of transitions.

A few other lessons from this reflection are worth emphasizing.

- Take chances early in your career by seeking out immersion experiences that enable you to lead before you know, make mistakes, and cultivate intuitive knowledge.

- Organizations need to support as well as be aware of the overinvestment of social entrepreneurs. Their capacity for high productivity at relatively low cost is not a sustainable business model for organizations or for individuals.

- Pick jobs and projects throughout your career that have an element of risk and that test your limits, but have an explicit conversation with yourself about potential personal and family impacts.
- Treat your risky career investments (including misadventures) as a treasure trove to be mined throughout your career, especially as you take on the roles of coach and mentor.

5

Building on Personal Assets (Deficits)

> I must say that ... my constitutional shyness has been no disadvantage whatever. In fact I can see that ... it has been all to my advantage.
>
> —*M.K. Gandhi*

My childhood was comfortable, and I rarely lacked anything I needed or wanted. At the same time, my parents communicated that self-sufficiency was almost as important as godliness. They counseled me not to depend upon others, to take care of myself, and to live within my means. I absorbed these parental nostrums and transformed them into a philosophy of living on the cheap—no rent, no couches, no telephone, no car, and no fancy clothes.

This frugality paid unexpected dividends in the early years of my CED career when I worked for meager pay in exchange for experience and the chance to do good. Some of the circumstances were difficult, but I survived and prospered, and I could always visit my parents if I needed a good meal. This approach to life and work was certainly a function of my being young, without a lot of baggage, and unencumbered by family responsibilities. But it allowed me to work in some wonderful bad jobs.

I kept up this living cheap approach for a good fifteen years, with a few bouts of normal living. Even when I married, I was a reluctant investor in home furnishings and easily adapted to cross-country commuting and living in a closet-apartment by myself during the week. It became apparent that this trait that had been an asset getting started in CED was also preventing me from making a home for my family and myself. I realized I had to change my ways.

These days my frugality is tempered by the needs and wants of children and my own penchant for book buying. I admit it: I have become a consumer. But I remain frugal at heart and still embrace a personal philosophy of self-reliance. That outlook has also shaped how I approach CED. But I have also learned that what I consider to be personal assets can end up being liabilities. Likewise, traits that others may see as liabilities can prove to be quite valuable. This chapter explores that lesson.

It's critical that new and established leaders lead from their strengths, which may include a strong vision, an ability to communicate values, good strategic thinking, organizing prowess, charisma, or relationship-building skills. These assets are not sufficient, by themselves, to achieve all objectives, but they are reliable resources to draw upon when facing situations of risk and uncertainty. Leaders need to build confidence—their own as well as that of others—that the tasks at hand are doable. Once started down the path of action, however, other skills and resources are needed, but breaking the inertia of standing still is a pivotal step. Some efforts never advance beyond the starting line.

These strengths or specific talents are seemingly hardwired into who we are. In *Now, Discover Your Strengths*, authors Marcus Buckingham and Donald Clifton have identified thirty-three such individual talents like arranging, input, or empathy. If you buy the book, you can take an Internet-based self-assessment of your talents that spits out your *Top 5* talents in seconds. This assessment of talents is not all you are, nor is it all that is required to be a good person, parent, or leader. But it does give a sense of your, I must say it, natural talents.

Personal attributes other than these conventional strengths have been equally important for my leadership and problem-solving over the years. These personal attributes, however, are frequently thought of as deficits or quirky features that are tolerated but not admired. Peter Han, in *Nobodies to Somebodies*, quotes Scotts Company CEO Jim Hagedorn, "I think that really, I've just found a legal way to use my delinquency." Discovering the positive power of these ignored and undervalued attributes takes time and self-confidence, and demands we acknowledge that good outcomes can come from atypical leadership resources and styles.

In this chapter, I argue that leading from strengths requires valuing and using perceived weaknesses. Many of these so-called deficits actually embody unrecognized skills and require the development of compensatory strengths. Two of my undervalued strengths are that I'm an introvert and that I suffer a mild version of attention deficit hyperactivity disorder (ADHD).

As you read this chapter on turning deficits into assets ask yourself the following questions:

- What are your unusual leadership strengths that some perceive as weaknesses?
- How have you turned these traits or behaviors into more intentional assets?
- How have you used these unusual assets as a civic leader?
- Are there side effects from these unusual assets that you have to manage?

I'm an Introvert

Let me start with my unmistakable introversion. I've taken the Myers-Briggs test several times, and friends and colleagues, more experientially, have assessed me as an introvert. Even my father assessed me as an introvert, as "retiring," in his words; he advised me to marry a woman of means because he didn't believe that I had the necessary extroversion to strike gold in the labor market. Introversion is a temperamental style whose characteristics exist along a continuum: there is no single, universal version of being an introvert. Marti Olsen Laney, in *The Introvert Advantage*, recounts a common experience, "The way my brain worked puzzled me. I couldn't figure out why I could think of lots of comments after the fact." And, it must be said, introverts are in the minority in society and in most organizations, one for every three extroverts. Former GE CEO Jack Welch concludes in *Winning* that "the world generally favors people who are energetic and extroverted." That's why I often joke that I'm a leader of the ILF—the *Introvert Liberation Front*.

My energy and personal renewal derive from a healthy and regular dose of solitude, not from group interaction. This is the defining characteristic of introversion for me, and when I don't get enough, I feel it. Recharging my batteries is often my most creative time. At times of personal and organizational stress, I need to find the space to catch my breath and steady my feet. This makes me a homebody, but it's not that I close my coffin lid on the noise and chaos of social interaction. I like to know that people and communities surround me as I'm alone.

Mulling is my way of doing homework in private rather through the display of messy early-stage thinking. Some folks need to try on for size their half-thoughts in public in order to refine them and maybe even to decide if they really believe them. At its worst, this comes across as logorrhea, the unstoppable flow of words. For me, that is an imposition on other people's time and patience, especially for early-stage thinking, and I rarely pontificate at will. I would rather sit back, listen, and begin mulling. But things are never that simple. If I'm clear on my role, familiar with folks around the table, in a small group, or talking about one of *my* topics, I can explore out loud with the best of the extroverts.

Me and My ADHD

My ADHD is another story. I've never had a test, diagnosis, or long talk with the family doctor about my symptoms. My ADHD is, for the most part, a retrospective understanding of self, and, admittedly, it is as much a metaphor helpful for my self-understanding as a clinical insight. The underlying pattern of behavior that made me adopt this metaphor in midlife is that I have a difficult time concentrating on any one topic or task. I have trouble sitting still, standing in line, walking slowly, or listening. A focused, narrow present quickly begins to feel claustrophobic, engendering a physiological reaction of squirminess, clamminess, and slight nausea.

My ADHD made school difficult; sitting still in the classroom was an awful experience when combined with my shyness about speaking up and introversion. I'm surprised I made regular progress because the inability to sit still contributed inevitably to acting out and getting into trouble. Hobbies, chores, and homework all presented challenges—almost before I got started I felt as if I needed to move on to the next topic, to the next project. This was a big problem for me in my adolescence and early adulthood—I had the bad habit of quitting jobs and dropping courses, unable to concentrate, and always tantalized by something new.

As I grew up, this lack of concentration matured into what might simply and painfully be called impatience. Always grappling with my own inability to focus and stay focused, I became increasingly impatient with the pace of the problem recognition and problem-solving of others. This trait, in general, has been bad. Getting things done and on time is a good thing; sometimes it helps organizations move to action and overcome roadblocks. However, irritable impatience over big and small things makes relationships difficult, undermines people management, and reinforces a disposition for anger.

My Talents and Challenges

These personal attributes—introversion and metaphorical ADHD—have shaped the contours of my shadow self that I have come to recognize and understand only as I grew up. It has taken decades to turn these quirky attributes into assets. And, for most of this time, I was just surviving, making do with the materials of life that were mine to deploy. That was just who I was. It is only in recent years that I've realized how much time, trial and error, and creative adaptation have been required to transform these attributes into positive leadership qualities.

My introversion and ADHD present four challenges for my leadership in organizations and communities. One challenge is the difficulty I have in passionately communicating mission and meaning, as well as the exuberant pitching of new ideas and development opportunities. The effective communication of meaning requires a compelling description of important problems and opportunities, using powerful images, metaphors, and stories. Leaders must communicate more than the importance of an issue; they must convey the realistic belief that we can do something about these problems and opportunities. Leaders must convey a sense of credible and reasoned judgment.

Another dimension of this communication challenge is what I call the *P.T. Barnum* ability to sell problems, solutions, and new innovations. Here the tone is one of exuberant optimism, not high seriousness and well-wrought arguments. In situations of high importance and uncertainty, such optimism may outweigh the doubts of even the most trenchant skeptics, who are always on the lookout for *snake oil* salesmen. Enthusiastic advocacy for a course of action can be infectious, helping to build confidence, buy-in, and a willingness to act with dispatch.

In part, I suffer from a terminal case of brevity that, at times verges on the cryptic as I pack meaning into my short, rat-a-tat-tat sentences. I even grow weary of my writing as my sentences trail off into the void of scribble. To say more is to get outside of my comfort zone and requires elaborating early-stage arguments that I'm afraid of showcasing because they always seem too tentative and undeveloped for my inner logician. My brevity is not without admirers, however. I'm a legend in the Casey Foundation for bringing home the PowerPoint on time in a nest of extroverts who love to talk.

One of my editing remedies for my brevity is to add words, context, and split up highly compressed sentences, sometimes expanding my thoughts and sentences over days and weeks. Although I don't give up my vacuum-packed thoughts without a fight, if I'm steadfast and lucky, a comprehensible picture emerges. Surprise, surprise—communication occurs.

Brevity and skepticism occurring together sometimes conveys a critical person who cuts little slack for human vagaries. Luckily, my version of skepticism contains a streak of levity that, at its best, creates a cushion for my sometimes pointed, and always brief, remarks. Of course, when levity descends into smart-ass commentary, the opposite effect is unwittingly achieved. Irony almost never works in public.

Another challenge is my impatience with details and my inability and/or lack of aptitude for concentrating on specific topics for long periods of time. My work in CED over several decades, including writing articles, editing books, and giving speeches about workforce, economic, and community development, certainly qualifies me as an expert in most circles. But, frankly, most of the time I operate at a fairly high level of generality about specific subjects, whether job training or business development. I'm not a negotiator of deals, a financial underwriter or whiz kid, a statistical expert able to tease out meaning from a pile of numbers, a sophisticated theorist who paints a picture of the future, or a patient observer and ethnographer of the details of community and family life.

Another challenge for me has been the management of people in project teams, organizations, partnerships, and coalitions. It has taken a long time for me to recognize that I can get the best from staff and colleagues by giving of myself and seeking to walk in their shoes. My perpetual mistake, in spite of all that I intellectually know, is that I think everyone I work with should be like me: self-motivated, self-critical, to the point, hardworking, never needy, and always seeking relevance.

Most of the organizations I have worked for over the years reinforced this bad behavior. Start-ups, turnarounds, and political transitions all generated the pervasive feeling of emergency, battlefields, and important values being at stake. My expectation was that we needed people who could figure things out without a lot of hand holding—inventing solutions and processes, unclogging bottlenecks, and working incredibly long hours. They were burn-out jobs, I now know.

Each of these organizational situations eventually demanded more leadership. Start-ups calmed down, turnarounds added new staff and programs, and I found myself managing a department of staff who were mandated to work together on a common agenda. My *limited* leadership resources were taxed and strained. Each time I would leave a job, I would promise myself that I would not manage people again, only to be coaxed back into it because of opportunity or the startling reality that there was nobody else who was going to do it any better. Luckily, I learned some tricks of the trade along the way, particularly how to manage my introversion and ADHD in a more positive way to enhance rather than detract from my ability to lead. Even with a commitment to change myself, I would be less than honest if I didn't admit that managing people continues to challenge me daily.

My impatience has its positives and negatives. To my detriment, impatience reinforces the perception of me by some colleagues as arrogant, rigid in thinking, and sure that my way of understanding the world is the only valid approach. Impatience is a problem for many people; it rarely contributes to good leadership. I must constantly remind myself to establish more *process* to facilitate communication, help folks understand what I'm trying to say, and encourage staff and colleagues to help state what works best for them.

Unusual Strengths and Skills

What seem like deficits can be turned into strengths and assets that add value for colleagues, projects, and organizations. To do this requires creative adaptation, self-reflection, and, above all, a commitment to practice, over and over.

Distracted by ADHD, I've developed the ability to synthesize disparate materials. I'm able to discern patterns amid the jumble of facts—across bodies of work, generations, and places. My squeamishness has helped me cut to the chase about key themes, overwhelming patterns, and models. Indeed, the work I've enjoyed the most—the project management I've relished—is that of a designer. Designers combine disparate knowledge to create new things.

Another strength related to my metaphoric ADHD is my ability to keep lots of *balls in the air* through what I call *cubbyhole* management. I've turned my inability to focus for long periods into an iterative, rotating focus on a whole array of tasks, projects, and ideas. What I do is simple: I pull out cubbyhole A, spend some time on a particular problem or task, close the cubby, and then move on to cubbyhole B. The key is to keep moving and to turn off emotionally to the cubby content once the cubbyhole is closed. And then I move on to the next one and the one after that. I demonstrate relentless focus, but only for short periods and then iteratively over time. I was born to be incremental. This is a productive use of the unhealthy personal habit of compartmentalizing life. What happens when I can't move on causes emotional stress and anxiety, a problem I discuss below.

A related strength is the ability to hold multiple contradictory ideas at once, a common definition of what constitutes an intellectual. Some might call this critical ambivalence, being wishy-washy, or indecisiveness. For me, this represents the belief in what William James named a "pluralistic universe" that defies simple, unitary systems of thought and action. Some of the most interesting American reformers and critics have occupied the uncomfortable ground that Arnold Kaufman called *radical liberalism*, simultaneously embracing markets, participatory democracy, and the welfare state.

My introversion also serves as a protective factor. My introversion has protected me from many of the temptations associated with running organizations; having power over people, money, and contracts; and having audiences that pay attention, frequently too much attention, to what I say. A common temptation is to believe one's own rhetoric about accomplishments and become captured by the enticing opportunities to advance personal career and agenda. My distaste for huge amounts of face-time and social networking, as well my reticence about touting my accomplishments, has saved me from this temptation of narrow self-absorption, careerism, value displacement, and, at times, conflict of interest. Some would say that I've missed the opportunity to tell my story and harvest the benefits. I would say that I've stayed on course.

Another strength is allocating extra time to accomplish specific tasks and projects. Because I can't focus on one thing for long periods or go deep on a specific issue, I have to spend more time in order to complete projects while, at the same time, skipping around to feed my ADHD. Some folks focus completely on their work between 9 and 5; they avoid all distractions—even talking on the phone to friends and loved ones—but when work is done for the day, it's done. My work metabolism couldn't be more different; I'm nibbling on projects all day until I fall asleep, and even in my dreams. One important byproduct of this approach is that I get things done on time or early.

Allocating lots of time and working in small chunks also have proven helpful for writing projects, including this book. It's important to break down complicated projects into outlines, themes, scenes, and paragraphs rather than getting anxiously hung up on the big outcomes—the paper, the chapter, and the book. One must take advantage of small amounts of time to make progress, even small amounts of progress. For example, my penchant for arriving at movies ten or fifteen minutes early is useful for taking notes, creating outlines, or even jotting down a few sentences on credit card receipts that I find in my wallet. Of course, my kids complain about arriving so early and then waiting.

Another strength is knowing the kinds of environments in which you thrive. I do best in organizations with strong values and leadership that encourages innovation; that have a clear value orientation for improving results for low-income communities; and that are willing to take on the tough challenges of changing public and private systems. My work prospers when I work in tandem with a boss, board president, colleague, or partner who is a *rainmaker* for new projects and innovations and who communicates persuasively the mission of the organization to inside and outside audiences. I count myself lucky to have worked with Robert Mier at the City of Chicago and Douglas Nelson and Ralph Smith at the Annie E. Casey Foundation, who embodied this approach to organization building. In addition to being rainmakers, these leaders played the role of P.T. Barnum—exuberantly advocating innovative solutions.

I'm not helpless when I'm on my own or working in the context of a different type of leader. Neither do I ever want to work for leadership that seeks to micromanage me to be an extrovert, as if that were possible. My recommendation is to find the organizational garden in which you do best and that takes advantage of and nourishes your strengths.

From Challenges to Assets

Turning personal challenges into leadership assets is an essential part of developing yourself as a leader. It requires digging deep, but also focusing attention on how you do the work. The recent craze of interest in "emotional intelligence" calls attention to the importance of the intelligent use of emotions for all aspects of life, including organizational life. The authors of *Primal Leadership* state, "[T]he fundamental task of leaders ... is to create *resonance*—a reservoir of positivity that frees the best in people. At its root ... the primal job of leaders is emotional." Leadership competencies based in emotional intelligence include self-awareness, self-management, social awareness, and relationship management.

One aspect of emotional intelligence—the self-management of emotions—has been a struggle for me. Learning how to control impatience, and sometimes anger, has been a lifetime struggle. What makes anger so debilitating is that it is like adult-onset asthma. I really didn't have it until I began to manage others, to have relationships, and to get married. These new situations created *in-your-face* confrontations with difference and the deep-seated instinctive response to protect psychological and personal space.

Being an introvert set me up for a big and unexpected discovery. Anger came like an unforeseen squall out of my depths, exploding into the present and then disappearing. Anger is toxic in relationships and in the workplace, but it is also a great teacher about one's *hot buttons*, the physiology of emotion, and how to let go.

As I build personal assets from perceived deficits, I apply emotional intelligence in ways that differ from conventional usage. I'm increasingly aware of how I use emotions—anxiety, gut reactions, and clarity—as tools for management. Some of these emotions relate back to my introversion and ADHD, but the source of my emotional makeup is more complicated, a matter of being hard-wired as a part of *homo sapiens*. I'm curious about how I use emotions in this way. Emotions serve simply as sentinel indicators for when things are going well and when they are not going well.

I experience *clarity and balance* when I understand the risks and returns of a specific course of action; I physically and emotionally relax. The method I frequently use to develop clarity is playing *devil's advocate*, testing assumptions, options, or alternative hypotheses in a group setting. This Socratic dialogue helps me understand whether team members have a full grasp of the details, opportunities, deal breakers, and *over-the-horizon* threats. I gain clarity not from being assured that we have all the answers, but by understanding that we have a full grasp of the salient questions. Of course, staff and colleagues may feel tortured.

I have a problem when I can't close a cubbyhole, my tires spinning on ice as I am unable to move to the next cubbyhole. I feel *dissonance and danger*. It could be staff misunderstanding, an unexpected change in the environment, questionable performance, or a new X factor coming into play. Dissonance turns into anxiety, usually the kind that wakes you up in the middle of the night. I obsess, working my way back to a reasoned response as I imaginatively role-play worst-case scenarios.

Over the years, I've developed fairly good skills at assessing the strengths and weaknesses of different kinds of partners. My *gut reactions and intuitions* have proven to be accurate in too many cases. My introversion functions as a "canary in the mine" for new players who want to control more than is appropriate or who rely upon talking a good game, without the capacity to deliver results. This is not a rational assessment of skills, experiences, and résumé; it is an uncontrollable, automatic, emotional set of reactions.

Recently, I realized that I no longer could manage a complicated community-building project on the West Coast because I no longer had a *feel* for the site and community. I had lost a sense of the rhythms, dynamics, and local context, in part because of the sheer increase in activity, relationships, and complexity. Without a feel for the site, I felt increasingly anxious, not only that I didn't know what was going on, but also that I no longer had a compass for guiding and informing my leadership decisions. I soon realized that I was in danger of making unproductive mistakes. That made me more anxious.

Many of these skills can be thought of as intuitive knowledge, the ways we "translate experience into action," in the words of Gary Klein. In *The Power of Intuition*, Klein offers a number of tools and exercises, like the *premortem* before a new project start-up, for strengthening our intuitive knowledge. In other words, intuitive skills can be honed without waiting for the accumulation of lived experience. In the end, the right combination of intuitive and analytic knowledge for the right situation is needed.

A final emotional dimension that I've talked about with colleagues is the feeling of *ownership*. Ownership is that gut reaction that one should make another pot of coffee when taking the last cup, do the dishes without being asked, or pick up litter on the street because it keeps the neighborhood clean. Ownership, in the leadership context, is waking up in the middle of the night to obsess about a problem or opportunity. It's about starting each day asking what strategic and priority actions would make my project or organization succeed. It's about doing the hard things.

Avoiding Bad Debts

Anger is like a bad debt. In the field of family financial asset building, bad debts include out-of-control credit card bills, rollover payday loans, and the epidemic of medical debt. Bad debts drag families down, eating up scarce income, lowering credit scores, and preventing other types of asset building. Bad debts result from poor decision-making about finances; but these decisions are a response, in most cases, to a lack of affordable credit products, lack of health insurance, and the structural deficits in family budgets that result from the lack of good job opportunities.

Everybody has some bad debts and always will; it's a part of regular living and the consequence of the unexpected—loss of jobs, sickness, or other family transitions. Good debts, in contrast, help families build assets and wealth (homeownership), get and keep jobs (owning a car), and invest in lifelong learning (student loans). Of course, predatory lenders serving each of these types of good debt can strip family income and equity; the point, however, is that good debts help build wealth. They are indispensable. Families with good debts build credit histories, improve credit scores, and are able to build assets to invest in family education, make emergency expenditures, and pass on resources to future family generations.

This may seem like a convoluted path for continuing our discussion about anger, but the analogy between anger and bad debts is illuminating. Anger may be unavoidable and even the right thing to do at times; however, anger doesn't build relationships and has a corrosive impact on family, friends, and colleagues. Buddhist educator Robert Thurman writes that anger is "one of the three root poisons (along with greed and delusion) that constitute the real cause of the life of suffering, the ... endless life cycle of unenlightened frustration." As in financial asset building, it's a good idea to minimize bad debts like anger and maximize good debts like integrity, understanding, and love.

Anger, like a bad debt, is deceiving because it seems to help you obtain what you want in the short run, and quite efficiently, to boot. In the early 1990s, when I directed the Southeast Community Organization in Baltimore, we were a part of a campaign to launch resource recycling in Baltimore. We opened up our rear courtyard as a drop-off site for bottles, cans, and newspapers. It operated all week; most business occurred on Saturday, when cars lined up and volunteers directed traffic, unloaded cars, broke glass, and stacked newspaper. The City of Baltimore's Department of Public Works provided large dumpsters for the recycling materials and dropped them off in our courtyard every week.

At one point, during the early stages of the recycling campaign, the city decided that it couldn't provide the dumpsters at the frequency we needed them. Unfortunately, this would have shut our site down and resulted in the pile-up of broken, wet, and smelly recycling materials during days and weeks when there was no container. It seemed like an utterly bureaucratic excuse from an agency that was supposed to be promoting recycling. Consequently, I phoned the city's recycling director and launched into a tirade, full of high-pitched anger and condemnation. It was mostly a put-on, but the recycling director was taken way off guard by this flash of anger that was outside of his normal experience and expectations. After all, we were environmentalists. He caved in to our wishes for regular dumpster delivery, and I learned something important that day. I learned that angry rages are outside the normal patterning of communications for most people; hence anger is effective in making people acquiesce, give up, agree, go away, and meet your demands.

Casualties pile up along this path of anger. Sure, there is success, but relationships are fragile and tentative, particularly with colleagues and friends. Very little good credit ensues from anger as bad debts accumulate in terms of organizational morale, legitimacy, and memory. Angry leaders find that they have minimal cachet with important stakeholders. Leadership change frequently is required before organizational strategies and culture can be retooled. Angry leaders eventually bite the dust, or do they?

I have three pieces of advice about handling anger on behalf of good debts and organizational health. Try to understand your triggers for anger, like impatience, stress, and loss of control, and how these triggers play out in different situations. A part of this awareness is to understand anger accelerants, such as diet, alcohol, and stress of all kinds, which lower thresholds of anger explosions. Recognizing the onset of anger and learning how to ratchet it down before it picks up too much speed and takes over is a critical skill. This is the art of de-escalating anger. Taking a walk and doing meditative breathing are good techniques for calming anger; self-awareness of anger dynamics can also stop anger before it goes too far by recognizing more explicitly what is happening. Walking away or delaying responses to anger-triggering situations can prevent anger in the first place. And, as uncomfortable as it may seem, apologizing for angry outbreaks is always a good move.

Anger is a bad debt that accumulates in fear and distrust, not only at the individual level, but also for societies. Its apparent short-term benefits are not worth the possible losses in the long run—lost relationships, personal frustration, and cultural enmity. We cannot eradicate anger in all its forms, but we can sometimes prevent its outbreak, prevent it from becoming habit forming, and control it when it does spill over our defenses.

Celebrating Deficits

It is a myth that people are born with personal strengths that hardwire them to be effective leaders. In fact, I hope I've been convincing in demonstrating that peculiar attributes can be turned into assets for leadership, family, and community. These assets are not only good for leading and making a living, they are also good for you and how you think about yourself, a part of your own personal reconciliation with the skin you occupy everyday. To discover, nurture, and develop these undervalued attributes, however, requires personal commitment to self-awareness and practice—a commitment to emotional intelligence.

The story of undervalued, unrecognized strengths offers a larger moral to a story that's worth embracing. If undervalued assets exist for each of us among our distinctive characteristics and behaviors, and function as critical success factors for leadership, think of unrecognized strengths that you might find in the people you work with as well as with family and community members. John Kretzmann and John McKnight describe it in this way: "This basic truth about the 'giftedness' of every individual is particularly important ... It is essential to recognize the capacities ... of those who have been labeled mentally handicapped or disabled, or of those who are marginalized because they are too old, or too young, or too poor."

There is a larger story about building upon the assets of people and communities as a way of solving problems, creating opportunities, and nurturing community. Some assets are *diamonds in the rough* that need some creative polishing. Good leaders do this for themselves, but also, more importantly, for others.

I've drawn several lessons from adopting this lens on myself.

- Use every opportunity to learn about your temperament and personal strengths and how they relate to work and life through self-reflection, testing and assessment, and mentoring feedback.

- Organizations need to invest wisely to understand the conventional and sometimes unconventional strengths of their staffs and ways that these strengths can be recognized, deployed, and supported.

- Get inside the metabolism of your everyday work life to understand how you translate personal characteristics (including weaknesses) into effective approaches for solving problems, completing tasks, and building relationships.
- Understanding the limitations or downsides of your temperament in organizational settings will guide personal growth, help you develop new self-management skills, and make you a more effective leader.

6

Time: Obstacle, Friend, Tool, and Teacher

○ ○
It is not that we have a short time to live, but that we waste a lot of it.

—*Seneca*

For three years, from the late 1980s to the early 1990s, I taught a two-day summer workshop on CED at Tufts University. Each year, fifteen to twenty community developers starting out in the field would learn about new ways of thinking and investing in CED. I always began the workshop by discussing the evolving timeline of a commercial development project that I was working on in Baltimore. This project represented what most community developers were up against back home, the opportunities and the challenges.

Each year I would come back and present new steps and creative approaches we had undertaken. I conveyed my frustration and worries about whether the project would proceed. The presentations garnered great interest from the students and stimulated discussions about similar CED projects they had worked on or had observed. Meanwhile, in Baltimore, the project struggled. A few years after I stopped teaching at Tufts, the project collapsed.

This failed commercial development taught me many lessons. But what remains most remarkable is the amount of *time* we expended on the project.

Time is an important topic for CED practitioners and one that is rarely discussed. That is unfortunate, since the passage of time is frequently an obstacle to CED success. CED projects—especially unconventional projects in tough neighborhoods—take a lot of time, frequently three or four years from conception to opening the doors. In reality, real estate development of all kinds takes time, usually more than initially projected. The types of development I'm talking about eat up more time because of challenging issues related to land assembly, financing, politics, and tenant commitments. And the deals keep on coming undone the closer they get to breaking ground. Time means new obstacles and new solutions.

Managing time involves self-control and personal choices. Understanding time as a friend and obstacle is a skill worth developing because time is a resource, a constraint, a force, and a tool. Being skillful in using time well seems like an easy task, but it is not. This chapter delves into the sometimes mundane ways we spend our time and how we could do a better job using time to our advantage. Learning how to stick around for the long haul is essential for CED practitioners because the challenges are long-term.

Ask yourself the following questions as you read this chapter on time:

- How has time been an obstacle in your CED or nonprofit experience?
- How has time been a friend, tool, or teacher?
- What are your secrets for using the powers of time?
- What have you learned about sticking around for the long run?

Meaning of Time

Time is certainly about duration. Time is about B.C. and A.D., leap years, eras, Gregorian calendars, technology, clocks, modernization, rural and urban, center and periphery, hard times and good times. Time is a cultural phenomenon—not an objective given. Time is space, and space is time, according to cosmologists. Some very important, world-changing events have taken very little time, like the Wright brothers' first flight of twelve seconds; yet the Erie Canal—a big dig transportation innovation of the pre-Civil War era—took eight years, three months, and twenty-three days to build. Time is always relative.

In the 1980s, when I worked for the City of Chicago, we funded a study of CED in partnership with the Local Initiatives Support Corporation (LISC), a national intermediary supporting community development corporations (CDCs). We found that CDCs played a distinctive community-organizing role mobilizing public and private institutions, in addition to identifying and packaging development deals. CDCs shepherded nascent projects through the gauntlet of time and the unexpected. Projects that get stuck for too long are in jeopardy of losing backers, momentum, and feasibility.

How do CDCs manage time? They require organizational capacities and competencies for managing the unexpected disruptions of time. These capacities include flexible staff resources, the ability to mobilize political power to influence institutions and decisions, access to technical and financial resources, and having *on-call* champions to push things forward when facing unexpected obstacles. Good judgment must direct these capacities because political backfiring is a constant pitfall. The ability to stick with complicated but feasible development deals long enough to reach success is sometimes hard to distinguish from unflagging allegiance to a bad deal that should be abandoned.

Time is not just an obstacle, however. It is a friend, tool, and teacher that should be used well. As in cooking, long, slow roasting frequently produces the best taste. The same is true for designing and implementing breakthrough CED projects. Unfortunately, many public, private, and philanthropic investors have short time horizons and are captive to fashion cycle grant-making that changes from year to year. In the world of CED, there never seems to be enough time to get it right.

Having the Time

After all the research and hand wringing has been done about what contributes to strong families and healthy children, spending time together comes out on top as an explanation and recommended strategy. Spending time together means sitting around the dinner table, working on homework, playing Scrabble, doing chores, and enjoying downtime. That seems easy enough, and we could all do a better job on some of these fronts. Spending time together becomes more difficult if a parent is single, works multiple jobs, experiences transportation difficulties, or must spend lots of time at multiple locations accessing services and work supports. Time is a precious resource that is in short supply for many families. Tim Russert, in the *Wisdom of Our Fathers*, writes, "If real estate is about location, location, location, fatherhood is about time, time, time."

Two examples of social investing at the Annie E. Casey Foundation illustrate the importance of *having the time* in the world of CED. The Foundation made the realistic assessment that public and private systems do not change overnight, nor do families reach self-sufficiency by participating in a single social program for one year. Indeed, healthy and competent adults are nurtured from pre-natal care through parental love and nurturing, early childhood education, and transition to adolescence. Too often social investors don't allow enough time.

Casey's *Jobs Initiative* sought to connect young adults with children to good jobs and careers. This eight-year initiative articulated a set of key design principles and promising practices and challenged six participating cities to develop their own investment plans based upon these principles as applied in their communities. From the outset in 1995, we expected robust job placement, job retention, and career advancement results as well as solid steps forward in making workforce systems more effective. At the time there was a lot of skepticism about whether workforce development represented an effective intervention; many policymakers thought that workforce development could produce only minimal gains for families.

In a policy or practice arena in which there is no consensus about change strategies, sometimes *trial and error* combined with the best available knowledge is the only way to proceed. The *gift of time* that the *Jobs Initiative* provided to its sites was the opportunity to fail small. Usually one- to three-year grants don't even provide enough time to fail. And failure itself is a prohibited activity. Without the time to learn from failure and go back to the drawing boards and try again, community developers are unlikely to develop durable and effective social innovations. This is particularly true in the arena of workforce development, in which uncertainty remains about the most effective interventions, the impacts of changing labor markets, and the cycle of new and evolving public policies.

The other aspect of the *Jobs Initiative*'s *gift of time* is that complex interventions made up of many interacting parts require time to unfold and play out the dynamic of trial and error and learning. Many social interventions rely upon the sequential accumulation of experience and learning, building step-by-step rather than all at once. Job sites, for example, really couldn't learn about job retention in a practical way until they had placed a sufficient number of people in jobs; likewise, learning about long-term job retention (twelve months or more) could be pursued only after enough time had elapsed so that workers could be assessed for their job retention experience. Learning had to be developmental. One of the *Jobs Initiative* sites, Seattle, was thoroughly embarrassed when it finally saw that its job retention numbers were far below its expectations. It immediately launched a continuous improvement effort to understand and improve job retention performance. Because it had the time, it was able to fail and then to succeed.

Casey Foundation's *Making Connections* initiative is a ten-year effort to build strong families and neighborhoods in ten cities. *Making Connections* is a charter member of the species known as comprehensive community initiatives (CCIs), which embody the notion that communities need to change a lot of things at the same time if outcomes for children and families are truly going to change. The assumption behind this idea is that most factors in the lives of families and communities are interconnected—jobs, housing, health, education, and safety. While some of these factors are more likely to be *root causes* than others, changes made to only one or two of these elements rarely make things better for large numbers of families. In short, a lot of things have to be improved at the same time if staying put in a neighborhood is going to be a reasonable decision. And that's the rub.

Making Connections required several years of start-up in each site to avoid the pitfalls of prematurely choosing partners, strategies, and investments. The initiative began by focusing on relationship building, seeding ideas and pilots, exploring communities to find points of agreement, and identifying partners who could lead the way. It chose not to lead with dollars and a fast-track planning process; rather, it offered ideas and the *gift of time* so that folks could get to know each other and perhaps even work together. Only then would it be time for planning—after action and not before.

Time and Leadership

The above stories convey the multiple meanings of *time* for project design, implementation, and continuous improvement, and might be best understood under the broad rubric of *time management*. Time is an obstacle, friend, and tool for leaders, increasing the pressure for results, but at the same time making quality action possible. Learning about the various dimensions of time and your own time practices is time well spent.

How often have you heard the tiresome advice that *timing is everything*? In 1983, I received the chance of a lifetime when Chicagoans elected Harold Washington mayor. Several years before, I had left Chicago to pursue a doctorate, feeling that politics would never change for the better in Chicago. Now some of my best friends had joined the Washington administration and had offered me a job to come back just as I was completing my studies. Who would have thought it was possible that a progressive, smart, charismatic mayor would be elected in Chicago, of all places? And who would have thought that I would jump off the traditional dissertation track and opt for a commuter marriage?

Peter Han, in *Nobodies to Somebodies*, studied one hundred diverse leaders to discover how they spent their twenties and crafted pathways to success. One strong pattern among these leaders was their intentional thinking about *when to stay and when to leave* a job, even a good job. No one length of time was optimal, but these leaders were very attentive to the advancement and learning opportunities in their jobs. A finding from our *Jobs Initiative* and other workforce programs is that workers frequently need to switch jobs to move up, but switching too often or for the wrong reasons can be a mistake. For most of my career, I've held jobs for five to seven years. I've been envious of those CDC directors who never leave, but that hasn't been my job tenure metabolism. Of course, things change with time; I've been at my current job for fourteen years.

Time management requires big and small choices. For instance, a distinctive part of my leadership persona is that I'm an *on-time* guy who gets to meetings at the appointed hour and submits deliverables by close of business. I'm predictable and reliable. This habit has served me well in a variety of jobs and roles. As I've said, I arrive at meetings, airports, and movies far earlier than required.

The advent of new technologies, especially e-mail, gives new meaning to the platitude, *take a breath* or *cool down* for a moment. This is a leadership and life skill worth remembering. How many times have you or a colleague succumbed to the temptation of an immediate and emotional retaliatory response to an aggravating e-mail, frequently failing to distinguish the "reply all" from the "reply" button when firing off the hot response? Suddenly, a larger audience gulps at the expression of honest, tortured emotion expressed over the Internet. The advice to take a moment and cool down is equally important when confronting the micromanaging of a boss, the obdurate actions of an employee, the disconcerting inquiries of a reporter on deadline, or the left-field expectations or perceptions of a board member or stakeholder. This is the basic stuff taught in job readiness classes for new workers—take your "emotional elevator" down a few floors and *take a breath*.

A contrasting application of *taking a breath* relates to writing, a staple skill and time commitment for nonprofit leaders. Over the years, I've discovered that good writing, for most of us mortals, requires multiple and sometimes endless revisions, because writing is a process of thinking, not simply the recording of prepackaged profundities. We have a natural human tendency to fall in love with our own prose and, as a result, are blinded to its imperfections because we lack emotional distance. One way to edit more efficiently is to let drafts sit for a time. As the drafts age, imperfections magically rise to the surface. Of course, if we had instantaneous emotional distance, our nasty internal editor would slash through our sentences moments after we put them on paper or on the computer screen. Nothing would get done. Time, however, allows us to see our words of clay in all their awkwardness and infelicity.

Impatience is a complicated gift. Impatience helps me get to the point, focus on results, and manage a meeting, but is less helpful when relationship-building and symbolic acts of unity are called for. Working for a departmental commissioner in city government taught me unforgettable lessons about getting to the point in memos, elevator conversations, and presentations. You've got to cut to the chase—there's simply not enough time for a lot of foreplay if you want to get a point across to busy people. As Malcolm Gladwell argues in his provocative book, *Blink*, "The power of knowing, in that first two seconds, is not a gift given magically to a fortunate few. It is an ability that we can all cultivate for ourselves."

Meetings are organizational building blocks, even though we rarely acknowledge their artfulness. Sharing information and making group decisions require the using of time well. Peter Drucker provides a memorable description of good leadership when quoting a professional musician commenting on his orchestra conductor: "He doesn't waste our time." The orchestra leader respected and valued the time and priorities of his orchestra members.

Think for a moment about the CED project described at the beginning of this chapter and the hundreds of meetings that went into its planning and implementation. Negotiating obstacles, staying the course, and keeping morale up can only be enhanced if these meetings are run well. This really came home to me in a personal way when I became a customer of so-called *learning* meetings, not a producer of meetings. As I found my time wasted, I reflected on whether I had valued the time of my customers (i.e., sites) in our *Jobs Initiative*. Probably not!

Rarely have I experienced pushback as a meeting facilitator when I've invoked our mutual agreement to be on time. Talented people can always fill the empty space left by poor meeting design or facilitation, but this doesn't mean that this is their preferred way of spending time. In fact, they would prefer making their own time management choices. Learning how to plan and support effective meetings is one of those mundane skills that will win admirers and produce big payoffs.

Develop time management skills through practice. I spent several semesters in doctoral seminars presenting on a weekly basis classic articles and arguments about urban theory. One had to figure out what was important and how to convey these gems of wisdom as quickly as possible while our omniscient professor nodded from the front of the room, always ready to cast a grimace our way if we went off track or committed an unpardonable interpretive *faux pas*. What I remember most about these readings was not the ideas but the regular practice—the same kind of practice of getting to the point that occurred day-to-day when I staffed a commissioner in city government.

An unnerving but creative work time is the period *in between* big projects or assignments. One experiences simultaneously accomplishment, letdown, and uncertainty about the future, whether you are a greenhorn or an experienced hand. It's about starting over. The rhythm of work changes dramatically. You ask yourself, What is my job? What is important? What's so disturbing is that several days before you were swept away by the flow of creative engagement and accomplishment.

So what does one do in these *in-between* moments? I go domestic by cleaning my desk and office, sifting through piles, making lists, and answering neglected e-mails and phone messages. This activity is analogous to straightening one's bedroom, workbench, kitchen, or garden—preparing for the next round of projects and life.

At these times I make special lists of the most important things that I should do to prepare myself for the next big project, to build capacity in my organization, or to perform organizational duties that I've put off, like asking a new colleague to lunch. This *in-between time* is special because it inevitably builds momentum for the next round of action. Tilling and sifting produce new, exciting, and unexpected connections and opportunities. The neural synapses start firing. I scope out the next campaign—writing outlines, gathering ideas, and bouncing ideas off of co-workers. After a week, if I'm blessed with that much in-between time, I'm ready to re-enter my normal, messy, world of work.

As I've grown older and more experienced, I've observed a new dimension of my own *time management*. Time management is frequently the downfall of many promising staffers; they just can't get things done—and on time. Taking the standard time management seminar helps, but my sense is that everybody needs to come to grips with what they need to get things done and what obstacles always mess things up. And, as Jim Collins cautions, we must be "clock makers" as well as "time keepers."

In addition to overallocating my time for projects, I start early and work incrementally, piece by piece, breaking down tasks and setting objectives and due dates. I now have a better intuitive sense of how much time it will take to complete most tasks. I still overallocate by starting early, but I have developed a kind of *muscle memory*, or *intuitive* sense, that allows me to cut things a bit closer, just as a tennis player, after years of practice and tournaments, moves around the court in seemingly automatic and efficient ways. This sense derives from practice, trial and error, and a better visualization of what is really expected—what is the threshold and appropriate level of success for a particular assignment. By starting early, I'm also unconsciously or semiconsciously mulling over the nature of the assignment, the logic of the presentation, relevant examples, key decisions, and recommendations. By the time I'm ready to write the memo or report, I've already done the heavy cognitive lifting; then I just have to make sure I get to the point. One might call this the productivity of experience—*time well spent*. Of course, I have to admit that a little voice in the back of my head still warns me that maybe this time I'm cutting it too close.

Seeing around corners anticipates how projects, partnerships, and people evolve. It is an intuitive, strategic skill based upon scores of situations, stories, and mistakes as well as applying analytic tools of collective action and game theory. The skill is to focus on one or two key variables that shape change. Dual leadership of project management, for example, almost always falls apart because of miscommunication, competition, or the exit of one leader. Coalitions that don't spend the time to develop common values and beliefs almost always remain superficial. Staff and consultants have come up to me after the fact and said, "You were right about the future. I just couldn't see it." Of course, sometimes I miss the boat entirely. And I have a penchant for seeing what obstacles can occur rather than seeing clear pathways to success. But as Robert Grudin, in *Time and the Art of Living*, observes about football, "Good interceptors have the art of reading almost instantaneously the direction of a play as it takes shape and of moving into positions where they will be most likely to prevent or minimize offensive gains. In these positions they are also most likely to be where errant passes drop."

Sometimes a good tool for seeing around corners is to *let the process unfold*. Process can make things go away, reveal the real issues, stop things in their tracks, or build consensus for more timely action. Process can be as short as sticking your toe in the waters or as time-consuming as group visioning. Deploying process is also an old trick that can be used to preserve the present or dissipate opposition.

Time and the Long Haul

Sticking around and the *long haul* are about the importance of continuity for project implementation, organization building, career development, and social movements. Sticking around means staying with projects to help them stay the course; it also means being there to harvest the recognition and learning. Social movement historian John D'Emilio describes the pace of much social change as "creeping" or "leaping." Unfortunately, it's not uncommon in multiyear foundation initiatives for no one to be around at the end who understands why the investment was made in the first place.

But sticking around is more than just remaining in place a bit longer. It's about reinvigorating and reinventing oneself so that one is a vital and engaged presence for the long haul. Time has the unfortunate effect of smoothing the edges, promoting complaisance, and leading us to avoid conflict, even creative conflict. This is especially the case if our passions run so hot in the short run that we literally burn out. As we grow older, we become more concerned with other aspects of our lives—not just time well spent at work. A big-time leadership question for all of us is how to remain engaged and committed over the course of a career—the long haul.

The long haul is a new and distinctive lens for me to look at life over two, three, or four decades. I get a special feeling when saying I've been in the field for twenty-five to thirty years. Those of us who stick around long enough have a unique perspective on the making of CED history. No one else has that. Added responsibility comes with longevity in the field. We must resist the temptation to rewrite history, become captive to favorite war stories, or lapse into cynicism because so many personal projects and organizations have bitten the dust.

Neighborhood development as a form of CED has existed since the founding of settlement houses, like Chicago's Jane Addams Hull House, more than one hundred years ago. Comprehensive approaches to neighborhood development, however, have been around only for the past fifty years, starting with urban renewal and Model Cities and evolving into Empowerment Zones and CCIs like *Making Connections*. Although place-based development strategies have many flaws, Robert Halpern, in *Rebuilding Urban Neighborhoods,* argues that neighborhoods still represent the only effective scale to work with families and communities.

Three neighborhood sagas from Chicago and Baltimore show how the passage of decades brings problems and challenges into focus. The North Lawndale neighborhood saga is about the trials and tribulations of a west-side Chicago neighborhood that declined from 140,000 in 1960 to a population of forty thousand residents in 2000. This incredibly shrinking neighborhood was the outcome of a complicated process of ethnic succession, racial blockbusting, community organizing, the birth of the northern Civil Rights movement, a first-generation CDC, urban riots, Model Cities, the relocation of Sears headquarters to downtown, the underclass debate, the federal Empowerment Zone, faith-based development, mixed-income housing, and a homegrown Chicago CCI. The story of North Lawndale in the past half-century represents a journey of thousands of people, billions of dollars, and an encyclopedia of urban development ideas and policies.

What does time teach us about North Lawndale? Things had to get very bad to begin getting better. Most of our urban development ideas were holding actions at best, or stepping-stones that helped people to escape. Small successes are better than big ideas and policies that are impossible to implement. There was an absence of the political will to stop or ameliorate the ugly process of neighborhood disinvestment and racial change. Some people, however, stuck around and made a go of it. Yet the path to modest success has been built on so much human pain and physical deterioration. There had to be a better way.

East Baltimore is similar to but different from North Lawndale. It's a largely African American neighborhood surrounding the Johns Hopkins University Medical Center, the largest employer in Baltimore and Maryland. The neighborhood has been troubled for more than fifty years. The late James Rouse, the builder of malls and waterfronts and the founder of the Enterprise Foundation, helped invent the tools and policies for urban conservation in the 1950s in this neighborhood by supporting housing code enforcement and housing rehabilitation. The community also supported an early version of faith-based, self-help housing similar to Habitat for Humanity, the War on Poverty, Model Cities, and urban renewal. More recently, in the 1980s and 1990s, East Baltimore experienced Seedco's community/hospital partnerships, an Enterprise/CDC-designed CCI, a feasibility study for a clone of South Shore Bank of Chicago, and the inclusion of East Baltimore in Baltimore's successful Federal Empowerment Zone application. Needless to say, not much positive change occurred because of these investments, and East Baltimore remains one of the poorest neighborhoods in Baltimore with one of the largest economic engines sitting in its midst.

What persisted over decades was the poverty of the neighborhood, the protracted insularity of the Johns Hopkins medical complex, and the inability and unwillingness of the community and medical complex to work together. A new redevelopment effort is now underway, under the leadership of Johns Hopkins, the City of Baltimore, the state of Maryland, and the Annie E. Casey Foundation, to leverage significant community change from the building of a new life sciences complex. This ten- to fifteen-year project is projected to create six to eight thousand jobs, build or rebuild twenty-two hundred homes, produce two million square feet of commercial space, and cost upwards of $1 billion in public, private, and philanthropic resources.

Whether this ambitious redevelopment effort will help the neighborhood and the medical complex break out of a time-honored failure to work together is too early to tell. Repeated failure has induced major public and private investors to join an audacious attempt to invent a "humane form of urban renewal," displacing African American families, for their own good, that of the city, and certainly that of Johns Hopkins University. A decade from now we may conclude that the story of East Baltimore has again repeated itself: big institutions running over poor communities.

The saga of SECO/SDI, also of Baltimore, offers an organizational perspective on the passage of time. Here the historic pattern is not about persistent failure.

Rather, the story is similar to that of a successful company that becomes an unchanging "cash cow" and then a crippled organization. That's when I came into the picture, and things looked up for a while, but over the past decade SECO/SDI has continued its downward path.

In contrast to North Lawndale and East Baltimore, SECO/SDI's long-term downward trajectory was a function of its success. It helped preserve the neighborhoods of southeast Baltimore from the highway wrecking ball, influenced the city to expand and continue neighborhood development, and helped give rise to a plethora of neighborhood associations and development organizations. All this success created a role mismatch between the community and policy environment and the niche of SECO/SDI.

Time and Timeless

An even broader application of the long-term perspective is found in utopian thinking and utopian dreams, an often unspoken dimension of CED. Utopias are timeless inventions of the imagination that portray, in holistic detail, the way societies could (or should) be organized if we would only adopt the right ethical, economic, and political or design principles. Utopias include Plato's *Republic* and Thomas More's *Utopia;* utopias of the nineteenth and twentieth centuries include the Transcendentalists and Brook Farm, Edward Bellamy's *Looking Backward*, kibbutzim, and even hippie communes. There are conservative utopians like objectivist Ayn Rand and believers in the utopia of unfettered, decentralized competitive markets. And, in a way, contemporary CCIs are utopian in how they seek to rebuild whole communities.

Utopian, timeless thinking is viewed as either the work of crackpots, the outright dangerous, or as work essential for inspiring hope and alternative visions that disrupt the weight of the present. Those who see utopian thinking as dangerous advocate incremental reform, free markets, and a slower pace of change; they remind us of the incredibly inhumane outcomes of "blueprint" utopias like the Soviet Union or Cuba. Utopian thinking, in their minds, leads to totalitarianism as captured in dystopian novels like George Orwell's *1984* or *Animal Farm* and Yevgeny Zamyatin's *We*. Soviet-style totalitarianism tried to stop time.

Today's utopians argue that we are trapped in a present of narrow possibilities controlled by elites, war, unfettered globalization, economic inequality, ethnic cleansing, economic degradation, and political oppression or turmoil. Utopias represent other possible paths that are, at their best, built upon the bedrock of human rights, free institutions and democracy, and economic self-determination. Russell Jacoby contrasts the non-blueprint with the blueprint utopians as "those who dream[ed] of a superior society but who decline[d] to give it precise measurements." The utopian spirit is timeless.

The opposite of utopia is, in the words of Francis Fukuyama, *the end of history*. He argues that we have exhausted the long dialectical march of history through beginnings and middles and have now reached the end. Liberal democracy and modern capitalism represent the end of history; we can't improve upon this context for achieving political and material well-being or for encouraging and protecting the creative spirit of humanity.

Memories

If utopias evoke the future, memory retains and accentuates the passage of time and the vividness of present moments. Memory is not just something that happens inside our heads, but is evoked and embedded in our landscape, relationships, and language. A real discovery for me, when I worked for SECO/SDI in the 1980s, was that older people preferred to "age in place," in *naturally occurring retirement communities*, or NORCs. Lots of factors played a part in this frequently stubborn commitment to age in place—financial resources, fear of the unknown, not wanting to place burdens on children, and memory.

We would often ask older key informants in southeast Baltimore why older residents preferred to stay in rowhomes ill-suited to meet their everyday needs. Rowhouses have narrow and steep stairs, bathrooms on the second floor, and sometimes even basement kitchens. We heard many stories of older residents crawling up stairs for a bath. We learned that staying put had to do with the intertwining of biography and place; home, block, and neighborhood; the laughter and pain of full lives reflected in the landscape, evoking stories, relationships, and values. This web of connection is a part of community, the accumulation of daily habits, walking to the store, greeting neighbors, putting out the garbage, or looking out the window at the world going by. Memory is a stabilizer and a source of identity and belonging.

Memory is also the backbone of my favorite form of narrative writing—the autobiography. The autobiography is a narrative of time and memory as understood from one person's point of view, telling stories of coming of age, survival, discovery, humility, persistence, and renewal. The voice of autobiography is—allowing flaws, lapses, and biases—the quintessential reflective narrator, living and thinking about life, an act of discovery and memorializing. The autobiography, in this sense, is a model of a thoughtful life, whether or not the words reach paper.

Autobiographies influence my life, even though I may remember only a fragment or glimmer of feeling that they evoked for me. Eugenia Ginzburg's *Journey into the Whirlwind* and *Within the Whirlwind* reveal an indefatigable humanism amid decades in Stalin's camps in the Kolma region of Siberia. Richard Wright's *Black Boy* is an autobiographical adventure of a boy surviving the harsh realities of the South and his family and telling how he escaped to become a writer. Alfred Kazin's *Starting Out in the Thirties* is a coming-of-age story in which a Brooklyn boy expands his horizon to the whole city and culture and beyond. Andre Gorz, in *The Traitor*, explores with painful persistence the nagging question of how one becomes who one is out of the murky combination of personal predispositions, family life, environment, history, and chance. Of course, the point is to escape the paralysis of these questions and chart one's own direction.

Memory can be a call to action and renewal in the present based upon a key event, person, or anniversary. In 1991, SECO held a ceremony along the waterfront of southeast Baltimore that celebrated the twenty years since the defeat of the "Road," the highway that would have destroyed the neighborhoods and Baltimore's economic renaissance. We brought back old staff and board members to remember the origin story of SECO, a major community victory, and the new challenges of upscale development paradoxically made possible by saving the waterfront from a concrete six-lane highway. The ceremony took place on a parcel of vacant land that was the result of the demolition of a swath of rowhomes before the highway was stopped. The meta-message of the event was that SECO was still alive and well—an organizational presence taking on contemporary neighborhood challenges.

In 2003, the Egan Center of DePaul University convened a symposium in Chicago to commemorate the twentieth anniversary of the election of Harold Washington as mayor of Chicago. But the DePaul event had its eye on the future in two ways. It brought together writers who had studied and written about cities where mayors had pursued equity policies in the 1990s combining new forms of workforce and economic development, citizen empowerment, and neighborhood development. The sponsors were interested in the next generation of progressive mayors as well as the relationship between good economic times and social and economic policy. The symposium focused on the decades ahead for major cities in the twenty-first century, on what lessons could be learned from Harold Washington and other cities to inspire and direct municipal equity policies of the future. Celebrating the past was a way of preparing and mobilizing for the future.

A Life of Time

I conclude this chapter about *time* by emphasizing the importance of the present. To meet the challenges of the long haul, overcome unexpected hurdles, and stick around long enough to make a difference, we need to take time off to rest, renew ourselves and prepare for the future. A wonderful thing about Americans is our work ethic, but in too many instances this devotion to work drives out other important uses of time—family time and spiritual time, for example. Carl Honore, in *In Praise of Slowness*, writes, "Remember who won the race between the tortoise and the hare. As we hurry through life, cramming more into every hour, we are stretching ourselves to the breaking point."

My sense that I'm really taking serious time off occurs when I realize I have forgotten what day it is. When I return to work, I ask myself how I can lose track of time, outside of the occasional week's vacation, in order to improve my overall quality of life. This is not about getting rid of clocks and time management; it's a question of living for the long haul. My best advice derives from my imperfect knowledge and practice of Buddhism—to clear the mind and be absolutely in the flow of the present; quite a contrast to being swept up by time-driven stress or with one's head in timeless utopian thinking. Christopher Titmuss, Buddhist thinker and writer, says, "Part of the problem is that we have such little regard for the present moment.... Life is here in this moment.... This moment is all we have; everything else is abstraction." Not surprisingly, it takes practice to let the ennui of daily life pass through us like a steady breeze. In search for the present, time can be an obstacle, friend, tool, and teacher.

Thinking about *time* offers many lessons.

- Make sure you understand how time functions as a friend and as an obstacle in your nonprofit and CED efforts. Sometimes you need the time, sometimes you need no time, and sometimes you need to persist over time.

- Organizations need to be much savvier about the multiple meanings and roles of time and how they can help staff navigate these differences in their projects and investments.

- Learn how to use time to get things done, improve quality, and prepare for the next round of projects.

- Managing time means recognizing dreams and memories as well as struggling to be fully in the present.

7

Managing Messiness

o o o o o o o o o o o o o o o o o o o o o o o o o o o o o o
Is there some design
In these deep random rain drops
Drying in the dust.

—Richard Wright

When I arrived in China in 1997 to adopt a baby daughter, I was flabbergasted by the car, truck, and motorcycle traffic that jammed the streets of Guangzhou without apparent reliance on traffic signals or stop signs. Occasionally a policeman waved wildly, seemingly with little effect, in the middle of a rotary intersection or tended to the remarkably rare collision on the side of the road. The maddening traffic produced an incessant, disorienting cacophony of beeping horns. It assaulted the senses and appeared chaotic. But, somehow, it all functioned. What was I missing? As I listened more closely to the beeping horns during the next few days, I sensed a pattern in the constant chirping, a cadence and rhythm like birds in early-morning manic conversation. But I couldn't make the cultural translation. Was this my imagination, or were these fanatical drivers really communicating? Only ten years later, when I read Anthony Bourdain's *A Cook's Tour*, did I discover that it wasn't a mess at all. "A beep means 'Keep doing what you're doing, change nothing, make no sudden moves, and everything will probably be fine.' It does not mean 'Slow down' or 'Stop' or 'Move to the right' or 'Get out of the way …' The horn means simply 'I'm here!'"

As with the Chinese traffic, I have learned that the CED field, as well as other areas of civic leadership, can look quite messy to outsiders. I have learned that messiness can stop progress in its tracks. But I have also come to appreciate that messiness is not always such a bad thing. Learning to deal with messiness is essential for the CED toolbox.

Messiness implies disorder, mayhem, and confusion. Messiness has some quite different meanings in the realm of civic leadership. I'm referring to the often messy world of organizational and environmental change. Leadership philosopher Warren Bennis argues that our present and future is about complexity: "The fact is that there are too many predicaments, too many grievances, too many ironies, polarities, dichotomies, dualities, ambivalences, paradoxes, contradictions, confusions, complexities, and messes." And, as in my example of car traffic, messes are sometimes in the eyes of the beholder.

This is not to say that old-fashioned messiness is not a problem. Confusion disorganizes the best of efforts and can cause accidents and produce paralysis. And sometimes the way we conduct our lives is "all messed up." Disorganized communities are frequently unhealthy and have low levels of morale and of confidence that they can solve the tough problems that they face.

Messiness challenges the ways we go about solving problems. Planning theorist John Forester writes, "Messiness is important because it teaches us that before problems are solved, they have to be constructed or formulated in the first place." In this chapter I reflect on good and bad messes, how to navigate messes, how to combat their negative side effects, and the pros and cons of simplicity. I must sheepishly confess at the outset that, in spite of my fondness for messes, I recently tested as somewhat intolerant of ambiguity on a self-test in Gary Klein's *The Power of Intuition*.

Before I launch into another story, remember to ask yourself the following questions as you read this chapter:

- What messes have you experienced in your work?
- How do you distinguish creative from destructive messes?
- What tools do you use to make sense of messes and take productive action? What's your tolerance for ambiguity?
- How have you incorporated simplicity into your life and work?

Messes and Community Building

For three years I had the good fortune to manage the start-up of the Casey Foundation's *Making Connections* initiative in five cities. Start-up is tough work that combines relationship building, marketing, strategic planning, and arm twisting, all pursued in short visits every month or so. *Making Connections* recognized that multiple factors—jobs, health care, housing, and family support—influenced family life, and that these interdependent factors required change simultaneously if the cycle of neighborhood disinvestment was to be transformed into a virtuous cycle of community building. The problem was how to invest in this multifaceted, long-term effort in a way that spawned local creativity, co-investment, and ownership.

Several features distinguished the start-up of *Making Connections* and our support for local creativity and ownership. The overall approach was to keep the process open and organic, but anchored in some fundamental values. We emphasized that we were leading with ideas, not money; but ideas meant touchstones, not exact blueprints for action. In our minds, kids do better when they were in strong families, and families do better when supported in their communities. Neighborhood family strengthening, as we called it, involved the weaving together of economic opportunities, social networks and supports, and trusted and appropriate services. We used the powerful metaphor of *connections* to underscore how many low-income families are disconnected from the mainstream economy, transportation, the Internet, banking institutions, and each other.

We chose not to begin with a protracted planning process or grand collaboration. This approach to community building risked, in our minds, excluding family participants and unpopular ideas as well as promoting competitive group politics and planning paralysis. Instead, we began with a three-year period of relationship building and seeding of small-scale projects. We hoped to anchor the work in neighborhood leadership, connect with major policy players, experiment with promising family-strengthening interventions, join forces with others to promote and communicate family-strengthening messages throughout the community, and identify and enhance local capacity to use data for communications, policy advocacy, program design, investment decision-making, and evaluation.

We didn't hand off *Making Connections* to any one local organization as we had done in other demonstrations, such as the *Jobs Initiative*. We found that no matter how good and effective a particular organization was, most nonprofit leaders couldn't resist the temptation of trying to make a big foundation investment, such as *Making Connections*, all their own. Intermediaries would try to do all the work themselves, discourage the use of partners, stand between the Foundation and the community, and convey—at times unconsciously—that this was their initiative. Again, stakeholders, ideas, and ways of working and thinking that were not in the comfort zone of the designated intermediary would be left out, undermining long-term community buy-in and sustainability.

A major consequence of not handing *Making Connections* off to local intermediaries was that Casey Foundation staff had to play larger and more intensive roles than they had in managing past initiatives. This approach had several impacts, both good and bad. On the one hand, it implicated the Foundation as an institution in a fundamental way so that it intimately experienced successes and failures: it couldn't hide behind an intermediary, and staff couldn't jump on planes and go home when things weren't going their way. This made the Foundation more sensitive to local conditions and the practical implications of different types of decisions and strategies. At the same time, this management approach encouraged the Foundation to make available to its site teams the full array of lessons that it had learned from its investments in the fields of child welfare reform, community building, and workforce development, for example. This had been a long-term organizational goal, but had been difficult to achieve because the Foundation had its own knowledge and funding silos. On the other hand, Casey staff and their varying skill sets launched this complicated effort in cities that they did not know well and that were thousands of miles away from the home office. Imagine how the difficulties of doing this for one city were compounded by launching five sites at the same time.

An inherent risk for *Making Connections*—its ideas and start-up—was that it opted for openness and creativity rather than transparency and structure. In a sense we decided to "embrace confusion," or messiness. This became all too evident in the ways in which local folks reacted to *Making Connections*. It was like a Rorschach test for social policy innovation.

Making Connections made one group of local folks very nervous. They said it was unclear and confusing without someone in charge and with no obvious structure or application process for grant seekers. All the skills and capacities that good nonprofit organizations were taught proved to be of only modest help in cracking the *Making Connections* enigma. Yet grants were being made, and to unconventional, grassroots groups. Sometimes these established organizational leaders would say in frustration, "We already know what residents want." Or "We are the residents." At its worst, this group of established organizations accused the Foundation of ignoring or disrespecting leading nonprofits and their array of programs built up over decades. In this light, *Making Connections* was doing harm. Their perspective embodied at least one bit of truth: I had to spend a lot of time for each of my five sites saying "no" to numerous large and small nonprofits—with and without professional development officers—who contacted us for funding by mail, phone, or personal advocate.

Another group of folks had a quite different reaction to the way we started *Making Connections*. They said something like the following: "Oh, I see, you're inviting us to be a part of a discovery process about family-strengthening. You're asking us to help define family-strengthening for our community, advise you on how to make sure residents are at the center of the work, and identify other partners with similar beliefs to join the parade. Nobody has ever asked us to be at the table so early." This group saw an opportunity to shape an initiative, its problem and opportunity statements, its messages, the key ingredients for family and neighborhoods, and the *Making Connections* investment process. These folks saw that the opportunity of *Making Connections* was not to fund one more set of programs, but to change a whole way of doing business about community building. The Foundation was asking them to the table.

This story about *Making Connections* design, planning, investment, and governance is essentially a story about messiness. In this case, we felt that embracing messiness had greater payoffs than relying upon linear, highly structured blueprints and decision-making processes. The assumptions behind this choice were simply that creative messiness was a natural state of all communities—a bunch of loose and moving parts—and that messiness meant that we didn't have family-strengthening all figured out in advance. That is, embracing messiness allowed the community to create more authentic statements about the problems that they were trying to solve.

As I confronted the challenge of messiness in *Making Connections* sites, I sought advice about how to proceed from Peter Plastrik, co-author of *Banishing Bureaucracy* and *Fieldbook for Reinventors*. He replied, as good consultants do, "Oh, you're interested in self-organizing systems." By this he meant systems that eventually generate their own direction, momentum, and power. He said we should first identify a set of leaders who shared *Making Connections'* ideas about family- and community-strengthening. Then we should involve these leaders in pilots and experimental projects related to family-strengthening. After some experience, we should convene these leaders to share what they had learned, suggest next steps, and identify other leaders. Over time, Plastrik counseled, credible principles, themes, and strategies would begin to emerge from this creative stew, as would a group of engaged stakeholders willing to take *Making Connections* to the next level.

This approach to supporting self-organizing systems and investments was successful in shaping the start-up of *Making Connections* in my sites, although it required folks to board a different type of community-building train. In the words of the evaluator Carol Weiss, there is "nothing as practical as good theory" to make sense of messes and to invent next steps. What has discouraged me, though, is how powerful the linear, highly structured approach to comprehensive community initiatives (CCIs) can be. When leaders are asked to say what made

Making Connections most effective, they are likely to name a specific program element rather than our distinctive investment approach. Even though our investment process worked, it was uncomfortable, unnatural, and difficult to explain.

That local leaders revert to conventional explanations for their success suggests a paradox about innovation. At the early stages of innovation, we have creative messes—a thousand flowers blooming, lots of assumptions, hypotheses, and guesses in play. As we begin to develop credible strategies, however, our creative messes become simplified. At the point of success, we proclaim the viability of a model and take pains to dismiss alternative, competing approaches. These other ideas recede without attention and nourishment. This simplification of approach allows us to pursue efficiency and scale. We've created a winner. The problem comes when the environment shifts, new problems and opportunities present themselves, or there is a fundamental paradigmatic shift in values, customers, or technologies. We have traded our creative messes for standardized designs and now find it almost impossible to recover our innovation footing in unexplored options and alternative pathways. Not surprisingly, other innovators take the lead.

Understanding Messiness

Understanding and managing messiness, as in *Making Connections,* requires a distinctive approach to social problems that includes a willingness to experiment, make mistakes, and learn. Although a lot of lip service is paid to developing these capacities, they remain relatively rare and difficult to develop.

Messy, or *wicked,* problems, in the words of planning theorists Horst Rittel and Melvin Webber, represent contentious and unresolved questions about social values such as the relative importance of intact, two-parent families compared to single, female-headed households. In messy situations, we don't even know what the problems are that we are trying to solve.

The private sector often turns to prototyping (as have the nonprofit and public sectors more recently) to "fail small" while learning more about the underlying assumptions of potential solutions for messy problems. The mantra of prototyping is "ready, fire, aim," an approach I learned more about from the Rensselaerville Institute. Design is not a one-time event; rather, design is the "incremental process of successive approximation." How will American consumers react to a new consumer product or service such as the polymer doors of a Saturn? Will job coaches enhance the ability of inexperienced, low-income employees to keep their jobs and advance? Paper-and-pencil planning will not yield useful solutions without action-oriented experiments.

Two existential approaches help make sense of messiness. The late planning theorist Donald Schön described the practice of reflection-in-action. Schön argued that planners facing messy situations must embrace an iterative process of design, in which new and emergent alternatives, relationships, possibilities are revealed through action. Planners must be prepared to learn as they go, questioning assumptions, absorbing new data, synthesizing new designs, and receiving new and often unwelcome feedback from reality. Schön states, "In reflection-in-action, rethinking ... leads to on-the-spot experiment and further thinking that affects what we do."

Living and working with messes—creative or otherwise—demands unusual personal attentiveness. The Buddhist practice of mindfulness provides a useful guide for navigating messiness. Awareness in the present moment allows us to see and feel the connections, overlaps, synergies, and possibilities. Thich Nhat Hanh, the Buddhist teacher, counsels, "While washing dishes one should only be washing the dishes, which means that while washing the dishes one should be completely aware of the fact that one is washing the dishes." The concept of *mindfulness* is also used by organizational theorist Karl Weick to identify the skills and attention needed to "make sense" of complicated and messy organizational environments. Weick and co-author Kathleen Sutcliffe, in *Managing the Unexpected*, caution, "When people function mindlessly they don't understand either themselves or their environments, but they feel as though they do."

Messes are abstract nouns like time, organizations, neighborhoods, or society, as discussed in Chapter 1. No one perspective does justice to the complexity of these phenomena; they are like prisms with many different edges, faces, and combinations. Robert Grudin, author of *Time and the Art of Living*, offers a methodology for making sense of these messes:

> Like students of art who walk around a great statue, seeing parts and aspects of it from each position, but never the whole work, we must walk mentally around time, using a variety of approaches, a pandemonium of metaphor. No insight or association, however outlandish or contradictory, should be forbidden us; the only thing forbidden should be to stand still and say, "This is it."

Metaphors make this reading of messes possible because of their power of invoking analogy, association, overlap, and contradiction. In Chapter 1, in the world of CED, the metaphor of the *leaky bucket* is illuminating by calling attention to the inflows and outflows of resources from neighborhoods, some of which could be better captured for enhancing economic opportunity. Alternatively, *building connections* calls attention to the isolation of neighborhoods from the broader economy and political world.

At times, the frozen, one-dimensional meanings of abstract nouns like *community* have to be exploded in order to acknowledge the messiness. Take neighborhoods, for example. In the past, conventional definitions of neighborhood referred to slums, homogenous ethnic enclaves, networked communities, or administrative planning units. Chuck Bowden and Lew Kreinberg, in *Street Signs Chicago*, remind us that neighborhood is just as often a fiction imposed by those who want to control the chaos of immigrant workers, underground economies, poverty, or residential hyper-mobility for the purposes of keeping the peace or of pacifying neighborhoods so that they can be plundered by new social groups, developers, and politicians. Bowden and Kreinberg argue, paradoxically, that there is no such thing as a neighborhood.

Ethics and Messiness

Navigating messiness is also a challenge for social and ethical development. Early in planning school, I became enamored with something called "adventure playgrounds" developed in post-World War II Amsterdam and London by advocates like Lady Allen of Hurtwood. Most playgrounds of the past (and the present, for that matter) consist of single-purpose, predetermined, immovable apparatus—swings, seesaws, slides, or jungle gyms. Individual equipment is typically separated from each other, sunken in a sea of concrete or asphalt, surrounded by a fence, and guarded by social norms that narrowly define swinging and sliding. Of course, today's designers have improved play environments by building interconnected play landscapes.

Adventure playgrounds start from a premise radically different from that of conventional playgrounds—one as much about learning as about exercise. Adventure playgrounds are workyards that contain an untidy mess or jumble of materials—tires, beams, barrels, spools, logs, and rope—that children are allowed (and encouraged) to assemble and disassemble in any way they want. War-ravaged cities had an abundance of what some would call junk, but had far fewer fixed and formal playground environments. This is another case of building upon unusual assets. The role of supervisors is to keep kids safe in adventure playgrounds as well as to offer building advice, as opposed to making sure that kids don't use the play equipment in some unintended way—like climbing up slides rather than sliding down. Nancy Rudolph, in *Workyards*, states, "Adventure playgrounds are places where children are given free rein to develop their abilities."

Creative play is about constructing and building, exercising vision and teamwork in the world of loose parts and messiness. This is the story of life. This doesn't mean that kids don't want to blow off steam by running and swinging to their hearts' content. They do, and that is good. But kids frequently like to do this in the context of imaginary scenarios that they construct in their fantasies and in reality. How much better when kids can actually construct these theatrical scenes out of everyday materials—even if they are made from junk. Ellen Handler Spitz writes of children's rooms in *The Brightening Glance* as "Messy in the most delightful way, in the sense that each child had construct[ed] the most complex scenarios, bricolage, and displays." Unfortunately, playground gatekeepers in the United States have not showed much openness to adventure playgrounds, citing such intractable problems as insurance, noise, and supervision.

The late architect planner Kevin Lynch, who wrote so insightfully about urban design and environmental perception, confirmed for me the underlying genius of adventure playgrounds in his studies of childhood and play. After numerous interviews with kids and adults, Lynch concluded that the favorite play spaces of kids were not formal playgrounds but *naturally occurring* adventure playgrounds—alleys, railroad right-of-ways, dumps, or abandoned buildings. All of these places are characterized by their distinctive messes as well as by being places forbidden by adults. For me as a kid, my favored play spaces in the burgeoning suburbs of central New Jersey were of the same ilk—construction sites, streams and creeks, the dump, and the woods—all fully stocked with moving parts. Play at building was endlessly engaging.

This function of loose parts and play evidenced in adventure playgrounds is true for our interactions with nature, our first adventure playgrounds. What natural ecologies provide, in addition to a rich array of loose parts, is grounding in the spiritual and scientific fundamentals of life. Without this grounding, we risk losing an anchor for balancing our lives. Richard Louv, in *Last Child in the Woods*, argues that "healing the broken bond between our young and nature ... is in our self interest ... because our mental, physical, and spiritual health depends upon it." In other words, messes are engaging and may be vital for our survival. A journalist recently described Bob Flowerdew's three-quarter-acre organic garden in UK's *Gourmet Gardener* as a "mess, but it's a charming garden once you look beyond the strangeness of it."

As a summer intern in 1975, I worked with a group of Pilsen kids to build a small, adventure-like playground on an empty lot. First we had an abandoned building that was a fire hazard torn down. Kids broke all the rules by sitting on the lap of the judge as he signed the demolition order. Then we had to overcome parents' fears that fixing up the lot would attract bad elements, a sad but common commentary on the threatening role of improved open space in densely built, low-income communities. We then worked all summer with the kids to forage logs and wood chips from nearby parks, tires from junkyards, and donated hardware. We built a simple playground and workyard from old materials.

Adventure playgrounds represent a "theory of loose parts," as coined by environmental planner Simon Nicholson. Many types of educational, organizational, and community environments can be designed that encourage self-direction in the assembly of parts to fit specific needs and aspirations.

Our Common Messes

If adventure playgrounds offer the opportunity for kids to build castles out of messes, then old-fashioned, multi-ethnic, bustling twentieth-century cities (and now twenty-first century global cities) provide playgrounds for citizenship and moral development. Think of these cities as creative messes containing a jumble of different people with vast differences and remarkable commonalities, rich and poor, friendly, threatening, or indifferent. These cities are full of noises, smells, traffic of all sorts—cars, pedestrians, motorbikes, and, of course, taxis. Land uses change and intermix in a stew of enterprise, varied walks of life, and vernacular landscapes. Walking through these messes called cities is an unfolding adventure full of surprises, the unexpected, twists, and turns stretching one's frames of reference, personal experience, cultural competence, and repertoire of social moves. As Tony Hiss explains in *The Experience of Place*, our innate skills in simultaneous perception allow us to "take in whatever is around us—which means sensations of touch and balance, for instance, in addition to all sights, sounds, and smells."

Let's not get too romantic about cities, however, or at least let's have a sense of the downside of messes. Nineteenth-century Western cities and today's global mega-cities of the developing world share acute problems caused by the messes that result when many people congregate in the same places over incredibly short periods of time. Lack of water and sewage systems cause disease; the lack of housing produces shantytowns and homelessness. Planning was invented to clean up these messy aspects of cities; the same problems that now plague many global cities.

The simple benefit of experiencing the messes and disorder of cities is that diversity is healthy for human development. It teaches tolerance, encourages curiosity, requires adaptation to uncertainty, and promotes an ethic for navigating public space. And sometimes city streets are frightening and require flight. Overall, however, walking through messy cities builds civic commonality in the context of urban anonymity in which people show respect without knowing each other. By learning about co-existence and difference, we build personal and community resilience. In *The Conscience of the Eye,* Richard Sennett conveys the ethical messiness of cities as "a place where different ages, races, classes, ways of life, and abilities crowd together on streets or in large buildings. The city is the natural home of difference."

Unfortunately, in the United States, far too few cities and urban places exist in which one can take a stimulating walk through diverse urban neighborhoods and districts. The advent of post-World War II suburbs, public housing, and urban renewal accelerated the separation and dismemberment of mixed-ethnic, mixed-use neighborhoods. Urbanists like Jane Jacobs and Lewis Mumford bemoaned for more than fifty years the simplifying, separating, and sterilizing of the urban environment, all of which robbed it of its wonderful messy qualities. The worst examples of this type of urban landscape are high-rise public housing surrounded by empty fields and traditional, single-family, car-dependent suburbs in which only the woods and messy basements offer adventures for kids. This simplifying process is even evident in contemporary neo-traditional neighborhood planning and downtown revitalization, which have been heralded as restoring European-style urbanity. Ironically, Disney-like waterfront developments—as predictably cookie cutter as they are—have created new public spaces that encourage diversity and civic commotion. Moreover, the influx of a myriad of immigrant groups into suburbs and edge cities—old and new—has overwhelmed planning simplification and redesign and recreated some messy urban moments. In the end, people trump urban design as they recreate messes.

Old-fashioned central cities are now participants in metro regions in which they have declining influence. Self-protecting suburbs, the inability of many cities to expand their boundaries, and weak regional systems have created a messy patchwork of enclaves that shape social interactions, politics, and policy. Gerald Frug, in *CityMaking*, sketches provocative ways to advance community building in the context of metro regions and their disconnected places. He recommends new forms of cross-jurisdictional decision-making, financing, and voting as methods to bridge unnecessary boundaries and divisions and to promote common agendas.

Cities and regions are markets, central places in which goods and services, information, skills, and partnerships are exchanged and transformed into new products and services. This episodic role, as in occasional, seasonal fairs, became a permanent feature of towns and cities, and promoted voluntary and frequently messy exchange among many different kinds of producers, consumers, and traders. Over time, city markets moved beyond the simple exchange of goods to new roles that included adding value to raw materials, invention, manufacturing, and business services and coordination.

Markets are messes, but orderly messes, that are created by societies and exist within established rules and norms of behavior for exchange, payment, and future purchases. Markets require entrepreneurs of different types. My favorite places to visit in U.S. cities or around the world are public markets. Whether in Guangzhou, Mexico City, or Baltimore, public markets offer messy experiences of societies, cultures, and business life that never cease to engage and surprise. Think of the World Wide Web and blogosphere as the latest versions of a messy marketplace of ideas, products, and services.

Messy markets are not loved by everyone, however. The destruction of Maxwell Street in Chicago—a low-end retail district and flea market—is a case in point. It was just too messy and uncontrollable, and the city refused to invest in its upkeep over the years. Moreover, the University of Illinois at Chicago wanted to erect new dorms and classrooms on the vacant land. The City of Chicago had originally designated Maxwell Street a public market in 1912; it combined low-end retail district and flea market and was home to Eastern European Jewish immigrants. As the surrounding buildings fell under the wrecking ball in the 1960s and 1970s, Maxwell Street became a vibrant weekend market covering ten to fifteen square blocks and involving hundreds of small entrepreneurs. Blues musicians played on corners, ethnic entrepreneurs sold specialty wares and food, and vendors hawked everything imaginable, including what was stolen from your car the week before. What a wonderful example of grassroots, entrepreneurial economics at work. It was too good to last. Mayor Richard M. Daley destroyed the market in the early 1990s in a fit of urban cleansing and land grabbing and moved its remnants several blocks east to a more "secure" location.

Markets triumph, however. A recent visit to the relocated Maxwell Street made me realize that while the relocation of Maxwell Street was a land grab, the new market on Canal Street was healthy and thriving. It was also cleaner, a little less funky, more regulated, and better smelling. My skepticism was that of a preservationist, not of a marketer. I do wonder, though, what will happen to this new market location as high-income housing and commercial development continue to be built around it.

Cities are also the birthplaces of democracy—whether in ancient Athens, the free towns and communes of Europe in the Middle Ages, or New England town meetings. These days, however, the world of politics is talked about as being a mess in a negative sense—confusing, rife with money, driven by narrow self-interests, and ineffective. Yet, at its best, democratic politics as we know it is about building coalitions to achieve common purposes. While we share many commonalities in U.S. society, it's frequently difficult to identify the public good of specific issues without resorting to the topsy-turvy process of advocacy, bargaining, and negotiation. In other words, politics is coalition building to solve messy problems—important things about which there are much uncertainty and a host of value conflicts.

As in the marketplace, a tendency exists in the political world to shut off competition, multiple voices, and alternative policy formulations. Competition is great in theory, but is hard work and produces winners and losers. Simplifying politics occurs when one interest group secures advantage in the short run; the long-term danger is the monopoly power of specific groups, the worst case being an anti-liberal regime that curtails rights and responsibilities. In a more benign form, a myriad of obstacles are thrown up in our cities and towns to thwart voting, access to key information, and civic participation in decision-making. If we become separated from the messiness of interests and experience, however, our answers to problems become brittle, uninspired, and ineffective.

Messes and politics went together in Chicago during the first years of the mayoral administration of Harold Washington, what came to be called the period of "Council Wars," or "Beirut on the Lake." I believe that our most creative period of policy innovation, grassroots outreach, and coalition building occurred when the Washington advocates had only twenty-one votes in City Council to the majority's twenty-nine. Some critics called this situation a mess in a negative sense, but the political competition engaged and motivated everyone. When Washington ultimately secured a majority in 1986, I observed a pulling back from innovation, although the espoused rhetoric was that now we could implement a more comprehensive, progressive agenda.

Messiness Theory

Contemporary theorizing about complexity and chaos sheds light on the meaning of messes. Unfortunately, the abundance of complexity and chaos theories has given them a faddish quality that reduces their power of explanation. Nevertheless, these theories illuminate messes and offer important guidance for leaders in how to design effective interventions and organizations.

Complexity refers to the dismantling of the old paradigm of fixed, linear, hierarchical systems—what some have called the industrial paradigm. New and emerging environments, in contrast, are characterized by constant change, uncertainty, open systems, decentralization, networks, and information flows. These elements define what has been called the new economy, which has lost some of its glow from the dot.com meltdown. Elements of complex environments are bundled in new and unexpected ways—sometimes by farsighted entrepreneurs—and then continue to morph and evolve. Sound familiar—a creative stew, a mess?

Complexity and chaos refer also to patterns of order in messy populations or environments, like weather and cloud formations. Small changes can make huge differences when repeated and multiplied many times, giving new credence to the importance of incremental improvement as we lose faith in the possibility and advisability of big changes.

Provocative implications derive from this brief excursion into complexity and chaos theory. Messes are orderly, but difficult to discern easily within these environments. Likewise, small changes can make a difference in the ways that systems and environments behave if we can identify high-leverage, small changes. And the changes that organizations make are likely to reflect their past. Margaret Wheatley, in *Leadership and the New Science*, states that,

> Self-reference is what facilitates orderly change in turbulent environments. In human organizations, a clear sense of identity—of the values, traditions, aspirations, competences, and cultures that guide the operation—is the real source of independence from the environment.

Two organizational design strategies follow from complexity theory. Charles Handy, in the *Age of Paradox*, emphasizes the importance of *subsidiarity*, the devolution of functions and responsibilities to the smallest possible unit, whether level of government, business division or work team, or building block of community. Learning and adaptation occur at the front lines. Dee Hock, founder of VISA and author of *Birth of the Chaordic Age*, advances the notion of the inside/out corporation—that is, central functions are invented by member organizations or affiliates rather than by the center. Think of VISA or of how school systems should work. In both cases, the source of innovation is the periphery, not the center; command and control leadership is outmoded.

Encouraging simplicity and the cleaning up of messy complexity, however, has distinguished the European Enlightenment, the building of nation-states, and even the evolution of the market economy. Nation-states required the homogenization of languages, ethnicities, nations, currencies, time zones, and a whole host of administrative procedures. Bureaucracy, after all, is premised on *rule-based* action applied to many varied situations. Many benefits derived from simplification and standardization, whether governing formerly separate principalities, delivering the mail, bringing new products to scale, or creating new institutions like commodity markets. The enemy was local variation.

But, simplification can veer out of control, as demonstrated by totalitarian ideologies and regimes, dehumanized city planning (e.g., public housing high-rises), or mono-crop agriculture. As political anthropologist James C. Scott warns in *Seeing Like a State*, "Radically simplified designs for social organization seem to court the same risks of failure courted by radically simplified designs for natural environments." Oversimplification, ultimately, brings about instability and disaster, as when overplanting of a single crop year after year weakens the soil's structure and nutrient base, increases susceptibility to disease, and heightens risks of erosion.

Messiness Is Messy

Conventional meanings of messes explain much about people and communities. Messes, in this sense, refer to disorder, confusion, muddles, untidiness, and filth—a heap or jumble. I remember my parents' yelling at my sisters and me on more than one occasion, "Clean up that mess!" An article on a neighborhood fight in Baltimore over the re-use of an old church was titled "Holy Mess." Anthony Bourdain, in *Kitchen Confidential*, rightly observes that a cook's "messy station equals messy mind." This chapter has struggled valiantly to make messes into more noble things. Now it's time, at the close of this chapter, to acknowledge the full story of messiness.

The concept *tyranny of structurelessness*, coined by Jo Freeman in her classic 1970 speech and article on social movement organizations, describes a mess typical in many corners of organizational and civic life that prevents clear thinking and action and ultimately reinforces the status quo. Messes of this sort cleverly mask such intents by espousing the benefits of openness, lack of authoritarian structure, and responsiveness. Meetings go nowhere, goals are not plausibly connected to authority and action, and meetings adjourn without any clear understanding of who's in charge. These meetings have such numbing and confusing effects that attendees rush to escape without fully digesting the failure of the meetings to make progress.

Another version of messes in inner-city neighborhoods, identified by George Kelling and Catherine Coles in *Fixing Broken Windows*, calls attention to the impact of *visible signs of disorder*—broken windows, abandoned buildings, vacant land, burned-out cars, and young or seemingly homeless men hanging out on street corners—on civic, financial, and business development. People interpret these signs as indication that the neighborhood is too far gone; is a place to escape from rather than a place to stop and shop; and certainly is not a place to raise a family. Of course, such signs sometimes relate to inexperience with the messes of cities and mask conventional signs of order and stability that exist on the protected side streets.

A favored urban revitalization strategy, for example, is to rid downtowns of the homeless. The homeless scare suburbanites by acting crazy and by begging sidewalk café dwellers for money just as these neo-urbanites are imagining themselves in Paris or Amsterdam. Cleaning up downtowns involves relocating missions, shelters, and feeding programs so that occasional visitors don't have to witness poverty amidst plenty.

In some ways, social disorganization becomes most visible in the aftermath of natural and man-made disasters—floods, chemical spills, and nuclear reactor meltdowns, for example—that produce messes that are far-reaching. Sociologist Kai Erickson, in *New Species of Trouble*, observes the terrible and long-term impacts of these disasters, which resemble in many respects the human tragedies perpetuated by concentrated, intergenerational poverty.

> By collective trauma … I mean a blow to the basic tissues of social life that damages the bonds attaching people together and impairs the prevailing sense of community … a gradual realization that the community no longer exists as an effective source of support and that an important part of the self has disappeared.

What is so tragic about the Hurricane Katrina aftermath in New Orleans is the combination of a natural disaster with public sector incompetence and pervasive institutional as well as human poverty. Together an unprecedented mess has been created whose negative consequences have fallen most heavily on the residents with the fewest resources and fewest choices. A mess of this proportion continues to produce paralysis of action and human burnout. But as *Washington Post* columnist Eugene Robinson observes, "… the greatest natural disaster would have been just a messy inconvenience if not for the fumbling hand of man."

In light of messy messes, I can't count the number of times that advisors, bosses, and colleagues have counseled me, "Keep it simple!" The value of this counsel has been proven to me by my own proclivity over the years to offer the same advice to my colleagues.

In many situations we just need a simpler set of choices, whether for picking retirement investment options, making health care decisions, or even buying homes. A part of the problem is what is called *cognitive overload*; we just can't process too much information or do too many things at once. We want things simple, not messy. Habits are comfortable in part because we don't have to think. This means, of course, that we are taken advantage of now and again by the marketers of simplicity. That's okay because too many options guarantee that we do nothing or are preyed upon by unscrupulous vendors.

What makes "Keep it simple" such good advice? "Keep it simple" means take one step at a time and learn as you go. It also means picking two or three high-priority actions or changes that you and your colleagues want to be remembered for. *Making Connections*, for example, charts progress after six years in terms of neighborhood employment, family asset building, and children's readiness for school. We're even toying with the idea of a central management entity in each site to provide more coherence to implementation and long-term sustainability. "Keep it simple" means that good theories have the smallest number of moving parts, as the maxim known as *Ockham's Razor* advises. Parsimony is power.

Organizing Messes

Don't be afraid of messes; they can be your creative friends. Don't stand for lingering messes; they will undermine worthy efforts. There is no simple answer to this dilemma. We live in a complicated world that defies simple answers. But this world does need to be made legible and transparent if we are to act with confidence and credibility. Embracing messes and clarifying them should be twin goals for effective civic leaders. I offer a few lessons to help.

- Learn the difference between creative and paralyzing messes—their underlying dynamics, how to navigate them, and what your tolerance is for ambiguity.

- Organizations need to revisit their linear *one-size-fits-all* approach to problem-solving and service delivery if they are to thrive in the world of messes.

- Take small, incremental steps when confronted by messes to learn what they are about and to seed change. Big steps sometimes make bigger messes.

- Going simple has its merits, and simple things underlie much complexity, but simplicity, if taken to extremes, can become one-dimensional and oppressive.

8

Mistakes Are Your Résumé

o o o o o o o o o o o o o o o o o o o o o o o o o o o o o o
We pay a heavy price for our fear of
failure. It is a powerful obstacle to growth

—*John W. Gardner*

Early in my CED career, I experienced a failure that has stayed with me for decades. When I worked for the Eighteenth Street Development Corporation, we launched a spin-off construction company. It was a way to create jobs for our pre-apprentice trainees and take advantage of the home renovation market that we were helping to stimulate through counseling and loans. We undertook a business feasibility study, developed a business plan, raised capital, and hired an initial business manager to start up the new venture.

It was a failure. A part of the story was that the bright-idea guy (i.e., me) left the organization just as the new venture was getting off the ground. That was a blow to the effort, and I still regret my timing. But there were many other problems as well. Simply, the neighborhood construction work didn't materialize, and the business manager couldn't identify alternative markets. During this period, the early 1980s, federal housing programs were cut or frozen, further narrowing our intended market. Our timing was off.

Such failures are nothing new in the CED field. I have devoted much attention to analyzing and learning from failures and mistakes—either others' or mine. By mistakes I do not mean, for the most part, scandal, sudden about-faces in commitments and focus, premature withdrawals of funding commitments, or rogue organizations. I'm referring to what Eliot Cohen and John Gooch, in *Military Misfortunes: The Anatomy of Failure in War*, call "constructive failures," those failures that occur in spite of thoughtful design and implementation. Such failures somehow defy the best theories, past experience, and sound advice; they can call into question basic assumptions. Constructive failures can provide invaluable insights into problems and solutions and can, in theory, lay the groundwork for the next generation of investments. Yet many leaders in the nonprofit sector rarely venture beyond the rhetoric of learning to share their mistakes openly.

Paradoxically, mistakes galvanize the learning process much more than successes.

Mistakes may be the most important part of a résumé, even if you haven't written them down on paper. They represent the experience behind the words. As you read this chapter, take the opportunity to ask yourself the following questions:

- What have been your top three constructive mistakes?
- What mistake have you learned the most from?
- How does your organization view mistakes?
- Whom do you talk to about mistakes and the lessons learned?

Mistakes and the Nonprofit Sector

What has stayed with me for decades from that early failure experience is a sense of skepticism about nonprofit business ventures and social enterprises. For most neighborhood nonprofits, operating in the marketplace—even with a safety net—is not a slam-dunk pathway to success. Every city has spectacular nonprofit business failures to bear this out. In 1984, I wrote, in a *Neighborhood Works* article with Wim Wiewel, about nonprofit business ventures, "[S]ince most new businesses fail, neighborhood development organizations will have to confront the organizational consequences of losing ventures ... Failure affects credit ratings, credibility, staff morale, and relations with your constituency ... Can neighborhoods afford failures of this sort?"

I undertook three feasibility studies for nonprofit ventures when I directed South East Community Organization (SECO) in Baltimore: a concierge business linking downtown office workers to neighborhood vendors, a neighborhood resource recycling business, and a long-term health care co-op. None of them appeared sustainable. A few years later, after I had left SECO, a new director launched the health care co-op anyway, and, not surprisingly, it failed.

Yet nonprofit ventures do succeed, some of them truly awe-inspiring, like Pioneer Human Services in Seattle or Delancey Street in San Francisco. Somehow they combine effective business models, leadership, technical assistance, financing, and luck.

In the entrepreneurial business world, mistakes are an important part of your résumé. Thomas Peters and Robert Waterman, in their 1980s classic study of successful corporations, *In Search of Excellence*, write, "A special attribute of the success-oriented, positive, and innovating environment is a substantial tolerance for failure." For example, venture capital firms sometimes even require that you have one or two mistakes in your career history. Entrepreneurs pick themselves up and try again.

The nonprofit sector, however, is somewhat allergic to talking about mistakes. During the past several years, as I've begun to write about mistakes and philanthropy, I've encountered some strange reactions. Not surprisingly, communication consultants get all twisted up by the notion of talking openly about mistakes. You should be promoting your successes, they say. The technical folks reluctantly acknowledge the importance of thinking about mistakes, but then ask whether the time is right given the current political climate or the state of the nonprofit sector. A few brave souls have said, "Great stuff. Go for it!"

A number of individuals, organizations, and philanthropies, however, are grappling with the power of mistakes. For example, the failure of the Virginia Eastern Shore Corporation in 1999 yielded lessons about the perils of joining community economic development and environmentalism. Similarly, the failure of seemingly high-performing community development corporations (CDCs) has occasioned serious reflection about the support mechanisms for these entrepreneurial organizations by national intermediaries like LISC. Finally, a recent *New York Times* article reports that "many of the nation's largest foundations regard disclosing and analyzing their failures as bordering on a moral obligation."

Talking about mistakes, even constructive mistakes, is counterintuitive. Yet I believe that talking about mistakes is critical to develop authentic, risk-taking, organizational cultures that support innovation and continuous improvement.

The *Jobs Initiative*

In looking at mistakes, let's consider the Jobs Initiative. As I've said previously, the *Jobs Initiative* (JI) was an eight-year investment of more than $30 million by the Annie E. Casey Foundation. Started in 1995 in six cities—Denver, Milwaukee, New Orleans, Philadelphia, Seattle, and St. Louis—the JI supported jobs projects and workforce systems changes that created better opportunities for low-income young adults to acquire good jobs and career and become connected to regional economies.

Earlier failures and successes in the employment and training field shaped the JI design. The comprehensive Job Training Partnership Act (JTPA) evaluation published in 1993 concluded that few practices were successful in the workforce field, and what did work had minimal effects.

However, one exemplary program, the Center for Employment Training (CET), which produced remarkable income gains, was buried in the evaluation. Unlike other programs, CET was employer-driven, market-oriented, community-based, and job-centered. The JI embraced CET's core features and asked participating sites to invest in jobs projects that applied these principles in various industries and with different groups of job seekers. Paradoxically, subsequent evaluation studies have cast doubt upon the CET model.

At the same time, the historic inability to replicate effective social programs influenced the JI design—the tendency of cookie-cutter programs to fail when confronted by the idiosyncrasies of local situations. The JI adopted the thinking of *design replication,* in which the focus was on transplanting core principles into different environments, full of local nuance, rather than imposing a rigid program model for all situations.

Four additional elements of workforce development failure influenced the JI design. First, too few training programs focused on the needs of employers or on regional characteristics and did not fully grapple with the challenges of long-term job retention. Second, many job training programs gave short shrift to low-income, low-skilled men, even though they were hard hit by economic restructuring, incarceration, and family crisis. Third, local civic champions seldom adopted workforce development as a key element of their platform for community renewal. Finally, workforce development efforts have seldom accounted for the role of race, ethnicity, and gender in employer relations, retention, advancement, and the workplace.

The JI devoted its final four years to *system reform* strategies that built upon the experience and capacity of sites. Without this focus, small, effective jobs projects may never become adopted, expanded, and institutionalized by the fragmented institutions and funding streams that characterize workforce development. At the same time, by explicitly investing in systems change, the JI ran the risk of antagonizing a competitive, piecemeal system that always seemed ready to protect itself from outside reformers.

The JI recognized at the outset the likelihood of mistakes and the potential benefits of early mistakes. With the JI lasting eight-plus years, the Foundation provided time for sites to fail and to develop second and third plans of action in response.

The JI adopted an outcomes framework developed by the Rensselaerville Institute to guide its investments. This approach emphasized results, learning, and a prototyping methodology to test strategic assumptions and, when possible, to fail small and learn big. By focusing not only on connecting job seekers to good jobs, but also on long-run retention and career advancement, the JI pushed the envelope of established practices in the workforce field. Expanding the commitment to these results required new experiments and thus new mistakes.

Finally, the JI helped sites use quantitative and other relevant information to assess progress and to take corrective actions. Employment and training programs risk having, statistically speaking, *no effect* unless program implementers learn and continuously improve their programs.

Several typical indicators of workforce development success illustrate JI accomplishments and the areas in which mistakes and failures took place. The JI recruited twenty-two thousand harder-to-employ participants and placed twelve thousand by 2005 with over three thousand employers. One-year retention rates in forty-plus jobs projects ranged from a low of 20 percent to a high of 80 percent. Participants increased wages and hours worked, on average boosting incomes by $4,000 per year. JI participants more frequently obtained health benefits.

In sum, the *Jobs Initiative* led to three major insights about workforce development for low-income, low-skilled workers:

- Long-term job retention and advancement can be achieved through employer-focused workforce investments that combine job readiness and skills training, human service supports, and post-employment services.

- Effective workforce providers can be developed through a combination of flexible capital, technical assistance, outcomes-based design, and high-engagement investing.

- Achieving concrete workforce results can provide credibility to advocate for both workforce policy reform and new institutional arrangements that foster career advancement.

Four *Jobs Initiative* Mistakes

Not surprisingly, mistakes were made along the way, constructive mistakes, for the most part. Although I focus herein on site-based mistakes, we at the Foundation made some key mistakes as well: not focusing enough on long-run career advancement, not requiring more public sector engagement at the front end, and inventing a much too conservative definition of labor market retention.

Swinging for the Home Run. FOCUS HOPE of Detroit is an exemplary, long-term training program started in the 1980s that continues today. Its partnerships with the auto industry enabled it to develop an array of initiatives that included a manufacturing business, remedial help for high school graduates, machinist training, and courses linked to a four-year engineering school. Graduates of its sixty-week training program filled well-paying, skilled machinist jobs.

Philadelphia stakeholders attempted to replicate FOCUS HOPE. As part of the effort, the Ogontz Avenue Revitalization Corporation—a local community development corporation—purchased an old factory building in a North Philadelphia neighborhood to house the replication project. It also recruited key stakeholders to invest in the replication, including the former CEO of Crown, Cork, and Seal, The Reinvestment Fund (TRF), Philadelphia Community College, and the Delaware Valley Industrial Resource Corporation.

The Philadelphia Accelerated Manufacturing Education (PhAME) attracted major public, private, and philanthropic investment and formed partnerships with community colleges and local engineering schools. A major shipbuilding award for Philadelphia's naval yards promised an important economic development linkage. Most important, documented shortages existed for thousands of skilled machinist jobs at manufacturing plants in the region.

But the project failed. By 2004, PhAME had merged with the Delaware Valley Industrial Resource Center. Few prospects remain for recreating in Philadelphia the complex of job training programs that constitute FOCUS HOPE.

What were the mistakes? First, the timing was wrong. Second, overcommitment to a single approach prevented creative adaptation.

The timing mistake had two dimensions. The mid- and late-1990s were simply the worst possible moment to launch a long-term training program. Public policymakers rewrote the playbook for welfare clients and job seekers by requiring *work first* policies that put people in jobs, not job training, even if the jobs had no future. The economic prosperity and tight labor markets of the 1990s gave *work first* credibility.

This training model required full-time coursework for sixty weeks with the promise of high-paying machinist jobs. Not surprisingly, it sought more job-ready candidates with higher skills who could support themselves while out of work. But this was impossible for many lower-income, inner-city participants, the program's target group.

The project and its supporters launched a creative but ultimately quixotic advocacy campaign to solve this problem. Their answer was financial stipends for participants. PhAME found an ally in Philadelphia Interfaith Action (PIA), a metropolitan coalition of congregations. The combination of business leadership and African American pastors formed a potent coalition to persuade local and state officials to provide stipend dollars, first $2 million and then $5 million. In the short run, they achieved a victory; stipends brought in a new cohort of trainees with lower incomes and sketchier job histories. In the long run, however, the well ran dry for stipends as training dollars dwindled.

PhAME and its supporters scrambled to invent new financing mechanisms that would attract short-term capital to support the long-term wage and income gains that would result from sixty-week training. The timing and cost just weren't right, however, and the project eventually lost the ability to provide stipends. Participants as well as allies, including the interfaith coalition, drifted away.

Philadelphia also suffered from its overcommitment to a single approach. As the long-term training project was getting off the ground, the JI was working with local businesses through Philadelphia First—a coalition of corporate leaders—to design a short-term training curriculum for entry-level, semi-skilled manufacturing jobs. There were eight to ten thousand manufacturing job openings in the Philadelphia area, jobs that would pay $8-$10 per hour and required no more than six months of training.

As this shorter-term training program got off the ground, the private sector board chair of PhAME, also the chair of the corporate leaders group, Philadelphia First, raised strong objections. Concerned that the short-term manufacturing training project threatened PhAME's viability, he argued that the short-term project be subsumed under the longer-term training project. Not surprisingly, it eventually became the program that dropouts from PhAME fell into. Consequently, the short-term program, which cost less, did not require stipends, and addressed labor shortages, was undermined.

Yet the graduates of PhAME, as predicted, have had some of the highest retention rates and wage gains in the entire JI. Long-term training made a real difference, but it cost a lot.

Me and My Theory. JI site-based theories of change built upon the unique attributes of local investors, partners, and policy advocates in the ways they formulated strategies to connect low-income residents to jobs and careers. For example, TRF in Philadelphia is an experienced community loan fund, while in St. Louis, East-West Gateway—a regional planning agency—specialized in transportation planning. The Milwaukee *Jobs Initiative* and partners like the Wisconsin Regional Training Partnership (WRTP) had strong ties to the labor movement.

Local investors created working theories of change over time through trial and error. A common pitfall, however, was that sites often fell in love with their theories and did not easily abandon or modify them, even in the face of steep challenges and disconfirming evidence. Unfortunately, it's sometimes difficult to distinguish sites that held on too long to bad ideas from sites that held on to ideas that just needed longer to incubate.

The Denver Workforce Initiative (DWI), operated by a local Denver foundation, was the first JI site to start implementation. Early in the JI, the DWI drew two conclusions that led it to develop a distinctive theory of change. The first conclusion, derived from community focus groups, was that people obtained information and support from friends, acquaintances, and family, not from formalized community organizations and the formal workforce development system. The second conclusion was that job seekers, employees, and employers had to change the culture of work to achieve job retention—including changes in workforce expectations, problem-solving, and conflict resolution.

DWI's theory of change, which was based upon these two conclusions, called for informal community coaches to recruit and support job seekers; a set of job readiness and supervisory training curricula validated by business and community; and a work readiness index that helped employers and employees measure readiness to get and keep a job. Denver's theory of change required heroic efforts to build authentic community connections and to transform workplaces.

It didn't work. First, it was difficult to implement. A key problem was finding and training community coaches, who in turn were to find and support people looking for work. Second, few businesses were willing to assess the health of their organizations honestly and then co-invest in the transformation of their companies in order to accommodate the needs of entry-level workers.

DWI developed several nationally recognized tools for training and assessment. But the organization was unable to utilize the whole set of tools at even a modest scale. At the same time, it was concerned that the JI's focus on results hindered the implementation of their innovations.

Developing a viable theory of change was essential for the JI sites. But holding on too long to the theory led to problems when results didn't match expectations.

Self-Evaluation Is an Unnatural Act. A key assumption of the JI was that well-meaning people and organizations committed to the same goals would be willing to confront mistakes and poor performance in order to improve results and make needed changes. The JI called this self-evaluation, in contrast to the long-term assessment or evaluation of results by third-party researchers.

The JI promoted self-evaluation in several ways. At the outset, the JI sought to clarify and communicate the JI's givens, assumptions, and hoped-for results so that everyone was working from the same game plan. The JI's outcome management framework helped sites specify strategies, targets, and milestones, and develop data collection systems. By building into its funding agreements reporting protocols for data collection, learning, corrections, and penalties for inadequate data, the JI reinforced its expectations for self evaluation.

The JI identified key elements of self-evaluation and created incentives and opportunities for sites to engage in self-evaluation. Self-evaluation opportunities included quarterly reports, site visits, and site-leader meetings on such topics as job retention. Moreover, the JI did its own self-evaluation. It assembled experts to reflect on JI results; supported additional studies on cost benchmarking of strategies and results and ethnographies of twenty-five families; and convened meetings of participants and employers to give feedback.

The JI made two mistakes regarding self-evaluation. It underestimated organizational resistance to self-evaluation and did not sufficiently invest in the development of explicit models of self-evaluation.

Workforce providers, as well as the broader nonprofit community, are skeptical about evaluation—who does it, how it is done, what it costs, and how it is used. Many nonprofits still remember the harm done by the Job Training Partnership Act evaluations that failed to sort out what worked from what didn't in the early 1990s. Front-line workers often bear the brunt of evaluations, and many involved in the JI were not enthusiastic about doing them. Not surprisingly, skepticism about the concept readily emerged, even though self-evaluation was billed as "good medicine."

The fact that the major funder of the JI was advocating self-evaluation also influenced site reactions. Local program leaders questioned whether the Foundation could separate its participation in self-evaluation from its role as investor. They questioned the value-added of the Foundation, aside from the money, and of exposing their own weaknesses in a way that might influence funding decisions. The JI resources were guaranteed for the long term, but local leaders questioned the value of reflecting too much too early as they moved through the start-up phase to implementation.

At the same time, several sites preferred generating innovations rather than managing for results. Sites rightly expressed concern that premature self-evaluation could undermine innovation, demoralize staff who were being asked to do things differently, or narrow the focus of innovation to the very short term.

The JI's leaders believed that if they built a strong measurement system, the sites would use it to do self-evaluation. It did not happen that way, in large part because of a disconnect between goals and realities. The JI focused on keeping people in jobs for the long term, but could not measure retention, much less motivate staff and partners to do something about it, until enough participants theoretically reached that milestone.

Further complicating matters were the economic and policy changes of the 1990s, which created tight labor markets and *work first* policies. Sites had to work harder to employ as many people as possible, even though many of their jobs projects were designed to help more job-ready clients. Finally, the economy and job opportunities worsened with the new century.

Even when the time was right for self-evaluation, several sites balked. It was a foundation project, not something they needed. In fact, some sites kept double books so that they could report their results to local leaders in a more favorable way.

Most important, the Foundation failed to create and support a simple but powerful model of self-evaluation. The numbers were supposed to be only a start, not the finish. But the focus on building information systems elevated the importance of numbers. Lower-than-expected job-retention rates can stem from many things, including poor participant selection, inadequate job-readiness training, or lack of job-centered human services. Understanding poor retention results required talking with front-line workers, employers, and other service providers.

Self-evaluation is an unnatural act. It is also an essential task for workforce providers and intermediaries, but implementing it will meet resistance. While the JI took important steps to encourage and require self-evaluation, it was a mistake not to have had a clearer self-evaluation design and a strategy for nurturing its implementation.

Flying Without a Net. Community interests collided in the JI at its inception. Organizations formed partnerships overnight and made promises to compete for the JI, while the eighteen-month planning process raised concerns about who got the money and who got the credit. If things weren't challenging enough, the JI start-up heaped expectations on JI entrepreneurs. Inevitably, not everyone attained what he or she wanted.

In many, but not all, cases the JI was not the central activity of its lead organizations. The JI spanned organizational boundaries as it built partnerships; struggled to stay aligned with the lead organization's mission and operating culture; and became absorbed into the Foundation's culture and family of initiatives. In a few cases—in which the JI was an explicit partnership—staff existed uneasily inside sometimes ill-defined governance diagrams.

The JI mistake was in not understanding the JI's impact on lead organizations and project directors. The Foundation did not do enough to prepare staff and organizations for the stresses they would experience. Although the JI management team intervened many times, it could have done a better job spotting problems and preventing or ameliorating contentious issues.

One JI site story illustrates the problem of *flying without a net*.

The JI lead organization in St. Louis was a regional planning agency—East-West Gateway. Although not directly engaged in workforce development in the past, the agency became more involved in the 1990s by working to improve transportation options for inner-city residents seeking work in the suburbs.

What was not obvious at the outset, however, was that the agency's distinctive organizational culture was not a good fit for handling the JI. It was not skilled at implementing programs, especially those that required flexibility and partnerships. It preferred formalized competitive bidding and performance-based contracting. And it had a relatively low pay scale, which forced the agency to constantly replenish a young staff that supplemented a core group of transportation planners and engineers.

The St. Louis JI did not have a project director in its first several years; existing staff performed these functions. Implementation was slow to get off the ground. The site's workforce planning and competitive bid processes complicated the development of jobs projects and partnerships. Based upon this early experience, and under pressure from the Foundation, St. Louis chose a new project director from the East Coast with considerable organizing and development experience.

Almost from the beginning of the new project director's tenure, tension existed that led to divisions within East-West Gateway and a lack of consensus about the JI. The JI still reported upward to the staff person who launched the JI in St. Louis in the first place. Yet, the new project director represented the JI to the Foundation.

Nevertheless, the JI prospered in St. Louis with the new project director. In the Foundation's eyes, the site overcame economic and institutional constraints to exceed expectations. Yet, by June 2003, the project director was forced to resign. Why did this happen? Several explanations are plausible.

There's no doubt that the JI caused organizational tension within the planning agency. Situated on the margins, the JI staff became inwardly focused, an independent group trying to develop partnerships in a difficult environment. They were organizers, not governmental bureaucrats, and were more attuned to building relationships with external partners than within their own agency. Elsewhere in the lead organization, staff viewed the JI as a rogue unit that operated outside the usual rules because it received much of its money from out-of-town, philanthropic investors.

In retrospect, it is obvious that the JI management team, its technical assistance providers, and evaluation team failed to heed the signs that the St. Louis site was in crisis. Perhaps more importantly, the project director made a mistake by not "managing upward" at the agency during a time of transition. Finally, the agency itself failed in its oversight responsibilities.

Too often foundations and their initiatives target other institutions in the name of system reform, while they should also be focusing on themselves. Other JI sites experienced project director turnover for a variety of reasons. *Flying without a net* frequently comes as a surprise, but it is a predictable aspect of innovative projects.

Learning from Mistakes

These JI mistakes have three implications for social investing beyond the JI. First, many of the JI mistakes grew out of an inability to anticipate, learn, and adapt, at both the site and foundation levels. To minimize that, foundations and other funding groups must invest specifically in efforts that build ongoing capacity to learn and adapt. Investors must recognize that organizations need extra resources to overcome their resistance to self-evaluation. Clearing that hurdle will require long-term investments, tolerance for mistakes, peer learning, and investor self-evaluation. One important step is to develop a series of in-depth case studies about common and not-so-common mistakes in foundation initiatives. This has been done in fields like engineering.

Second, high-engagement philanthropy, as pursued in the JI, produces tensions and challenges that sites must negotiate and balance. With the JI, these tensions contributed to mistakes, which in the best of cases led to fruitful redesign and implementation. Foundations must understand and anticipate such tensions. Investors need to be as clear as possible about their basic assumptions; they also must communicate with grantees about the tensions produced by high-engagement investing. When possible, these tensions can be ameliorated or at least predicted.

Finally, foundations must anticipate mistakes. Although the JI mistakes were constructive in most cases, they could have been predicted. Others had faced similar problems. Investors need to have a greater awareness of the mistakes likely to occur as part of developing and promoting social innovations on the ground. This does not suggest that all mistakes can be avoided. But better recognition may mitigate the damage of mistakes and smooth out the process of learning and adaptation.

What's striking to me is that it takes confident nonprofit leaders not only to share their mistakes, but also to bet their reputations on taking corrective action or going back to the drawing boards. This is honest, high-risk leadership. I'm surprised, however, by how many high-profile leaders duck this responsibility and instead sweep their mistakes under the rug, deny their mistakes altogether, blame their failures on others, or make it a practice to identify the mistakes of others but not their own.

More Mistakes, More Learning

Sharing mistakes is good medicine. As Winston Churchill said, "Success is the ability to move from one failure to another without losing one's enthusiasm." But it doesn't feel good if you are in the thick of things, trying to make challenging strategies work in a complex world. Realistically, though, waiting until the final evaluation reports are submitted to discuss failures may make some knowledge stale and irrelevant. We can learn to read the environment better for potential mistakes and take action to avoid mistakes. Honest and open discussion of mistakes is the most important step and requires the nonprofit sector to ensure that it can happen in ways that do not harm risk-takers and innovators. The nonprofit sector is well suited to show how this can be done.

A few other suggestions for building upon the power of mistakes include:

- Create a portfolio of your favorite constructive and non-constructive mistakes and include what you and others learned from these experiences.
- Support staff in acknowledging mistakes and learning from them.
- Spend time thinking about why confronting mistakes is more engaging than contemplating success. How can confronting mistakes build capacity to recognize mistakes early to take corrective action?
- Form a mistakes support group to reflect upon constructive mistakes in the CED field.

9

Unusual Partners and Allies

o o o o o o o o o o o o o o o o o o o o o o o o o o o o o o
For millions of us, we share fates
and pursue a common good with other people
not necessarily friends or family.

—*Douglas K. Smith*

Working to prevent the Schoenhofen Brewery in Chicago from becoming high-priced condos and a high-tech arts center introduced me to a small printing firm owned by William Kellogg, III. Kellogg had operated his printing plant, located in the east end of the Pilsen neighborhood of Chicago, for decades and employed thirty-five people. The Brewery complex of fifteen buildings on twenty acres had long ceased being the home of Edelweiss Beer ("a taste of good judgment," according to late-nineteenth-century advertising). In the intervening decades, the complex had cranked out Green River soda and pickles, stored chemicals, and served as a chop shop. In the 1970s, it was turned into an orphanage in the movie *The Blues Brothers* and served as the escape route for Pope John Paul II when he visited in 1979.

Bill Kellogg first came on my radar screen during a survey of local Pilsen industries that I and other students at the University of Illinois at Chicago undertook for the City of Chicago as a part of the *Pilsen Neighborhood Plan* and a required planning school group project. Someone finally listened as this white-haired, Evangelical Protestant offered an earful about the horrible conditions at the Brewery complex—the garbage, crime, and dangerous building conditions. Even so, he wanted to expand his facility, which printed food-packaging labels, and create new jobs at a time when Chicago was hemorrhaging jobs and companies.

I learned from Bill Kellogg that although he was a businessman, he shared concerns and aspirations with low-income Pilsen residents. He wanted to create more skilled printing jobs; residents wanted good jobs. And he preferred hiring neighborhood residents—simply because they could get to work more easily by walking, especially important during Chicago's bad winters; residents of the area also wanted jobs nearby. He bluntly noted that the City of Chicago and local real estate development interests were not necessarily on the side of small business; in fact, they didn't listen and frequently made things worse for smaller entrepreneurs like him.

It was an important lesson, as I realized that the real-world behavior of people and institutions could upset my preconceived ideas. I was a product of the 1960s and looked somewhat askance at corporate institutions and the private sector in general. I was also completely naïve about the complicated interests of different stakeholders that frequently defied simple categorization. Today, though, I'm pleased that I was open to learning about unusual partners.

Community residents joined with Bill Kellogg to form the *Pilsen Housing and Business Alliance*. The Alliance sought to discover and build upon common values and approaches that would benefit all neighborhood partners. Not everyone always agreed, much less understood or approved of the ways different partners advocated their cases. Bill Kellogg, for example, didn't favor picket lines or rowdy behavior in community meetings, even when city officials were stonewalling residents and businesses. But over the next few years, these unlikely partners fought off developers, tore down dilapidated buildings, and convinced the City of Chicago to make some long-needed infrastructure investments in the Brewery complex. Along the way, Bill Kellogg expanded his printing facility and created additional jobs for community residents.

This chapter doesn't offer a secret recipe for forming effective alliances with unlikely partners. Rather, it tells several stories about unlikely partners from my CED career and draws out relevant lessons. The primary lessons are to be open to old and new partners, recognize your potential as a partner, and understand what it takes to make partnerships work. And, as in most endeavors, not every partnership works. While you read this chapter, keep the following questions in mind:

- What unlikely partners do you work with and for what purpose?
- Are you an unlikely partner?
- In your experience, what are the key ingredients for effective partnerships?

- Why do some partnerships never get off the ground? Why do some partnerships thrive through hard times?

Partners for Industry

A few years later—in the mid-1980s—I met many more Bill Kelloggs when I worked for the City of Chicago. These steelmakers, recyclers, printers, and chemical plants faced problems similar to those Kellogg confronted related to the destabilizing mixture of neglect and upscale real estate development taking place along Clybourn Avenue and on Goose Island, both historic Chicago industrial districts. Indeed, they faced a situation that Pilsen has faced only in recent years. Chicago's near north side was experiencing a real estate boom, which encouraged speculators to buy up old industrial loft buildings.

What happened next was predictable. When speculators bought old loft buildings with high-end commercial or residential uses in mind, they assumed that they could get zoning variances when needed because industrial districts typically did not permit residential uses. Obtaining permission was no sweat; after all, this was Chicago, and real estate development greased the wheels at City Hall. You just had to hire a favored law firm and talk to the alderman; everything else would fall in line. These developers also had the habit (and the nerve) of applying for a variety of public incentives to help make the financing packages for their speculative projects both feasible and lucrative—incentives like historic tax credits and federal Urban Development Action Grants (UDAGs), not to mention the hidden subsidies related to the public infrastructure of streets and sewers. With these incentives came promises of jobs, new businesses, and increased tax revenues. Whether there was really a viable market for these new uses at the time or not, this incremental speculation ate away at inner-city industrial districts, creating a self-fulfilling prophecy of empty industrial buildings and higher land prices. Businesses just moved out or chose not to move into these industrial districts because of the uncertainty and speculative prices.

As in the Brewery story, an unlikely coalition of businesses, neighborhood activists, local politicians, citywide advocacy groups, and labor unions came together to advocate for strengthening planning and zoning regulations for industrial districts like these that were under siege. In this case, I must have seemed like the unlikely partner, for now I worked for the City of Chicago, often the conscious or unconscious facilitator of these neighborhood changes because of the way it made business and infrastructure investments and processed zoning variations and appeals. Frequently having to fend off the objections and obstructions of City Hall colleagues, we fought rezoning applications building by building, replied to the media slogan that "manufacturing was dead" with our own research, produced reports that documented the thousands of jobs that were at stake, and crafted plausible legislation that allowed change to occur in a more carefully planned way. On its third mayor, the industrial protection coalition won.

In retrospect, these were the right fights at the right time. But Chicago's economy—as well as the global economy—kept changing, and it became tougher and tougher for inner-city manufacturing and its jobs to survive and prosper while being heckled by in-moving people who liked the industrial look but not the noise and smells. This situation was becoming a fact of life not only in Chicago, but also in cities as far apart as Seattle and New York. Yet many commercial businesses produced better-than-average entry-level jobs and needed a location that served expanding central business districts like package delivery services, office suppliers, and back office operations. Firms like these have moved in and remained. Maybe our unusual partners and allies in these fights to preserve manufacturing were looking backward, or maybe we were just trying to keep the playing field level for all businesses.

This was the first of numerous personal lessons for me about unusual partners. One thing was clear: this wasn't just about how to come up with new and undiscovered partners; it was also relinquishing blinders about who could be a partner and understanding that I could be seen as an unlikely partner in the eyes of others. Finding unusual partners meant looking at the world differently.

Unusual Partnership Ingredients

Shifting allegiances make the terrain of partnerships, likely or unlikely, difficult to comprehend. Mary Nelson, the venerable founding executive director of Bethel New Life on Chicago's west side, once paraphrased a famous quotation to me in the late 1970s: "Community developers have *no permanent friends and no permanent enemies.*" At the time, and for many years afterward, I had a lot of trouble accepting this view of the world. I was coming to understand how friendship was ephemeral as I became separated from the intense friendships of my college years. My basic problem was with the "no permanent enemies" part of the phrase. I believed that powerful institutions influenced the most important social and economic factors shaping the quality of life in our communities. People who occupied important jobs, whether bank presidents, mayors, union leaders, or real estate developers, ultimately became intertwined with the power of these institutions. Seldom would they support policies that conflicted with the interests of the institutions they led. Even after they had retired from their positions of power, they remained compromised, at least from my parochial point of view.

The Bill Kelloggs provided evidence that the world of power was not so monolithic. My experience of community-organizing campaigns over the years has given additional credibility to the phrase, "no permanent friends and no permanent enemies." Yet I still had my doubts: these victories and unlikely partners, no matter how impressive, were inevitably tainted for me by the whiff of opportunism and deal making.

I've learned during thirty years of mucking around as a community developer to reframe the "no permanent friends and no permanent enemies" phrase into a more positive embrace of small *p* politics as a way of achieving a modicum of good in the world. For the most part, I've learned this simple notion from talking to, observing, and reading about the community organizing and leadership of the Industrial Areas Foundation (IAF) and other community organizing networks like Gamaliel and ACORN. All of these groups, to different degrees, draw upon the community organizing heritage of Saul Alinsky, George Wiley, and Martin Luther King Jr.

Community organizing embraces several core beliefs about the world and politics. First, power in all its forms is a resource that *have-not* groups have to muster if they are to enter into politics and shape conversations, agendas, and decisions. Mobilizing people and directing their power in numbers in public ways creates a new platform for these communities to enter into politics.

Second, the world of cities has become more fragmented and contentious, whether we are talking about neighborhoods, the business community, or a school system. Businesses exhibit a wide array of interests and opinions. Government is complicated by federalism, branches of government, professional ethics, political appointments, and whistleblowers. This piecemeal, chaotic world requires organizing, focusing, and directing, sometimes by new civic intermediaries. Our beliefs about economics and politics blind us. As a result, we can envisage only large-scale social and political change or no change at all. We feel powerless or lash out in desperation. But this is not the world that we inhabit.

Civic observers argue that society has become more fragmented because of the falling apart of bridging mechanisms like political parties, corporations, governments, or labor unions in the context of increased economic mobility and change. Metropolitan leaders, for example, lament the loss of homegrown corporate leaders who in the past served as pillars of the local civic community, ready to champion important causes, whether school reform, fundraising campaigns, community disputes, a new piece of community infrastructure like an art museum, or the campaign to attract a major political or sports event. In the past, most cities had a small group of these business leaders, named the *Vault* in Boston or *Civic Progress* in St. Louis, that seemed to make all the decisions that mattered and then some. This wasn't democracy, but things got done. "Now, we wish there was a conspiracy to get things organized," observed Jeremy Nowak, CEO of TRF, about the state of governance and leadership in Philadelphia. In part a highly diverse "civic sector" has emerged over the past several decades to try to fill this gap, frequently forming new civic intermediaries to bridge fragmented and diverse constituencies.

Third, the folks who inhabit these powerful roles and positions actually have beliefs, aspirations, and goals. They are not stick figures without ethical backbones, nor are they puppets simply controlled by larger forces and institutions. They are concerned about making their mark in the world, leaving a legacy, or doing something good. This is not to say that there aren't bad guys with few scruples and powerful friends, like mayors in jail or corporate leaders who defraud employees and stockholders. And we shouldn't minimize real differences in values, constituencies, and policies. But many leaders read books, belong to religious congregations, are thrifty, and experience pain and dismay over social problems and inequities.

The only way you really know what kind of leaders you are dealing with is by trying to build a *relationship* with them. A relationship is not making a marketing pitch, meeting for coffee once a month, or saying good things about each other. It is two-way sharing and revelation that conveys something authentic about what makes you (and them) tick. Mary Beth Rogers, in *Cold Anger*, quotes legendary community organizer Ernesto Cortes as saying, "We teach people that the relationship is more important than the issue." I'm not suggesting that advocates and elites should fashion a new form of social action therapy; what I'm saying is that non-instrumental and non-superficial communication on a regular basis can help build the foundation of trust necessary to take risks together in supporting new and unconventional ideas and actions.

Finally, unusual partners and allies have to produce real actions that make a difference in the lives of families and communities. Embracing symbols or mouthing rhetoric, no matter how agreeable, doesn't meet the test of community organizing. Partners make change together.

Organizing Unusual Partners

Less than a year after I joined the Eighteenth Street Development Corporation in 1976, I began finding a diverse crew of nonprofit colleagues around the city rehabbing old buildings and confronting the same challenges I was facing. We all had a similar set of questions, as I recounted in a 1981 *Chicago Tribune* op-ed: "Where do you get cheap two-by-fours? What foundations are interested in funding housing rehabilitation? How do you walk a voucher through the bureaucracy?" After a little bit of planning, five of us called the first meeting of what became the Chicago Rehab Network (CRN), which still exists today. Cooperation had direct payoffs for apparent competitors.

In the early 1990s, in another example of organizing unusual partners, the Communities Organized for Public Service (COPS) community-organizing coalition in San Antonio, Texas, convinced the head of Frost State Bank to help them establish a new, long-term training organization, named Project QUEST. This was a big victory and a tribute to unusual partners, particularly since Levi Strauss had just shut down a local plant and laid off hundreds of workers.

QUEST adopted the premise that education and training had to be employer-driven, long-term, and ready to provide flexible supports to families. All of these ingredients ran against the grain of traditional workforce development, required key institutions like community colleges to change how they provided educational services, and asked businesses to commit jobs upfront. And, not surprisingly, the QUEST model cost more. It required the infusion of flexible state dollars and local training funds. Business partners like Frost State Bank led the charge in San Antonio and with the State of Texas across several administrations. What's important to understand, in addition to these early victories, is that QUEST and COPS advocate each year to keep the resources coming.

More recently, community organizations like ACORN and cities like San Francisco have formed unusual partnerships related to tax preparation services for the Earned Income Tax Credit (EITC). EITC is the $40 billion anti-poverty program that rewards working families and is administered through the tax code. As many as 80 percent of EITC-eligible tax filers access EITC though paid tax preparation services as opposed to relying upon volunteer tax preparation services or individual filing. H&R Block is the tax preparer with the largest market share.

The problem with using paid tax preparation services is twofold. First, these businesses charge tax filers $200 or more to submit taxes, the average EITC refund being $1,500. Some advocates object that low-income workers should not be charged to access public benefits. Second and more seriously, paid tax preparers provide tax filers with RALs (rapid anticipation loans) that allow them to get their refunds within days rather than have to wait a week through e-filing. This is where paid tax preparers really make their money—charging interest rates for RALs up to 400 percent, costing tax filers another several hundred dollars.

Lawsuits, boycotts, and a growing VITA (volunteer tax campaigns) supported by the Internal Revenue Service have made H&R Block increasingly uncomfortable. And, it should be acknowledged, the IRS itself is an unlikely partner for the growing number of community asset-building campaigns that are helping working families move ahead by becoming connected to the tax code. Who would have thought that the tax collector was an ally? These community tax campaigns have given RALs bad publicity as an example of how families are exploited for a benefit that they have earned. RALs do produce profits for the for-profit tax firms like H&R Block, but they don't produce repeat customers, the lifeblood of the H&R Block financial advising business.

Volunteer tax preparation campaigns have their own problems—particularly the challenges of reaching scale, sustainability, and quality. Simply, volunteer programs cost lots of time, money, and goodwill. They are not meant for scale, but for putting the scare of competition into the marketplace. With no predictable revenue sources, the most prescient volunteer campaigns are searching for alternative business models to generate income and partnerships while increasing quality.

ACORN, a national grassroots organizing coalition, reached a settlement (i.e., partnership) with H&R Block in 2004 for a number of cities. More ambitiously, the City of San Francisco, as a part of the Working Family Coalition, has created its own local EITC, funded in part with grants from H&R Block and using H&R Block to prepare taxes at a reduced cost along with free tax preparation sites. In both cases, an *enemy* became a partner as they discovered strengths in each other. This is the stuff of partnerships, even if many advocates in the field were horrified.

Long-term partnerships are not developed overnight or from a single event. One definition of partnership evolution identifies three phases—"storming, norming, and forming." Wannabe partners have to experience the pains of difference and the commonality of values and vision before they can begin to articulate and then negotiate shared expectations, rules of engagement, and investments. Not all wannabe partnerships make it through these phases; they go their own ways after experiencing what life would be like if they really partnered with "X." Other fledgling partnerships live hollow lives, unwilling to commit seriously, but unwilling to walk away.

Staying the Partnership Course

Partners come and partners go, and some partners never make it as partnerships. In Chapter 5, I told the story of losing some partners-in-the-making when

SECO—the community organization I directed in Baltimore—became involved in drafting and promoting local linkage legislation related to high-income waterfront development. The purpose of the legislation was to provide neighborhoods with a tool to shape and mitigate the impacts of high-income development to support increased affordable housing and community amenities. The real estate industry, including developers, building trade unions, and contractors, fight most forms of linkage legislation because they fear it will discourage development by making it prohibitively expensive or complicated.

At the time, SECO's home was a one-hundred-year-old parochial school in desperate need of renovation. We worked up a renovation plan that costed out at $500,000 for elevators, new bathrooms, air conditioning, internal room renovations, and site improvements. No one source of funding would get this needed work done; SECO would have to piece together multiple strands of financing.

Somehow we were adopted by the son of a local commercial property management and development firm. He agreed to help us implement our renovation plan and identify and seek out new sources of financing for the project. The first resource he brought in was a group of building union officials who agreed to provide volunteer labor for installing new mechanical systems in exchange for good publicity, training opportunities for apprentices, and the cost of materials. As the project gained momentum and we got to know our partner better, we learned that the development firm was also connected to a local family foundation. It seemed possible and even likely that SECO would receive a grant to support building renovation.

Our fledgling partnership fell apart overnight once the linkage legislation was filed. Suddenly no one returned our phone calls—the development firm or the unions. They dropped us like a hot potato. We never got through the "storming phase" and lost several hundred thousand dollars for the building renovation. Obviously, SECO miscalculated by mixing an inherently unstable brew of community organizing, development, and fundraising. SECO, the development firm, and the unions saw the world very differently, and there were no overriding incentives to keep the players at the table. SECO was a political liability, not the model, passive recipient of charitable benevolence.

Not all disagreements lead to partnerships' falling apart in the early stages as in Baltimore. The story of the Partners Group in the White Center, Seattle's *Making Connections* community building site, is a case of words before action. Beware of fledgling partners who name themselves as partners at the outset of the partnership-building relationship. Partnerships require more than words.

Making Connections—the neighborhood-based, long-term initiative sponsored by the Annie E. Casey Foundation—aimed to strengthen families and communities on behalf of improving outcomes for children. To accomplish this ambitious goal required that the ten sites attract a broad range of co-investors and partners willing to work together for common results related to employment, asset building, community leadership and capacity, school readiness, and improved education.

After several years of topsy-turvy start-up, a unique opportunity presented itself in White Center because of the relationships and networks of local *Making Connections* leaders. An experienced official with the State of Washington, stationed at the Seattle Chamber of Commerce for a sabbatical year, proposed that a group of state and local public agencies, along with the Chamber, form a Policy Committee to work with White Center *Making Connections*. Many reasons accounted for this proposal—the interests of the State of Washington in service integration and potential cost savings, the concentrated poverty and public investment in White Center, the attractiveness of long-term Casey funding, and a strong and long-term set of personal, working relationships.

This was an unprecedented opportunity for White Center *Making Connections*. The formation of the Policy Committee—including state human service and employment agencies, local school systems, public housing agencies, the Sheriff's Office, county government, business leadership, and community residents—demonstrated substantial public and private sector support at a time that the Casey Foundation was assessing whether *Making Connections* was taking root in its start-up sites. Serious engagement and support of this kind also showed to White Center residents and other Seattle-area stakeholders that *Making Connections* was a serious effort that was taking off after several years of bumpy start-up.

Unfortunately, this promising partnership, eventually renamed the Partners Group, stumbled over the next few years, struggling to live up to its potential. The main problem was that almost all the partners except the Casey Foundation were unwilling to spend enough time together to work through the "storming, norming, and forming" phases of partnership building. The Partners Group has never met more than two to three times a year for no more than several hours at a time, has held only one or two short retreats, and at the outset delegated most of the day-to-day work to a Deputies Group made up of staff who could not make policy or resource decisions. While there were strong and practical bilateral relationships between public agencies and *Making Connections*, a viable multistakeholder partnership always seemed to be on the cusp of formation.

One early disagreement produced a bout of mutual suspicion that was never overcome. The State of Washington official at the Chamber tried to position the Partners Group as the governance mechanism for *Making Connections*, micromanaging a strategic planning process of his design that would determine how future Casey Foundation investments were to be made. *Making Connections* staff responded that the strength of *Making Connections* was in engaging multiple partners, seeding innovations, and remaining open to new ideas and partners. It was committed to an open process of design and action. For *Making Connections*, governance of the sort proposed meant top-down decision-making and control; this was not seen as a viable path to community change. This disagreement almost brought the partnership to an end before it started. Tense negotiations occurred, and the leading state official eventually was reassigned to other duties. Unfortunately, this early "storming" experience was not analyzed, and it consequently increased rather than decreased mistrust over the long run.

Several of the White Center partners thought that their specific work was the priority, whether reforming public schools, modernizing public housing, or providing families with economic services. They would join broader partnerships if they believed they could attract others to invest in their projects; their approach was to come off as good citizens while minimizing their new investments. The partners saw the opportunity to direct Casey dollars, not give up control of their own scarce resources.

Progress in transforming the Partners Group into a real partnership has occurred. New resources and public attention have resulted from this coalescing of important public, private, and philanthropic stakeholders in White Center. But it remains difficult to identify new behaviors and commitments on the part of individual members or in the policies and programs of the Partners Group. Nevertheless, major players have remained at the same table while *Making Connections* has begun to achieve results. It's hard to walk away from the potential of a real partnership.

Results and Unlikely Partners

Another approach was possible for the Partners Group and other fledgling partnerships. Results-based investing and accountability is a technique for helping reluctant investors become engaged partners. Results' thinking usually focuses on short-term, programmatic outcomes, but couches them in terms of helping to solve larger social problems. While a neighborhood employment initiative, for example, may produce only one hundred job placements per year, project leaders tell their funders that their program contributes to lowering the unemployment rate in the neighborhood and city. Lowering the overall citywide unemployment rate, however, may require tens of thousands of job placements, not one hundred placements. By exaggerating the impacts of a neighborhood program, the initiative diminishes the belief that we can really do something about unemployment or any other big social problem. We have entered the world of "spin."

If we took the problem of the overall unemployment rate seriously, we would proceed in a different fashion. An important starting point would involve defining the unemployment problem—how many folks are unemployed and for what reasons. Choosing an indicator of progress for lowering unemployment might be defined as "closing the gap" between the rate of employment in the neighborhood and city and the employment rate in the county. The next task would identify all those investors and stakeholders, likely and unlikely, who could make solid contributions toward increasing the employment rate: employment programs, businesses, chambers of commerce, child care services, economic development agencies, community colleges, welfare programs, or staffing firms, to name a few of the most obvious contributors. While each of these actors alone could contribute specific results, together—as a partnership—they could make a much more substantial impact.

The moral of the story is to use a vision of results to bring stakeholders together to invest for the same outcomes. This doesn't diminish individual programs and priorities. It merely shows what we all know: we can't solve problems alone; we need partners.

Why don't these partnerships appear more frequently and stay together longer to achieve big results? One answer is that there are impediments, barriers, and disincentives to stakeholders coming together—what political economists call collective action problems. That is, it takes an extraordinary amount of organizing and focus to bring key stakeholders together, as in the world of workforce development.

Several barriers make partnerships of this kind highly improbable in the workforce arena without the exercise of extraordinary leadership, a factor that itself is in short supply. Workforce development produces uncertain and long-term monetary payoffs that accrue to individual workers and companies at best, not to the general public and not to the world of financing and real estate that is so important to local politics. At the same time, workforce development is frequently perceived as a small problem without a lot of resources in play. In other words, there is not enough on the *politics* table to encourage new behaviors on the part of stakeholders who tend to promote themselves. Business skepticism about workforce development and investing in low-wage employees is fueled by the free-rider phenomena, in which non-paying firms' take advantage of the workforce investments of competitor firms by luring away their employees with marginal wage and benefit improvements. Many firms would rather take their chances without public programs. Moreover, many institutions of the workforce world are more concerned with protecting their own jobs and prerogatives than with supporting workforce innovations, high performance, and robust results. Their goal is survival. If all this were not bad enough, the public perceives improving workforce development for low-income folks as a poverty program, not as a "public good" that benefits everyone. It's a small problem for a special interest group. This lack of support occurs in part because workforce development is inconsistent and confusing, having many different definitions of the workforce problem, funding mechanisms, and projected results. It's at war with itself.

All of these barriers contribute to the difficulty of workforce development to build large-scale, durable partnerships that make a difference. The exceptions occur when exceptional leadership by powerful political leaders, unions, business, or community organizations changes the underlying equation of the barriers preventing collective action. When this is done, unlikely partners come together to produce extraordinary results.

Unlikely Partners in the Making

Whether it's about reforming workforce development or encouraging revitalization in poor communities, developing unlikely partnerships is essential for cities and metro areas. As I stated in a 1991 op-ed in the Baltimore *Evening Sun*, "To meet this challenge requires more than bright ideas. We must design a workable civic process for getting to the future."

Creating viable civic partnerships is a particular problem for large projects. Big (or mega) projects like airports and convention centers are controversial because they experience substantial public scrutiny and require more explicit commitments for social and economic benefits in exchange for public investment. Mega projects provoke a range of problems and opportunities that in turn engage the emotions and resources of multiple stakeholders—environmental clean-up, residential relocation, land assembly, public infrastructure, environmental and social impacts, public financing, and an array of employment and business opportunities.

It's no longer possible for a strong mayor or business group alone to jam mega projects past a passive public, although many mayors still try this approach as an opening gambit. Witness the foundering of World's Fairs, Olympics, business attraction schemes, school reform efforts, and many other local mega projects that don't build upon solid and diverse partnerships. The biggest danger of the top-down approach is that nothing gets done in cities and metro areas that desperately need new investment and infrastructure.

A Baltimore story in progress demonstrates that timing, resources, and another partner were key ingredients for this new unlikely partnership. A good amount of "storming" is still going on among these partners, but the partnership has thankfully evolved into the "norming" and "forming" stages as well. Real progress is being made. This story about the East Baltimore Revitalization Initiative has familiar actors that I've talked about before—Johns Hopkins University, the City of Baltimore, the State of Maryland and the Annie E. Casey Foundation. Numerous residents and community-based organizations from East Baltimore play important roles.

The Initiative is a ten- to fifteen-year, $1 billion project to build an eighty-acre redevelopment area, focused on life sciences, with two million square feet of commercial space, twenty-two hundred new or renovated housing units, a new community school, a new subway stop, and many other neighborhood amenities. The Initiative is a mega project.

Three project elements are critical for understanding the challenges of this partnership. First, about eight hundred households had to be relocated, making the Initiative a form of urban renewal, or, given the demographics of the neighborhood, what activists in the 1960s would have called "Negro removal." Second, the vision for the Initiative is to create a mixed-income community that breaks up concentrated poverty by dispersing the poor and attracting high-income residents. Activists, in contrast, suggest that the Initiative is really a form of "land grab" that promotes gentrification, connecting up the Hopkins complex with downtown and the developing waterfront. Third, the implementation of the Initiative is predicated upon an "economic inclusion" agreement that will supposedly ensure that a fair proportion of the direct and indirect employment, development, and purchasing opportunities are obtained by minorities and low-income East Baltimore residents.

The background of the Initiative suggests both opportunity and caution. Hopkins employs more than thirty thousand people in Maryland, fourteen thousand in Baltimore, and one thousand new employees each year. Hopkins purchases $3.5 billion in non-construction services each year and is the largest grant recipient of the National Institutes of Health. Johns Hopkins is certainly an economic engine. Yet tension and bitter relations have characterized the relationship between the Hopkins complex in East Baltimore and the largely low-income, African American neighborhoods surrounding it for fifty years. Indeed, the history of the neighborhoods surrounding Hopkins is a microcosm of largely failed national and local urban policies—urban renewal, Model Cities, Enterprise Zones, and community development. Hopkins and a host of partners, such as the Enterprise Foundation and the City of Baltimore, have made numerous attempts over the years to break through these barriers. While modest short-term progress has been achieved, the larger problems and opportunities have remained unaddressed. One key barrier is the balkanized governance of Hopkins itself and the lack of community capacity to bring focus and oversee the implementation of community development in these poor neighborhoods. Hopkins is a medieval walled university city surrounded by poor neighborhoods. It's not a pretty picture.

So why be optimistic about the Initiative? A number of reasons suggest optimism, I believe. The Initiative is designed to make *scale* impacts on transforming these neighborhoods into better places to live and work. The project will make a real difference in the long run, as opposed to the piecemeal, short-term development that has occurred in the past.

In addition to Hopkins and the City of Baltimore, the Casey Foundation joined the Initiative as a partner. It has committed millions of dollars and significant reputational capital to make the project successful. Headquartered in Baltimore since 1994, the Foundation has made a hometown philanthropy commitment to strengthen Baltimore, but had never invested in a project as large as the Initiative.

The Foundation has facilitated four aspects of the Initiative that no one else was willing or able to embrace. It has supported resident involvement in project planning, especially the painful and potentially divisive discussion of residential relocation. It has invested in enriching the relocation benefits for the eight hundred relocating households and has challenged Hopkins to match its investments. It has provided substantial grant dollars, technical assistance, and staff resources to build a new intermediary organization—East Baltimore Development, Inc. (EBDI). EBDI oversees the physical development of the Initiative and is charged with ensuring the achievement of social benefits for community residents. Finally, the Foundation has provided capital, technical assistance, and high-level leadership to secure project financing and to entice other investors to invest in the Initiative. The Foundation's involvement has led to a substantial increase in community inclusion in all aspects of the redevelopment.

The Casey Foundation is taking a big risk by joining with partners who only partially share its values and commitments. The role of the Foundation—consciously or unconsciously—has been to provide the capital, ideas, and leadership that were missing in prior attempts to forge a viable development approach for East Baltimore. Early results show relocated families to be better off and that former renters are moving back into new, affordable housing.

All of this is not to suggest that the Initiative will be a complete success in the eyes of everyone. Already the economic, planning, and financing assumptions underlying the Initiative are shifting as land, relocation, and financing costs increase, especially in building affordable housing. A key indicator of success will be whether the unlikely partners stay together when mistakes are made and the going gets even tougher.

Partnerships for the Future

Thirty years later, Bill Kellogg's company is still located in the Brewery. Many of the businesses in the neighborhood have left, and developers have turned their buildings into loft apartments or live/work spaces for higher-income residents. But many working families remain in the neighborhood. My first unlikely partnerships taught me new ways of understanding my own potential as an unlikely partner.

We are inundated by talk of partnerships, collaborations, networking, and alliances. The new world of regions, economic and political decentralization, and customization means, however, that the process of forming bridging mechanisms, often with unlikely partners, is a necessity for almost any endeavor. We can't proceed merely on the basis of rhetoric and the heroics of single individuals. Given the political partisanship and ideological lockjaw that characterize much of our political scene, unlikely partnerships, especially those with the business community, can create a new center of gravity around which civic momentum can be built. Douglas Henton, John Melville, and Kim Walesh are audacious enough to call these unlikely partners *civic revolutionaries.* But maybe this phrase is just about right!

The following lessons and suggestions should help you find unlikely partners:

- Make a list of your genuine partners, past and present. How many of them did you consider unlikely? In how many of these relationships do you stand out as the unlikely partner?

- Organizations need to create a culture that values partnerships rather than an ethos of doing it all alone. Organizations can make this real by investing in an ongoing search for unlikely partners.

- Become explicit about how you go about building and sustaining the human relationships that eventually form the backbone of partnerships.

- Provide the space, glue, and leadership that encourage unlikely partners to come together on common agendas without initially having to make dramatic changes in how they do business.

10

Mentored and Mentoring

o o o o o o o o o o o o o o o o o o o o o o o o o o o o o o
This is what guiding lights do. We
show the way. And in doing so we
find the way.

—*Eric Liu*

In my last couple of years working for Mayor Harold Washington in Chicago during the late 1980s, I was assigned to the sports beat. The Chicago Bears wanted a new stadium to replace Soldier Field, the Cubs wanted lights at Wrigley Field, and the White Sox were threatening to move to the suburbs. Complicating the work was that much of it occurred in the spotlight of Washington's contested re-election campaign.

During that time, I received some rough-and-tumble mentoring. At the time, the Mayor had a volunteer business leader in his office, the owner of the largest Cadillac dealership in the Chicago metro area, who took the lead on all sports-related issues. I got to know him well, and his secretary and I regularly communicated about assignments and follow-up. Once I even took it upon myself to give her some tips on the next steps that we should be taking.

Several days later, I received one of those friendly but unmistakable pieces of advice from my boss that all assignments on sports issues ran downhill, not up. Only he used more colorful phrasing. The message was clear: don't poach on the time of the sports czar's staff. My boss may not have realized it, but he was helping me learn the ropes and, in that moment, was a valued mentor.

Mentoring of all kinds is hot these days. Depending on who's describing it, mentors combine the skills of teachers, coaches, old hands, consultants, therapists, sages, advisors, and gurus. It seems that almost anyone can be a mentor: spouses, siblings, parents, aunts, uncles, peers, and friends. A mentoring relationship doesn't last forever. Sometimes it's only situational, as when I got dressed down for overstepping my role with the mayor's staff. Other times the most effective mentoring takes place by observing and learning from role models or others in our lives who screw up.

In the CED field and the broader nonprofit world, mentoring can and does play a role worth discussing. In this chapter, I identify some of the key practices of good mentoring by exploring mentoring as it has played out in my nonprofit career—how I've thought about mentoring, how I've been mentored, and the mentoring roles I've taken. Reading this chapter requires that you reflect upon your mentors and mentoring roles. Keep the following questions in mind:

- Who are your mentors, and why are they effective?
- What issues or obstacles do mentors help you overcome?
- Whom do you mentor, and how has that worked?
- What skills and experiences do you have to offer as a mentor?

Why Mentoring

Several reasons account for the mentoring fad. Many young people are growing up without adequate parental, school, and community guidance and support about how to navigate a complicated world characterized by new family configurations, economic opportunities and constraints, and geographic mobility. It would be overly simplistic to say that young people need mentoring more now than in the past, but it is true that all of us have more options and choices to evaluate. That is one of the positive burdens of living in the U.S.

Experienced-based, informal knowledge transmitted by trusted adults helps us in our struggles to grow up, choose careers, pick ourselves up after failure, and find life partners. No explicit guidebook exists for successfully navigating these critical and frequently risky life transitions. Richard Ford's ruminating protagonist in the *Lay of the Land,* Frank Bascombe, pronounces that "the hardest thing to find in the modern world is disinterested, sound, generalized advice—of the kind that instructs you ..."

Three other aspects of modern life underscore the relevance of mentoring for CED and the nonprofit sector. Workplaces increasingly require critical problem-solving skills, effective work in teams, and emotional intelligence on the job. We no longer work alone or apart from our customers. This is why many businesses say, "We just need folks with *soft skills* who show up ready for work. We'll provide the technical training." Whether business involves customer service or cellular-manufacturing teams, today's employees need more than strong backs and minds. Mentors can help workers navigate the new business culture.

More and more responsibility for getting ahead economically is placed on the shoulders of individuals and families. The post-World War II-era safety net was a bit of an exception, and we're returning to more laissez faire times in which families manage their own financial services, health care, benefits, and retirement. HR departments, unions, community banks, full health coverage, and pensions are becoming things of the past. Every family is responsible for running its own family business—managing assets, obtaining credit for working capital, and generating diverse sources of income. The Internet has made the family business at once easier and more bewildering with all its new options and avenues of exploration and exploitation. On the policy and safety net fronts, debates fester about privatizing social security and the proposed payoffs of workers' managing their own personal retirement accounts. Everybody needs a financial advisor to navigate these financial and asset-building options.

Our world is more diverse in terms of ethnicity, race, gender, and belief systems. How do we sensitively and productively interact with this diversity in our homes, workplaces, places of worship, and communities? How do we become global citizens in our own backyards? No rulebook exists that provides adequate guidance. We need insider advice about these new opportunities. Mentoring shows others the *ropes* about behaving in these new situations and solving new problems. The need for mentoring has grown, not diminished.

My Mentors

I've chosen three colleagues, teachers, and friends who I can say, without hesitation, have influenced me. Lew Kreinberg is a retired community activist in Chicago who trained at the University of Wisconsin with the great American historian, William Appleman Williams. Rob Mier was an urban planner, teacher, and economic development official with the City of Chicago who died of lymphoma ten years ago. The late Barclay Gibbs Jones was a professor of city and regional planning at Cornell University who studied architecture, economic geography, and public policy.

By the time I befriended Lew Kreinberg in the late 1970s, he had been a Chicago community activist for almost two decades. Lew was a bearded hulk of a guy who wore a different hat every day and was ten-plus years older than most of us and worked for a wonderful organization, the Jewish Council on Urban Affairs (JCUA). He had been active in the northern Civil Rights Movement and the community organizing and development struggles of the North Lawndale neighborhood of Chicago. Looking for a new neighborhood to work in and a new community fight, Lew signed on to work with the Eighteenth Street Development Corporation of which I was the director in Chicago's Pilsen neighborhood. JCUA had a unique way of working with neighborhood organizations; it deployed Lew to work for long periods in one community, usually with one organization as the focal point. Lew stayed in Pilsen for more than five years, several years beyond my tenure. He was a coach for hire, but free of charge.

Lew taught me many things during these years. I learned that creative people defy and exceed linear job descriptions, particularly when you are not paying them. I made the greenhorn mistake of writing a memo to Lew that outlined the three or four projects I wanted him to undertake. The list included a feasibility study for a for-profit subsidiary, as I recall. That seemed reasonable; Lew's forte was supposedly as a researcher. I don't think Lew ever worked on, much less completed, any of these proposed tasks. He was too polite or oblivious to just rip up the memo.

Instead of pursuing my carefully outlined tasks, Lew bonded with all of us, put our projects and aspirations into a Chicago context of community struggles, and cheered us on like an older brother at a pee wee league baseball game. Meanwhile he collected reports, scraps of newspapers, city council minutes, and rumors about what was happening in the neighborhood or to the neighborhood. His back pocket was a treasure chest of clues and fugitive documents; he became our eyes and ears at City Hall and at the old Municipal Reference Library. Lew coached as we took on the bad guys and inevitably made mistakes.

Lew provided a safety net for younger folks working in the neighborhoods. This was really important for me when the gang banger ex-husband of our secretary threatened her and anyone else who supported her independence from him. Lew watched my back and understood how I was both afraid of this crazy person and a little shamefaced that I didn't retaliate by beating the guy up.

Arguing with Lew was a mainstay of our relationship as we walked Chicago or strategized after work in gritty neighborhood bars. Our argument was always the same. I emphasized the economic and policy *structural* impediments facing poor neighborhoods, like the way market economies create *bad* jobs and disinvest in poor communities. Trained in making sense of archival documents, Lew always put a human face on those who shaped neighborhood events—imperial development projects and the inevitable sleaze of Chicago politics. He was not an abstract thinker; real people made moral or immoral decisions in politics and urban development that had consequences. I didn't budge much at the time, although now I find myself in more agreement with him. But we enjoyed the arguments.

Lew liked me in spite of my limitations. He valued my commitment and saw potential in me for doing more good. At one point he asked me to participate on a panel discussion about neighborhoods at the JCUA annual meeting. I entered the downtown hotel after circling the block nervously several times trying to get up the gumption to go in. Lew saw me skulking around the lobby and winked. The problem was that I was deathly afraid of public speaking at the time, shy introvert that I was (and remain). My will soon gave out after I greeted Lew in the lobby. I hightailed it out of the hotel before the JCUA program had begun, probably to hide in a movie theatre for a few hours. The next day when Lew saw me, he laughed and laughed, now knowing that I was all-too-human. That was okay by him.

Mentoring is about sharing new ideas, giving honest feedback and advice, questioning assumptions, and providing support and networking. Lew was a mentor to lots of folks, including me, without knowing it. Rob Mier played the same role for me, another older brother type who mentored me right up until his death—and even beyond. I remember vividly our last time together early on a Sunday morning in February 1995. I whispered into his ear, "You are still teaching me," in the minutes before the cremation society came to pick up his body. Rob taught me about fighting disease, having hope, preparing for death, and dying with loved ones. I had been lucky in having a rather distant knowledge of death up until those weeks and months with Rob.

Rob Mier was in his fifties when he died in February 1995, the outcome of his exposure to Agent Orange while serving as a naval officer in the Vietnam War. Rob and I met in 1975 when he arrived at the University of Illinois at Chicago to teach urban planning as a newly minted Ph.D. from Cornell University who, like Lew, was older than most of us. I was in the second year of my master's program when Rob arrived, and I was already committed to CED. Rob's first impact on me was converting me to the belief and understanding that employment and "jobs" were at the center of every individual's and family's lives and thus constituted a proper and neglected focus of community economic development. Without adequate income, much else in life was more difficult for families. Up until that point, I had understood the conditions of poor neighborhoods largely from the perspective of the disinvestment in these neighborhoods by mainstream institutions, not in terms of their disconnections from labor markets and regional economies.

Over the next two decades, Rob and I developed a shared understanding about CED and Chicago. He was my thesis advisor, boss, co-author, technical assistance provider, and friend and, in addition, paved the way for me to pursue a doctorate at Cornell University in city and regional planning. He was also one of the invisible folks who recommended me for the Casey Foundation program officer position on jobs, neighborhoods, and economic development.

Once you joined Rob's team, he would sing your praises and send opportunities your way whether you wanted them or not. He had a clubby piece of advice about academic writing that conveyed how he valued and took care of his close-in colleagues; he counseled, "Always footnote your friends!" Moreover, he gave you feedback that stuck with you without putting you down. I remember one afternoon in his office when I was complaining about the ennui of my first marriage. He said rather bluntly, "We've all got problems!" This simple and obvious piece of advice has stayed with me through the years because it forced me to recognize that I was not the only person going through tough times. It meant that I should lighten up and toughen up. More humorously, when I took a job with the City of Chicago as a part of his staff, he made fun of my graduate student wardrobe of work shoes and old sports jackets that didn't quite fit. He helped me appreciate the new environment I was in where dress mattered, at least a little bit.

Rob's advising and coaching knew no boundaries, even personal ones. He helped facilitate my second marriage to another long-time member of his team who had worked with us in City Hall and had moved out east as well. And he told me in no uncertain terms, after she and I had had a relationship spat, that if I didn't treat her well, he would put a contract out on my kneecaps. Now, that's mentoring.

Rob hammered that race matters throughout his career. It's evident in how we interact and talk, in who gets what jobs, in what neighborhoods do well, and in who gets the attention of City Hall. Rob gave us books to read, led discussions, hired a diverse workforce, and invented his own simulation games for exploring the racial equity impacts of different types of economic development. He taught white professionals to observe who is in the room and who is not, the racial implications of decisions, and the biases inherent in public decision-making processes. In an article dedicated to Mier with Wim Wiewel, another Mier protégé, we wrote, "Mier equated social, political, and neighborhood equity with racial justice—the fair access by communities of color to resources, power, and opportunities."

Cornell University's doctoral program in city and regional planning was known for its focus on equity planning. So, late in August 1980, nearly thirty years old, I said goodbye to Chicago and drove out to western New York with the help of my youngest sister.

I had high expectations for remaking myself at Cornell. I planned to take Spanish and karate on top of a full load of classes. However, I soon discovered (or rediscovered) several disconcerting things about myself, Cornell, and my program of study. First, most of the so-called progressives were on leave or sabbatical, had departed for other universities, or were apostles of *high theory*, which was barely intelligible to an ordinary community planner like me. Second, I recognized rather quickly that I was a practical, applied guy who couldn't (or wouldn't) go deep on either theory or quantitative methods. That didn't make me a very attractive doctoral student in many respects, although the faculty seemed to value, at times, my five years of community experience.

By the second semester of my first year, I was hiding in my rented room, reading or going for long runs rather than attending classes. I needed some help and good advice. I was drowning, as was the fate of many doctoral students who lose their bearings. If I didn't do something quick, I was surely headed for a premature departure from Cornell and an unexpected return to Chicago. That really wasn't such a bad option, but I had set my mind stubbornly on earning the damned doctorate.

I made a tough choice that ultimately turned this situation around. I asked Barclay Gibbs Jones to be the chair of my doctoral committee. Jones was an elder statesman of the department who had founded the doctoral program, chaired the department, and trained many of its younger faculty. At one point, the young upstarts overthrew his rule in a fit of radical, or Oedipal, peeve. Barclay was conservative and skeptical of the activism of his former students.

To sign on with Barclay was both a peculiar experience and a common path for many students. The stacks upon stacks of dissertations and master's theses in his overstuffed office testified to his incredible productivity and effectiveness in advising students over the years. His well-regarded courses were seen as essential building blocks of the program, and his bow-tied, elegant style and strange office hours showed a professor who had given great thought to his point of view about everything. He was an inductive economist rather than theory-driven in a narrow sense and believed in the use of multiple research methods to illuminate patterns and discrepancies in the organization of cities and regions. He was skeptical about rationality, politics, and goal-driven planning.

The reason I chose Barclay as my advisor represented a healthy self-assessment and a careful consideration of limited options. As an older student with an applied background, modest preparation, and diminishing brain cells, I needed to be anchored in the empirical world of economies, cities, regions, populations, organizations, decisions, and projects. No other faculty member was a viable option. I signed up with Barclay—and eventually earned my Ph.D.

I learned a lot from Barclay about mentoring. He had a way of *sizing you up* to identify the dissertation benchmark that was appropriate for you given your strengths and weaknesses. In other words, he didn't impose an external or preconceived standard on students; rather, he tried to figure out how to customize the dissertation while still holding to general university requirements. For example, he didn't push statistical gymnastics if that approach was beyond your reasonable capacity and interest. This "customization" of the dissertation avoided wasting his time and ensured a high rate of completion.

Barclay instilled in me a curiosity about data, patterns, and discrepancies as a first order of business in urban and policy analysis. What are our expectations about the evolution of neighborhoods or cities? Were these expectations confirmed or disconfirmed through data analysis? What accounts for such discrepancies? The point was to investigate the world with an open mind guided by conceptual tools and not to be constrained by our own theoretical and analytic models.

Finally, the way Barclay worked with students at the end stages of their dissertations showed me that good advisors can have quite different styles. At a certain point in dissertation drafting, Barclay would schedule time with you from eleven at night until four in the morning. You would sit before him as he carefully read your material for the first time, pausing to make faces, leaning back in his captain's chair, or dashing off some editorial comment with the flourish of his pen. Occasionally, after staring into space for what seemed like eternity, he would jar you into awareness with a probing question that required you to mobilize all your wits. What this showed me, in addition to someone's unique eccentricity, was a faculty advisor who invested the time to mentor students to complete their dissertations. It worked.

Me? A Mentor?

These vignettes illustrate that mentors provide new ideas, feedback, advice, support, and connections. Sometimes this mentoring happens directly; it also happens indirectly through role modeling. And, as I've said, the impact of mentoring lives beyond the event, problem, or even the mentor's life. Mentoring, however, does not require you to be superhuman or superlative in all aspects of your life; my three mentors were real people with foibles, inconsistencies, and disorganized aspects of their lives. You don't have to be perfect, and, in fact, imperfections contribute valuable experiences and perspectives.

My three examples of mentoring others differ from my mentor experiences. It would be presumptuous of me to be specific about whom I have mentored—that is, naming names. What one person calls mentoring another may dismiss as bad advice or interference. As a general principle, I think it's a better idea for mentees to identify their mentors, not the other way around. So my three examples are more about mentoring roles and approaches that I have adopted than about personal cases. There is one big exception, of course; the first example is about my daughter, Emma, and my Bat Mitzvah advice-giving speech. Whether she has followed any of my advice is another story, especially now that I know more concretely, as a parent, the travails of adolescence. My two other mentoring roles are as a writer of book reviews for community developers and as a lead project manager for the Casey Foundation.

You would think that my words of advice to my daughter would come easily, but they didn't. I mused, pondered, and then finally drafted this short speech for her October 2002 celebration. I share the first part of the speech below.

> Emma, I want to share three things with you today. A story—with a point, I hope. A piece of advice, which I promise is not embarrassing. And then an added reason for celebration. In the end, these may all be about advice—but I can't help it. I'm a parent.
>
> The Story. As you know, my Great Aunt Fannie left me an antique rolltop desk about thirty years ago. It has lots of nooks, crannies, and little and big drawers. And it came with stuff already in it—old language books, pipe tobacco tins, and paper clips. This summer I brought the desk to Washington, finally, after all this time. It had sat in my parents' house. I would visit with it several times a year.
>
> When I got it set up in my bedroom in Washington and was able to look at it, I felt strangely relieved, light, re-connected to something I couldn't figure out at first. It looked smaller in my bigger room, and I soon added some new stuff. I love to look at it and rummage around.
>
> So, the point. Think for a moment about life as a desk, Emma—a rolltop desk. I realize that only someone with an academic streak or a love affair with stationery would pose such a question to his first-born daughter. But bear with me.
>
> My desk was filled with my life from about your age until college. Letters, papers, pictures, applications, newspaper articles, junk, and mementos. What

I found was a lot of stuff that was about my interests of the time, hobbies, books, friends, values and causes. Who I wanted to become, and who I was becoming.

Sometimes it's easy for adults to think that being a teenager is only about acting out and awkwardness. I'm sure that's true. It was for me. But what I found in my desk—looking back—were some of the building blocks of who I have become.

Today, and in days to come, Emma, you will be putting your own desk together. How you have studied for today. Your readings, your speech and many other things will be in it. You'll be adding a lot more in the next few years.

All I can say is that from the perspective of looking back from one's twenties, thirties, and forties and even beyond, you will learn about yourself as an adult by visiting with your past.

Not everything in your desk, however, will be about success. For example, I have three harmonicas in my desk from the old days: Your three-year-old brother, Jack, plays them better than I do. But I'm glad I wanted to be a harp player ...

A few years later, Emma commented on my mentoring speech at a family gathering, "Daddy, you compared me to a piece of furniture!"

Another of my mentoring roles has been as a writer. For almost fifteen years I wrote book reviews for the Neighborhood Library section of *The Neighborhood Works*, a publication of the Center for Neighborhood Technology in Chicago. For its fifteenth-anniversary issue in December 1993/January 1994, I wrote an omnibus review entitled, "A Decade (& More) of Neighborhood Books."

> Who keeps count? I hadn't until I rustled through my old files and piles of *The Neighborhood Works*. It turns out I've done 55 reviews covering 73 books since the fall of 1981, when I reviewed Lew Kreinberg and Chuck Bowden's *Street Signs Chicago*, a romp through Chicago history and contemporary community organizing.
>
> I soon developed a philosophy about what I wanted to achieve in my book reviews; I still follow it.
>
> This philosophy was born after reading a book by Russell Jacoby, *The Last Intellectuals*. Jacoby argues that our society is bereft of public intellectuals—people who are able to communicate effectively about important ideas to broad audiences. Instead, he says, the modern world is inundated by university nitpickers.

Well, this seems wrong when compared to my experience in neighborhood activism and community development. Many of the people I have worked with care about ideas, read books, argue philosophy, and, from time to time, put their thoughts down on paper. They fit the definition of public intellectuals.

So, I wanted my "Neighborhood Library" reviews to be critical summaries of books on urban issues useful to neighborhood activists, making ideas accessible and placing them in practical neighborhood contexts. The reviews have aimed to arm busy activists with ideas, concepts, arguments and perspectives that would be useful for proposal writing, organizing, strategy planning, and personal reflection.

More than half of the books I've reviewed dealt with the theory and practice of community organizing and development, biographies of Myles Horton and Saul Alinsky, "how to" books about credit unions and business incubators and evaluation studies of CDC accomplishments. There has been a wonderful mix of biography, history, and nuts and bolts books on community organizing published in the last decade.

Other topics revisited with some frequency in this space have been workers and workplaces, cities and nonprofit management. Although I did not review many books about race and gender, these salient issues crop up regularly in evaluations of other books.

Neighborhood activists are public intellectuals whether they know it or not. They are part of an ongoing social dialogue about the future of cities, nations and the world that takes place on the streets, in the halls of government, around kitchen tables, and in the books reviewed on these pages.

My other mentoring of folks has involved offering advice about getting one's life together, getting things done, being strategic, and assembling the pieces. I've mentored and advised friends, colleagues, employees, children, siblings, my spouse, bosses, consultants, and many others.

Getting one's life together covers a lot of different issues. I advised a best friend, for example, not to break up with his girlfriend, but to stick it out because he had a great thing going for him and didn't realize it. In other cases, I've advised folks to get divorced, get married, see counselors, or seek other relationships. I've given scores of "informational interviews" in which someone is asking you about potential jobs, careers, university programs, geographic locations, or networks of interesting people to interview. A variant of the information interview has been helping neophytes "learn the ropes" about organizational cultures, a type of job or community, what adopting children involves, or what it's like to negotiate divorce and child custody arrangements. It's amazing what one becomes an expert at while living one's life.

Getting things done involves coaching employees, colleagues, and students about how to complete specific tasks. This involves, at the outset, defining success and the ultimate results desired, a frequently neglected step. I've advised a number of students on their master's theses and served as a blind reviewer of articles and books and commented on how authors could make these submissions more successful. Having edited four books, I've built up quite a bit of "know-how" that I've shared with other would-be editors, usually to warn them about the frustrations of herding cats, that is, chapter authors.

Being strategic is a way of life. For me it involves asking questions: What is really important? What can I do to make a difference? What changes or next steps are critical to implement? What's over the horizon? Where are the problems or weak spots? Is there a mismatch of capacity and ambition? Are we (Am I) ready to take the next steps? Undoubtedly, more questions of this type qualify as strategic—all probing for higher-leverage understanding and action.

I'm surprised at how unnatural being strategic is for smart, experienced practitioners. I once advised my project directors to allocate specific time each week to ask and ponder strategic questions about projects and management. I advised them to ask similar strategic questions about the rationale and intended outcomes when planning meetings with key stakeholders.

Assembling the pieces is about putting together complicated partnerships, design processes, and social interventions. One must envisage multifaceted and evolving outcomes, move back and forth between present realities and future possibilities, redesign things that don't work, and build the capacity of people and partners. That's a handful because there is no preconceived right way to get things done in many cases. Because many good project managers are experienced in working on only one front at a time, they require a combination of coaching, nudging, and jumping in to get comfortable with the complicated world of assembling pieces.

Mentoring and Books

Before I plunge into a mentoring grand finale, I am compelled to discuss an unusual type of mentoring. For the most part I haven't met these mentors, and I'm sure they know nothing of me. A great many of them are dead, but not all of them. I visit with one or two different ones each week, occasionally revisiting particular mentors for more advice. I'm referring to books and authors, of course. Ever since I won an award in third grade for reading the most books in a year, reading has been a foundational aspect of my life. I read upward of one hundred books a year and scores of others via book tapes, and I carry multiple reading options with me at all times. Frankly, I would be lost without daily reading time.

What does reading have to do with mentoring? Well, from time to time, (i.e., every two weeks or so), I become enthralled by the narrative of a book and the skills of its author. I appreciate their craft, ideas, imagery, and questions. This happens for fiction, non-fiction, memoirs, biography, and travel writing. *Making a New Deal: Industrial Workers in Chicago 1919-1939,* by historian Lisbeth Cohen, helped me understand the cultural factors that shaped the unlikely multi-ethnic coalition that arose in the 1930s to support President Franklin Roosevelt and the New Deal. The author's skill and argument and the sweep of the book inspired me. Edmund Morgan's biography of Benjamin Franklin had the same impact by introducing me to a fascinating personage who is truly one of America's finest and brought alive for me the Founding Fathers in ways I've never appreciated.

From time to time I become fixated on one author or historical period and adopt a more focused reading agenda rather than my usual eclectic book selection. George Orwell of *Animal Farm* and *1984* fame is one of my favorite book mentors. What I've learned from Orwell goes beyond using simple language and the ups and downs of a writing career. As I've read biography after biography of Orwell, I've learned that flawed heroes (and mentors) are perhaps the best we can do. Orwell was unique in that he wrote and fought against class poverty, Stalinism, and imperialism, but was a highly fallible man of his times in his unmistakable strains of chauvinism, homophobia, and anti-Semitism.

My Executive Coach

I have one more story about mentoring—the executive coaching I've received at the Casey Foundation. It's yet another look at mentoring, but now as a professional activity and intervention, not as an implicit component of teaching, friendship, parenting, or management roles and relationships. This coaching experience encouraged me to write this book and this chapter about mentoring.

I wasn't looking for an executive coach when I asked the HR department at the Casey Foundation for help. I had a pressing personnel problem that was causing me anxiety and threatened to become worse. I had recently hired a new program officer, and after only six months we were at an impasse. We talked past each other; and as my anxiety about producing effective strategies and outcomes escalated, my feedback to the program officer became more intense and pointed. The relationship grew worse as other staff joined the fray. As a manager, I realized that it was my responsibility to solve this problem, no matter how much I thought I was in the right. Luckily for me, our HR department referred me to an executive coach.

Solving my immediate personnel problem prompted uncomfortable self-awareness on my part as a manager. First, I had to recognize that people are different, introverts or extroverts, work-centered or family-centered, concrete or conceptual thinkers. I knew this, of course, but I seemed to have forgotten about the implications of these differences in the context of project planning and implementation. I had a kind of *my way or the highway* attitude toward different work styles when it came to getting things done.

Second, I discovered that while I have a lot of strength as a conceptual thinker, I am impatient with anybody who doesn't grasp my brainstorms the first time around. When people don't grasp my conceptualization of a problem, opportunity, or plan of action, I am frequently unwilling to invest the time and energy necessary to ensure understanding and buy-in. I have little patience in helping my team advance from point A to point B, a remarkable problem given my role in management. My gut reaction is: Why don't they just get it? As I've said before, I have a version of ADHD and little ability to focus for a long time on one thing—like group understanding.

Dealing with personnel issues was a springboard for exploring more generally my role as a manager and leader and my own career development. As I look into the future, change is inevitable. I will have to decide what my next steps are: Do I have one or two big and new jobs left within me? Could I run a nonprofit again? Is it time to piece together consulting, teaching, and coaching?

These are uncomfortable options and questions for me. At this stage of my career, what is getting ready all about? Executive education? A new skill or two? My coach suggested that I spend time exploring what I know, what I don't know, what's happening in the CED field, and my natural and unnatural networks.

Mentoring Forward

This book grew unconsciously out of those conversations with my coach, and this chapter in particular, reflects our discussions. What is this practice called mentoring or coaching? Writing this chapter has convinced me that I have mentored many people and have been mentored myself. I need to better understand this "inner mentor" and what I've accomplished. Not surprisingly, as I've been thinking about coaching techniques, I've taken on new coaching roles in our projects and sites. The initial feedback has been positive.

Mentoring has many variations, as I have shown in this chapter, but it does embody some common principles and approaches. Mentoring requires commitment, truth-telling, and the centrality of those being mentored. Mentors coach, give specific advice, listen, serve as role models, make connections, and offer support. Most of all, mentors stick with folks. While it's useful and important to understand mentoring as a specific skill and even profession, I believe it is more important to appreciate mentoring as an integral and natural part of everyday life with friends, colleagues, and loved ones.

Here are a few lessons for developing a better understanding of mentoring in your life and work.

- Name the people who in big and small ways have been at your side, given advice and support, picked you up, and pointed you in the right directions. Whom have you mentored?

- Organizations need to build the capacity of staff, board, and volunteers to play mentoring and coaching roles, not only in supervisory situations, but also as a part of their nonprofit toolkit for making a difference in a diverse and complicated world.

- Mentoring requires listening; commitment to others; and digging deep to understand your own "know-how," intuitive knowledge, and practice stories.

- Find a coach who can help you learn the ropes of coaching so that you can refine your game.

11

Tell Your Own Story (Or Someone Else Will)

∘ ∘
There are only two or three human stories,
and they go on repeating themselves ...

—Willa Cather

In February 1991, Reverend Lee Hudson asked me to speak at the 10:00 a.m. Sunday service at Messiah Lutheran Church in southeast Baltimore's Canton neighborhood. Like so many other urban pastors, Lee was trying valiantly to save this old mainline Protestant church from closing its doors. Lee had built senior housing in the old church hall, joined community organizations like the South East Community Organization (SECO), and encouraged higher-income residents living in the new condos along the waterfront and in nearby renovated rowhomes to attend services and church functions.

Lee and I belonged to an informal group of community planners, developers, investors, academics, and activists named the Lewis Mumford Society after the great American urbanist. We met every few weeks for breakfast, read new and old books about cities, walked Baltimore neighborhoods, contemplated writing urban development manifestos, and took field trips to Philadelphia, Pittsburgh, and Chicago. Although we wanted to refine and share our point of view about vibrant cities and neighborhoods, our motto was that meetings of the Mumford Society required no preparation.

Lee occasionally invited Mumford Society members to offer our wisdom at his Sunday services. The story I told that morning revolved around the simple paradox that here I was again speaking in a church about the important role of religious congregations in urban life. This situation was paradoxical because I was religiously "tone deaf" and an adherent to a strange brew of Buddhism, Quakerism, and awe. Yet religious institutions and leaders had played a prominent role in my community development work. I have worked with religious leaders (as colleagues, friends, and mentors), held meetings in church halls, relied upon congregations to organize their membership for action, and depended upon the financial resources provided by religious denominations and orders. Religious institutions are one of the most reliable building blocks for community building and development in inner-city neighborhoods where many institutions have fled or given up. Today, thinking back on that long and broad support from the religious community encourages me to ponder my own non-beliefs!

That day in the pulpit, I was also sharing something personal about myself and my spiritual doubts—an unlikely Sunday morning message. But the lesson I hoped to share was that acknowledging personal paradoxes is important; beliefs don't always fit together in neat packages. In any case, it's important to *tell your own story*.

Stories convey personal and community change by providing the real detail of human life. Everybody has "war stories." No one, however, will tell your stories the right way. And stories can be warped by spin and selective use of sound bites or savaged by others who are coming from a different policy position. Good stories capture the messiness of real situations, events, and decisions. Planning theorist John Forester writes, "We're likely to find more stories ... than we will find opportunities to 'try things out,' to test our bets, to move and reflect in action."

As you read this chapter about *telling your own story*, think about your stories and whether you or someone else has done the telling.

- What are your key CED stories, and who has told them?
- If you didn't tell these stories, why not?
- What ingredients of good stories do you feel most comfortable or uncomfortable with?
- What stories have you been afraid to tell about life and career?

Stories and Personal Values

Take the current *"values"* debate! In January 2005, I was a discussant about *New York Times* journalist Jason DeParle's 2005 book, *The American Dream*, at the meeting of the U.S. Conference of Mayors. Robert Rector of the Heritage Foundation, a conservative think tank inside the D.C. Beltway, was a respondent as well. *The American Dream* follows three women and their families from Chicago to Milwaukee and through the tumultuous days of welfare reform in a state that would become the national model. The book challenges all assumptions—liberal and conservative—about welfare, work, and reform, but in the end the women are unmarried, on the precipitous edge of poverty, and have multiple kids who are not doing so well. Even those adults working hard and meeting social expectations were not miraculously lifted out of poverty; in fact, their kids were sometimes doing worse, not better, because no one was around.

My response after Jason DeParle summarized his book confessed that there were no easy answers to persistent poverty. I emphasized the importance of job training, work supports, and the need for economic development in Milwaukee, especially since the city had lost so many manufacturing jobs in the recent past. These tools were not used well or recognized by these families or by those charged with helping them, like welfare-to-work agencies and their case managers. Before Robert Rector launched into his stump speech about the transformative powers of marriage, he scoffed at my proposals for economic tinkering and accused me of reinventing the much-maligned *War on Poverty* of President Lyndon Johnson. Rector then pronounced that the problem for these welfare women was not economic, as liberals like me persisted in arguing; it was about the need for a *moral transformation* of low-income people that, at its core, requires commitment to marriage, responsible fatherhood, and informed, values-based child rearing.

This event was of no ultimate policy significance so far as I could tell, but it has stuck in my craw anyway. Getting skewered by Robert Rector is a liberal badge of courage, so this momentarily painful experience wasn't the source of the discomfort that bothered me for days and weeks after the panel discussion. I recognized that I had led with my chin on this panel as an inexperienced public policy pugilist and that I should have been better prepared to anticipate contrary arguments and opinions when I spoke across political divides, especially in today's Washington, D.C., policy environment. That was part of my self-discovery, but not all of it. The real discomfort was the knowledge that Rector had been correct in some respects; that bothered me not only because I hated to cede an argument to a single-minded opponent, but also because I had been reluctant to say what I really felt about social and moral values.

An untapped consensus exists in our country about fair play and what it takes for all Americans to succeed. Unfortunately, the dogma and dog-eat-dog rhetoric of the political left and right, the blue and red states, have too often drowned out this consensus and made real civic conversation, as opposed to incendiary sound bites, nearly impossible.

Whether to have a job has never been a choice for me; it has been the inevitable, seemingly natural course of events since I graduated from college, even in years before. That's my story, as it has been for many of my friends. Within days of returning home to Chicago after graduating from college, I took a job hawking medical books and supplies in Chicago and later toiled as a janitor in Philadelphia before deciding to pick a career and try out graduate school. I've never taken (or even applied for) unemployment insurance payments in between jobs or any other kind of public subsidy, like food stamps. I've used personal savings, family and spousal resources, and low-interest loans to help me through the inevitable (and for me luckily infrequent) transitions in life like graduations, dissertations, cross-country relocations, marriages and divorces, and births and adoptions. Since I had children later in life, I see college payments continuing into my golden years.

My father and mother felt privileged to be Americans and survive the deprived circumstances of the Depression era. Doing pretty well in life given where they had started was a function of hard work and good luck. My father's father died unexpectedly when he was thirteen, and my mother grew up in a garage apartment on her father's meager salary as a government clerk. My father used the GI Bill to attend engineering school after World War II, and my parents no doubt benefited from homeowner tax deductions and maybe even Federal Housing Administration-guaranteed mortgages as they moved from suburb to suburb. And for myself, I benefited from some of the same—good public schools, government-backed student loans, and a small inheritance from my great aunt that paid for one year of college.

The problem is that many liberals do not spend enough time saying what has worked in their lives—the values and resources that supported them through school, into jobs, and to owning their own homes. That's what everyone wants for themselves and for their kids. Too many liberals spend more time saying why things don't work, as I did in my response to Jason DeParle's book. This makes it difficult to build an unlikely coalition for increasing opportunities for those who haven't been as fortunate.

Personal Stories

Telling your own story can be a rite of passage for bonding with a group of friends, colleagues, or co-conspirators. I have to admit, though, that the male-bonding version of this storytelling is sometimes too much for my innate skepticism and short-windedness; but feminists have, in a more authentic way, used storytelling as a method for building consciousness, support networks, and action agendas. It is no wonder that storytelling is now being used more formally by evaluators of community efforts to get at the underlying dynamics of social change.

Oral history records our personal stories and places them in the larger historical context. When I directed SECO in southeast Baltimore in the early 1990s, a well-known community filmmaker and his crew sponsored by the Pratt Institute in New York came to town to record my story about SECO's history. SECO and its development arm were a part of the cohort of second-generation community development corporations, or CDCs, funded in the 1970s by the Ford Foundation. When the filmmakers asked me how I had discovered my avocation in the business of social change, I couldn't reply with a gripping story of personal or family hardship, ethical enlightenment, or a transformational journey. Rather, I talked about how my love for cities was ignited during my visits to my grandmother's two-flat building in Evanston, Illinois, an older suburban town on the northern border of Chicago, as I played in alleyways and snuck off to buy candy in neighborhood stores. I watched the faces of the filmmakers fall as I spun my prosaic story, but it was true. Lucky for them I didn't recount how the values of my Republican parents and my experiences in the Boy Scouts and on sports teams prepared me for dedicating my life to CED.

Personal stories are a key part of the ten-day community organizer training workshops conducted each year by faith-based organizing networks like the Industrial Areas Foundation (IAF) founded by Saul Alinsky in the 1940s. An important part of the training is for organizers and leaders to come to grips with what it takes to form enduring relationships with potential leaders, congregation members, and power stakeholders who control resources and institutions. Without relationships based upon shared values, it's nearly impossible to build the kind of coalitions and campaigns that are powerful enough to change public school systems, build affordable housing, pass living-wage ordinances, or win new infrastructure investments in poor communities. Uncovering shared values requires digging deep and exposing one's human pain, motivation, and bedrock beliefs. It's about taking ownership of one's past, present, and future, like owning the pain of being separated from one's child, suffering the loss of a parent, or experiencing the oppression of poverty. The IAF models personal storytelling about life as a powerful way of building relationships for the purpose of making change together.

COFI, or Community Organizing for Family Issues, is a quirky little organization in Chicago that has made big impacts while redefining the practice of community organizing. COFI training starts with storytelling in small groups about women's lives in families and how social change can't be separated from the day-to-day needs, aspirations, and leadership of families and their communities. Storytelling is an integral part of self-discovery; it establishes commonality through shared experience and helps the women take action together to promote community. More explicitly than groups like IAF, COFI views developmental leadership and network building as major victories.

Stories and Timing

Telling your own story is not just about speaking from your vanity, values, and experience; it also requires great timing and good luck if it is to reach a broader audience. Sometimes the best-laid plans for stories are derailed by somebody's *hit job* on your favorite project. At other times your favorite project is in the *groove* and you hit a home run.

The *Chicago Tribune* in late 1988, for instance, wrote an investigative series on how advocates—in the neighborhoods, city hall, and universities—were getting in the way of progress and real estate development at a time when Chicago desperately needed growth. There were certainly examples of obstructionist community organizations that opposed anything happening on their turf up until the point at which they finessed payoffs in exchange for supporting the project or for simply disappearing. But the series also knocked folks who wanted to preserve manufacturing by balancing old and new growth and who thought that real estate developers should pay their fair share for new physical infrastructure and other development costs. Although I had served as deputy commissioner of economic development during this era prior to leaving to complete my doctoral dissertation, the article dismissed me as a graduate student. Imagine my parents' surprise when their friends told them that their son really hadn't gotten his act together yet.

In 1995, the *Wall Street Journal* published an article by two young right-wing activists on the payroll of a think tank financed by conservative foundations. In this op-ed, they attacked Milwaukee's business community for supporting the *Campaign for Sustainable Milwaukee* (CSM) and its application to become a Casey Foundation *Jobs Initiative* site. CSM was a feisty coalition of unions, community groups, environmentalists, and public officials. The two young conservatives had infiltrated CSM and discovered, to no one's surprise except their own and the *Wall Street Journal*'s, that liberal activists not only had poor security, but also supported liberal causes and opposed conservative panaceas like school vouchers. The op-ed treaded the timeworn path of referring to the "Bolshevik" pasts of some of the CSM leaders, no doubt exotic political excursions during their college years. The Milwaukee business community and the Casey Foundation's UPS-dominated board came in for the unusual McCarthy-like criticism of being labeled as "dupes" of the radicals, those same folks who were so easily infiltrated. Luckily, the Milwaukee business community stood behind the effort, establishing appropriate safeguards and business oversight. Nevertheless, once a "hit" of this sort is made, it keeps circulating.

And then there are the *home runs*, or unexpected positive stories, even about bad news. As the holiday season approached in 1985, the Hasbro Company announced the closing of its Playskool facility on the west side of Chicago and the Christmas layoff of eleven hundred workers. This might have been just one more plant closing/relocation story in a time of industrial restructuring and globalization except for three things. First, Hasbro stole a move out of the "Grinch's" playbook by announcing layoffs at Christmas. What were they thinking? Second, Playskool had received a $1 million, low-interest Industrial Revenue Bond to create jobs at the Chicago plant, not to close down a profitable plant with name recognition as the best of children's toys. And third, Playskool stiffed its former business colleagues on the west side by giving no advance notice. The press had a field day with metaphors like "breach of trust" that staved off normal business opposition to any real or perceived restraints on business decision-making. Ultimately, the City of Chicago filed suit over the failed job creation, and Hasbro settled after several months, agreeing to delay layoffs, provide additional worker dislocation benefits, and help re-use the site for business and job-creation purposes. An important story was told that made a modest bit of difference for laid-off workers and arguably a bigger difference for policy discussions about corporate responsibility.

In 2001, I began investing in an initiative that eventually took the name, *Working Poor Families Project*, and attracted additional financial support from other foundations. Its purpose was to strengthen state-level policy advocacy supporting career advancement for low-income workers by making available annual fifty-state datasets from the American Community Survey and performance data about federal workforce, welfare, work support, and post-secondary education programs. By 2006, twenty-three states had written reports, established policy agendas, and advocated for specific policy and program improvements.

As the presidential election of 2004 loomed in the fall, we created a national report that addressed these same working-family issues, *Working Hard, Falling Short*. Our communications strategy was to release the report at a Washington, D.C., National Press Club briefing in mid-October with politicians, researchers, and advocates. We hoped to inspire dialogue throughout the country. To our chagrin, politicians declined to enter the domestic policy fray at this stage of the election campaign. So we launched Plan B—a targeted release of the report the week of the second presidential debates. As dumb luck would have it, *New York Times* columnist Bob Herbert featured the report in his syndicated column, and off we went receiving major national and international coverage, especially because he linked the report's unrecognized findings about working families to a similar lack of truth-telling about the war in Iraq. Even the presidential candidates and their running mates picked up the language and data from the report.

Conflicting Stories

Today's political partisanship has created a permanent condition of multiple and divergent stories about the same set of events and trends, like in the great film, *Rashomon*, by the renowned Japanese film director, Akira Kurosawa. Listening to these perspectives as refracted through the television media forces one to digest equally plausible (or equally implausible) points of view about subjects that differ, often dramatically, about basic values, premises, facts, and conclusions. Each combatant paints a story with a different brushstroke of detail and nuance. One is tempted to throw up one's hands and declare, "I give up!" Such stories no longer enlighten; they contribute to the paralysis and division of our country.

Conflicting viewpoints about the 1960s is a case in point. Many contemporary critics have dismissed the counterculture, youth movements, and policy agendas of the 1960s as variously inciting an age of sexual and cultural permissiveness (and hence the destruction of the family); driving blue-collar, white, ethnic Democrats to become Republicans; supporting the last desperate gasp of the New Deal; seeding the growth of an addictive drug culture; and contributing to the materialism, narcissism, and victimization that have overtaken our culture. These critiques have forever marked the baby boomer generation as permanently immature.

My story of the 1960s, in contrast, is about growing up and transformative changes in our political culture. Folk and rock music, civil rights marches, and anti-war politics blended with leaving home, going to college, having girlfriends, and starting out on my life. The spirit, values, openness, and excitement that I felt and experienced in the 1960s have stayed with me and continue to provide motivation and a reference point of experience. The violence, sectarianism, self-servingness, and superficial spirituality during these years also provided a host of lessons about human frailty, democracy, and social movements. Indeed, as a shy introvert, I never completely let go of my inhibitions (or good upbringing), and at the same time I always kept a skeptical, critical distance from the crazy-quilt of life taking place before my eyes. No matter the story of the 1960s that historians and cultural critics assemble, the *sixties* was my jumping-off point into my future, the beginning of my story as an adult.

In a more prosaic realm, job retention in the field of workforce development offers another *Rashomon* story. Job retention is arguably one of the most important workforce development outcomes—along with wage gains and career advancement—that measures whether low-income workers have achieved long-run attachment to the labor market. It's not just about getting a job, but about keeping the job and moving ahead. This is the success story that most public and private investors want to tell.

Unfortunately, we are rarely able to have an intelligent conversation about long-run job retention across different workforce programs, much less a national discussion. Job retention means different things to different people and institutions: it can mean three-, six-, or twelve-month retention in specific jobs or, alternatively, in multiple jobs in the labor market; it can mean working most of the time or only when one gets the lucky follow-up job retention phone call; and it can mean that retention percentages are based only on those program participants who are found rather than upon all those who were placed. And these variations are just the tip of the job retention iceberg.

Inconsistent counting is reinforced by facts of life. Federal workforce funding frequently encourages *creaming* of the most job-ready candidates by rewarding states and cities that show good retention numbers. Harder-to-employ folks are left behind. Few investors invest in workforce service providers to collect and analyze data about job retention for the purpose of improving performance. Somehow service providers are expected to figure all this out by themselves. And many workforce funders punish providers for telling the real story about what it takes in effort and money for folks to keep jobs. So all we get is a cacophony of job retention stories that have only a modest connection with reality.

Sometimes success stories are really about power and assertion rather than the facts. As relationships with colleagues, project sites, and consultants grow frayed over the life of long-term social initiatives, the disaffected speak loudest about what went wrong, what the powers that be really think, and how the world ought to evaluate the effort. There will always be painful truths to grapple with in such initiatives, but I'm surprised by the debunking of these naysayers. The lesson, of course, is that you must *tell your own story* early, often, and forever! On the other hand, I'm amused how people of all sorts claim to have been there at the beginning of a successful project, when in fact they were nowhere to be seen. I say let them tell their story. In this case, it's a sign of success.

What Stories Are Made Of

I want to digress momentarily to consider the vagaries of words—the building blocks of stories. This digression is especially relevant given my continuing tour of duty in the world of philanthropy, a chief source not only of flexible financial resources, but also of ever-changing and incomprehensible jargon. Foundations are purveyors of neologisms in part because they honestly believe that it really is difficult to give money away. Random acts of kindness don't usually satisfy the fiduciary requirements and impact (making a difference) ambitions of most foundation boards of trustees. Foundations spend a lot of time, to the consternation of their grantees, assembling and putting forth strategic frameworks for guiding their investments. This is when the special words come into play. As Balzac's Monsieur Bernard questions incredulously in the *Wrong Side of Paris*, "Can this be true? Can philanthropy be something other than mere vanity …?"

A few observations about foundations help clarify their function as word factories. Foundations are relatively unaccountable except to the Internal Revenue Service, meaning that no one is making them be clear about what they are doing or saying. National foundations have largely freed themselves from the geographic origin or focus of their founding benefactors or businesses, like Detroit and Ford Motor Company or Pittsburgh and Andrew Carnegie. Foundations compete with each other by identifying unique niches for their signature investments. Just listen to the taglines of national foundations on National Public Radio. What could a foundation possibly mean by "innovative impacts," for example? At best, foundations are social investors that operate between the university and think tank worlds of knowledge and the practitioner worlds of action. Preoccupied with incubating, replicating, and spreading good ideas, foundations sometimes establish elaborate rationales for investment or engage in never-ending cycles of strategic planning and reorganization—potent symbols that they are thinking and acting.

Foundations are prolific inventors and disseminators of jargon. Tony Proscio in *Bad Words for Good* explains how clueless foundations are about the effects of their jargon on normal discourse. "The only charitable answer is that they don't realize what they're saying and writing. All that leaden verbiage means something to them, or so they believe, so it comes to them as a bit of a shock when no one else can guess at their meaning."

So beware! We now enter the world of foundation words—or jargon. One of the tinniest-sounding of foundation words—*unpack*—is exactly what we are going to do when we try to decipher the mysterious vocabulary of foundations.

Unpack is a domestic metaphor apropos the world of philanthropy travels. *Unpack* refers to the need to break down complicated concepts or patterns into simpler parts. Yes, *unpack* means analyze. But foundation folks prefer to say *unpack* because, like archeologists or botanists of the nineteenth century, program officers collect ideas, programs, and the like on their many voyages into the field and bring them back to the home office to display and show off. Analyze is something you do in grad school.

The social investing of foundations is undertaken to achieve *outcomes*, the all-too-scarce currency that helps one reach, if lucky, return on investment for precious foundation dollars. To say that outcomes are results would be too simple, and that's not good; outcomes refer to longer-run, fundamental changes in the behavior of individuals, families, communities, and institutions. To achieve outcomes is not easy; foundations must first have a *theory of change* or road map of what to do and where to go. Following convoluted pathways represented in theories of change, however, requires extra capacity; that is why many foundations place such a high value on *capacity building*, a process that combines growing up and levitation. Having capacity is the ability to achieve outcomes, and capacity building is the training and *carb-loading* regimen needed to achieve capacity. Of course, much more needs to be unpacked to understand fully how capacity fuels the theory of change, which in turn produces outcomes.

Achieving outcomes, sadly, brings its own veil of tears. Good, innovative social investments are constantly in danger of being labeled as *boutique*—small, exceptional, and difficult to replicate. Boutique projects too often are left behind when foundations, in a frenzy of overdrive, issue a clarion call to *scale up*. What this means is simply to get more outcomes faster. When investments show promise in this regard, they are said to be "moving the needle," or, more powerfully, "turning the curve." For projects that are confidently on their way to scale, we say that they have reached a "tipping point."

If scaling up isn't enough, many high-performing projects are then interrogated to find out if they are really *sustainable*. Being sustainable means lasting for a very long time. But lasting for a very long time, most foundation experts argue, can be achieved only if these projects attain or contribute to the nirvana state of social investing, *system reform*. But, alas, to understand what system reform means requires us to return full circle to *unpack* this loaded concept. And, unfortunately, this takes more time than we have; and, anyway, we really can't talk to our boards of trustees about system reform. That just sounds too much like social engineering.

Harry Frankfurt in his provocative little book, *On Bullshit*, offers many insights that are relevant for understanding foundation jargon. He writes, "Thus the production of bullshit is stimulated whenever a person's obligations or opportunities to speak about some topic exceed his knowledge of the facts that are relevant to that topic. This discrepancy is common in public life ..."

Good stories ultimately require simple, authentic words and, at their best, are free of jargon. Stories are powerful because they transport us into worlds that are unfamiliar to us, yet that ring true. In these new worlds we are able to see ourselves and others in new ways that allow us, in turn, to plumb our own depths and generate new insights about our own life and the life around us. That's what the Bible does. That's what *Moby Dick* achieves. Harvard psychiatrist Robert Coles, in *Call of Stories*, writes that stories "remind ... me how complex, ironic, ambiguous, and fateful this life can be, and the conceptual categories I learned.... are not the only means by which one may view the world." As the novelist Mario Vargas Llosa writes in *Letters to a Young Writer*, "[Stories] are good because thanks to the effectiveness of their form they are endowed with an irresistible *power of persuasion*."

Stories and Evidence

Not everyone, however, thinks that storytelling is a good thing. In the early 1990s, when I directed SECO in Baltimore, we designed and implemented a school-based family literacy program. It combined adult learning, child learning enrichment and homework help, and family reading time together. This holistic approach addressed multiple issues and opportunities at the same time—school performance, adult learning, and family strengthening. Family literacy programs require multiple partners, face difficult implementation challenges, and are relatively expensive compared to individual child or adult learning initiatives. We included a formative evaluation in the project design to capture early impacts and lessons.

We set up a meeting with a local foundation and its wizened director to spread the good news. After we told several stories about specific families from this family literacy project and how grades, attendance, and family well-being seemed to be improving, he turned to us and sternly said, "We must guard ourselves against anecdote."

This deflation of our program *high* typifies an ongoing debate in social policy about evidence and how we make change. Counterposed to anecdote is the *gold standard* approach to evaluation, which involves random assignment research designs that weed out contributing factors other than the treatment interventions, such as family literacy, that may confound program impacts. The problem with gold standard evaluations is that they are expensive and long-term and work best with relatively simplistic (and powerful) interventions. These types of evaluation designs are not so useful for understanding messy, community-building efforts or investments that promote systems change. Yet the title of a recent Public/Private Ventures (P/PV) publication says it all: *Good Stories Aren't Enough: Becoming Outcomes-Driven in Workforce Development.*

The story thing gets even more confusing. The spin doctors of Capitol Hill offer contrary advice. Their targets and bosses (senators and representatives) don't read a lot, so the media gurus counsel. Just tell them a few good stories about people in their states or districts because that's all they remember; otherwise, you lose their attention. Another way of saying this is that sound bites are more powerful and effective than the honest portrayal of complexity. Let the spin begin! It has to be an elevator conversation, a three-paragraph memo. On the other hand, a new current in left-of-center communications strategizing counsels advocates to avoid using personal stories because they sometimes reinforce the image that poor people make bad decisions that they should be held responsible for. It's their fault. Instead of personal stories, we need advocacy narratives that reveal how *structure* and *policy* shape economic and social disparities, as well as personal choices, whether the lack of good jobs or cuts in important federal work support programs like childcare.

The story of our *Jobs Initiative* (JI) is a case in point. We gathered lots of data, albeit non-random assignment, that suggested powerful income impacts from well-crafted program interventions combining human service supports, job readiness training, education and training, and targeting of good jobs. We contracted with ethnographers to study these impacts in more detail for twenty-five families—our success stories. In *Jobs Aren't Enough: Toward a New Economic Mobility for Low-Income Families*, Roberta Rehner Iversen and Annie Laurie Armstrong show the ups and downs of these families over the years as families are in and out of crisis, as labor markets change, and even in the aftermath of Katrina, since New Orleans was one of our JI sites. Their ethnography was rigorous and comprehensive, anything but the usual storytelling; it raised serious questions about what *success* for these families was really about.

Stories and Metaphors

Good stories not only use authentic language, but also rely upon sturdy tools of the trade, like metaphors. Nonprofit leaders need to gather a few metaphors that help them tell their stories. Metaphors are figures of speech in which one thing is talked about in terms of its resemblance to something else. Metaphors create analogies, overlapping meanings, rich ambiguity, and a bit of mystery.

Two uses of metaphor take us in seemingly different directions about storytelling. George Lakoff, linguist and metaphor philosopher, has built upon his seminal studies of metaphors to understand the basic "frames" that underlie contemporary Republican and Democratic values and policies. Think of a frame or metaphor as a lens through which one sees the world, or at least a part of the world, and as a means for formulating interventions. Lakoff believes that differences in beliefs about family structure and functioning frame much of current partisan debates, the argument he makes in *Elephant in the Room*. For conservative Republicans, the family is about obedience—patriarchal and demanding of discipline and responsibility. Sins are punished. For Democrats, the family is nurturing, forgiving, and more egalitarian in the roles of parents and children. Republican parents protect us from the "axis of evil." Democratic parents provide us with a "safety net." Lakoff believes that most of us contain some portion of each. The trick for policy organizing and campaigning is to mobilize those folks who, depending upon one's point of view, are solidly in one camp or another or in the middle.

Generative metaphors draw upon the powers of comparison to create new possibilities and meanings. A good example is the timeworn phrase, "a glass half empty or half full." The half-empty glass leads to talk about what hasn't happened, deficits, or mistakes, while the half-full glass speaks to opportunities, achievements, and assets. In turn, deficits and assets are metaphors—drawn from the world of finance—that call attention to values and attributes when applied to people or neighborhoods. For many years, for example, experts talked about low-income neighborhoods from the deficit perspective as full of problems and needs. Sometimes they named them *slums*. Planning theorist Donald Schön observed that once you defined the problem as a *slum*, the inevitable policy response was slum clearance or urban renewal. More recently, experts have taken an asset-based point of view, which identifies the unrecognized resources, skills, and experiences in neglected neighborhoods. These neighborhoods have become a story of untapped opportunities. The challenge becomes how to build upon these assets.

Who Tells the Story?

I conclude this chapter about stories by contradicting myself about a bold statement I made earlier. At the beginning of this chapter, I said that no one could tell your story as well as you can. There is a lot of truth in this advice, but it doesn't cover every situation.

As I've shared before, I had the good fortune to be a part of the mayoral administration of Harold Washington in Chicago during the 1980s. He promoted a progressive municipal agenda that emphasized social equity and open and professional government in a town that had at least perfected the political machine, if not invented it. Washington was a feisty, charismatic, and thoughtful leader who loved politics and never backed away from a good fight. A lot of special initiatives succeeded under Harold's leadership, and I'm proud to have been a part of the movement that helped him get elected, govern, and win re-election. Yet the Washington administration had its flaws. Activist friends on the left said we were *sell-outs*, too timid when it came to taming plant closings. Critics to the right called these years "Beirut on the Lake" or "Council Wars." Academic colleagues said that we really hadn't achieved, in four short and tumultuous years, significant individual impacts and enduring change that matched our rhetoric. Obviously, the Washington years might be thought of as another *Rashomon* situation—multiple stories about the same set of events.

Which opinion is correct? Well, I've written or edited multiple articles, book chapters, and books that document and celebrate the achievements of the mayoral administration of Harold Washington. Several years ago, however, I said to myself, "I'm done. I have nothing more to say about this seminal experience. Leave it to the journalists, historians, and political scientists to tell the more complete story. I don't have enough of a knowledge base or enough time to do the research, and, frankly, I'm just too biased. I don't have the objectivity this story needs." Sometimes social and political stories are so complicated and long-term that it is impossible for any one participant or observer, however smart, well intentioned, and central, to tell the whole story. They can tell a piece of the story, and that is vitally important, but they can't tell it all.

Stories are powerful ways to engage diverse audiences in community building, program design and implementation, and social entrepreneurship. The color, texture, and evolving nature of stories can be more persuasive than lots of data or a press release about a point in time. But telling a good story around the campfire of life and career takes practice—both in the telling and the listening. Good storytelling is a lifetime's effort.

Here are some further suggestions that will be helpful for telling your own story.

- What stories about CED and about your personal values do you care most about getting right? How have you gone about telling these stories?

- Organizations need to be more conscious of their stories and supportive of the story-making skills and aspirations of their staff. Sharing stories is about learning and celebration.
- Learn about the building blocks of successful stories as well as the roadblocks and pitfalls that await all of us—like bad timing, jargon, and not sticking around.
- Knowing when someone else should tell the story rather than you is a good sign that you have done your work and that the experience deserves another set of eyes.

12

And Now What? The Adventure Continues

> Storybook happiness involves every form of pleasant thumb-twiddling; true happiness involves the full use of one's powers and talents.
>
> —*John W. Gardner*

Anyone who has directed a CDC or CED organization has engaged in Mondragon daydreams. The Mondragon Cooperative Corporation, located in the northern Basque region of Spain, is the largest and most integrated family of worker co-ops in the world, comprising as many as 150 co-ops in the 1970s in manufacturing, agriculture, and services, employing upward of twenty thousand workers, the vast majority of whom are worker owners. The Mondragon complex also includes a development bank, research organization, and health and welfare co-ops. Today Mondragon is the seventh largest corporation in Spain, with thirty or more overseas plants and far fewer worker members. Some of the luster has worn off as Mondragon has sought to survive and prosper in a globalizing world, but it still remains the stuff of daydreams.

Just mention Mondragon in a CED conversation and folks get bug-eyed. It's the nirvana state, the end of the rainbow. It's why we got into the CED business: scale, local ownership, integration, adaptability, and asset-building. Study tours and reading groups about Mondragon abound among wannabes as daydreaming spreads. And if Mondragon doesn't quite suit your daydreaming tastes, substitute the entrepreneurial and social-capital-rich Italian region of Emilia-Romagna or the self-employment generated by the Grameen Bank of Bangladesh led by Mohammed Unus, the recipient of the Nobel Peace Prize of 2006.

I believe daydreams are important. They are not just fantasies about impossible futures or golden pasts, nor are they slippery escapes from real work and committed vision. Daydreaming helps us relax, solve problems, negotiate relationships, visualize change, and envision the future. Daydreams help us make sense of the world. Sure, I've daydreamed about being an over-the-top basketball player and blues guitarist, but my daydreams are just as likely to be focused on the thorny issues of management as on the next version of Mondragon. I am pleased that I still can daydream about the next wave of CED, the focus of this chapter.

Let's begin by going back to the 1960s and 1970s, when a large-scale commitment to CED seemed politically feasible. Such a commitment would be built on a vision that integrated community control, local ownership, human services, and entrepreneurial investment in inner-city neighborhoods and rural regions. Despite the narrowing specialization of CED in ensuing decades, a reaction in part to the withdrawal of support from a bolder CED vision, a practice of comprehensive and integrated CED has remained alive in the field. Today we have impressive examples like Cooperative Home Care Services, Good Faith Fund, New Community Corporation, Coastal Enterprises, FOCUS HOPE, Pioneer Human Services, and Shore Bank.

A macro version of daydreaming Mondragon envisages a *third* or *social sector* that exists between markets and government and is a partial alternative to them. In its most ambitious form, as in Christopher Gunn's *Third-Sector Development*, advocates count up all the ESOPs (Employee Stock Ownership Programs), consumer and producer co-ops (including farm and rural electrification), credit unions, and municipal enterprises, as well as more conventional CED organizations, to arrive at some startling figures about what comprises the third sector. It's enormous, at least in a relative sense. A commonality of values and principles in this sector focuses on community benefits, worker rights, and environmental sustainability. If we add public pension funds and labor union financing, we've got quite a movement. The problem is that the third sector in its most ambitious form is as much a construction of third sector theorists as a reality. Oddly, the third sector of CED organizations is sometimes treated like the "slumbering proletariat" of old. If only it would awaken, become self-conscious of its powers and role, and then take the lead in contesting the imperatives of the public and private sectors.

My daydreaming about Mondragon has diminished considerably during the past decade. I'm as likely to sigh in frustrated disbelief at one more reference to Mondragon, and *third sector* talk inevitably makes me roll my eyes dismissively.

I've had to pinch myself to stay open to the possibility that one more proposal for a temp services worker co-op might actually be a viable source of jobs and income for undocumented workers. In the past year, I've had an unusually large number of people ask me, "Well, what about co-ops?" I've reacted in several ways. Sometimes I think that dreaming of Mondragon is a way of avoiding taking advantage of real opportunities in the present, as if making good on bread-and-butter jobs were somehow less important for families and communities than posing the bigger social change agenda. I believe in practical action. Alternatively, as I've participated in international meetings on economic development, *social economy* initiatives and cooperatives are a mainstay and are presented as if they are relatively easy to do. Maybe I need to go beyond staying open to at least partially embracing this social economy approach.

Now I'm daydreaming about why I'm not daydreaming about Mondragon. Is this a sign of advanced middle age in which taking new risks requires more psychic energy than I can muster? Has my investor role so enmeshed me in the world of current practice that I no longer can envisage major social change or breakthrough social innovations? Maybe I've witnessed too many failures of co-ops, worker buyouts, and all the rest to get excited by one more go-round of interesting innovations launched against stacked odds. I'm also less vulnerable to slick proposal writers and proselytizers who argue that a new, alternative paradigm is incubating in our midst, if only we would embrace it and feed it with free money. Getting to scale, our long-term investor hang-up, makes me skeptical about boutique projects that seem to be swimming against a tide of markets, even though a few exemplars still inspire me with the possibility. And then there's the question of political feasibility: the current political scene and budget woes draw us to crafting win/win partnerships with markets and the private sector, not wholesale alternatives.

Hegemony of Market-Based CED

The story of Mondragon during the past several decades is an instructive introduction to market-based CED. Surviving recessions and global market pressures forced Mondragon to make wage, benefit, and ownership adjustments, focus more on external markets, change its sector and product mix, centralize and coordinate investment, and move production overseas. Mondragon remains a source of inspiration, but its balance of costs and benefits is much different from what it was in its growth period of the 1960s, also a challenging time in the final days of Franco's authoritarian regime.

The emergence of market-based CED in the United States has multiple origins in addition to the factors facing Mondragon. As a backdrop, the past thirty years have witnessed a period of sustained economic structural change, federal and local budget cuts, and policy shifts that have encouraged more emphasis on individual responsibility and public/private partnerships. Affordable housing production, for example, now relies largely upon federal low-income housing tax credits that leverage substantial private investment rather than subsidy programs for community-based housing developers. The tax incentives of federal and local enterprise zones of the 1980s and 1990s supported private business expansions and hiring rather than the entrepreneurial investments of CDCs. And welfare reform placed much of the responsibility for dependence upon individuals, mostly women, rather than upon the lack of accessible good jobs and careers.

The mental models upon which CED was built in the 1960s embodied several limiting assumptions that have changed over time. CED was a targeted response to the withdrawal (or historical absence) of financial, economic, and organizational capital from inner-city communities and rural regions. In short, CED responded to uneven development. In many situations, this withdrawal of resources occurred almost overnight, especially for African American communities. The withdrawal of economic resources, often characterized as disinvestment, fatally combined racial steering, political exclusion, lack of information, demographic change, and the geographic restructuring of places and industries. It occurred in specific urban neighborhoods, but it was also happening for cities, older suburbs, and rural regions. This was misleadingly referred to as the urban crisis. The first generation of CED strategies sought to replace disinvested financial and organizational capital with CDCs and an alternative set of investment criteria that more explicitly counted community benefits and social impacts in the economic development equation. At the same time, the community-organizing strand of CED sought to curb the abuses of disinvestment and promote reinvestment, its crowning achievement being the Community Reinvestment Act (CRA) of 1977.

A number of factors contributed to altering the assumptions underlying CED and encouraging more market-based approaches. A first group of factors deals with successes and failures. On the success side, CED demonstrated the viability of urban neighborhoods, affordable housing production, and the profitability of private sector investment in inner-city neighborhoods. In a broader sense, many cities rebounded by the late 1990s, stemming population losses and showing budget surpluses in cities that were only a short time before written-off rustbelt fiscal disasters. CED became the commonsense way of doing business.

On the failure side, CED failed to solve urban and rural poverty and, in fact, became a target of blame for sustaining dependency and wasting precious public resources. This is a controversial argument. CED advocates have forcefully replied that CED has never been supported by bold policies and adequate financial resources. It is fair to say, however, that CDCs have proven to be an imperfect vehicle for stimulating economic development in neighborhoods, even though they have done a good job overall with affordable housing. Too often, CDCs have become mired in a grants-and-program mentality and have been unable to capitalize on neighborhood economic assets or connect their neighborhoods to broader regional economies. In many cases, CDCs have become the creatures of new ethnic-based political machines or have been encouraged to proliferate by public and philanthropic investors at a non-sustainable scale. Most cities have stories of CDC failures, while few places have put together the investment and management infrastructure to support CDCs' becoming high-performing and financially sustainable.

Another related debate challenges the efficacy of targeted geographic development for the purposes of poverty alleviation, the approach adopted by most CDCs. The policy choices posed in the 1960s—*gilding the ghetto versus opening up the suburbs*—have become transformed into a growing preference for encouraging mixed-income neighborhoods and the dismantling of ghettos rather than lifting up low-income neighborhoods. This preference builds upon the failures of place-based development and the negative effects of concentrated poverty on children and families. Mixed-income neighborhoods, in contrast, promise high-quality services, neighborhood retail, asset-building from rising market values, civic engagement and problem-solving, and a diverse mix of role models and social networks. *Hope VI* reconfigurations of public housing developments and housing mobility programs are the preeminent form of the mixed-income approach to community development. Even the Casey Foundation—a leading advocate of community building in high-risk neighborhoods—has embraced mixed-income development and what it calls *responsible relocation* for the dual purpose of dispersing poverty and supporting the land assembly needed for large-scale community redevelopment.

A larger policy failure, documented by Alice O'Conner in *Poverty Knowledge*, has been the shift away from structural economic explanations for poverty to programs and policies that emphasize individual deficits and personal responsibility for change. The new consensus holds individuals accountable for moving ahead while letting private firms lower wages, move offshore, and disinvest in communities—all in the name of maintaining economic competitiveness. It is no surprise that some of the most promising CED strategies emphasize community organizing that advocates for living-wage ordinances, family self-sufficiency standards, and community benefits agreements. Yet globalization has encouraged the reign of market forces.

A second group of factors encouraging market-based CED relates to new development, or at least to new opportunities, created by other economic development successes. Despite the economic recovery of many cities, regional economies are where more and more of the economic action takes place and where most people live, including more diverse populations and a larger proportion of low-income families. Indeed, many new immigrants to metro areas bypass traditional city ports of entry to locate in the suburbs. Michael Porter and his Initiative for a Competitive Inner City (ICIC) recommend that cities connect inner-city firms to regional economic clusters, thus building upon their infrastructure and labor supply advantages. At the same time, regional advocates are seeking to promote urban development by limiting the public investments that support the proliferation of suburban sprawl.

The mantra that regions are what is important for global economies has meant that CED applies to more than low-income urban neighborhoods. Equitable and tolerant regions are seen as a precondition for attracting and keeping "creative class" and give communities a competitive edge. This evolution demonstrates the success of CED, but also a shift of geographic focus.

Yet low-income urban consumer markets still did not receive sustained attention from market researchers until recent years. Some businesses, such as Pathmark Supermarkets or CVS Pharmacies, have stumbled upon untapped urban consumer markets. Other firms have been attracted to city neighborhoods because of the application of new information-gathering and technology by groups like *Social Compact* that portray the high density of consumer demand in urban neighborhoods. No better indicator of the viability of these markets exists than the proliferation in urban neighborhoods of so-called predatory mortgage and consumer finance companies that have filled the gap that mainstream financial institutions left.

The new attention to asset-building approaches to poverty alleviation reinforces the focus on individuals and neighborhood markets. For too long the predominant affordable housing strategy has been to concentrate subsidized housing in low-income neighborhoods, effectively suppressing market values and limiting the ability of homeowners to gain from housing value appreciation. Yet, for most Americans, family wealth derives primarily from homeownership and appreciating values, except in the case of African Americans, who have in many cases been confined to economically stagnant neighborhoods. Making neighborhood housing markets appreciate requires mixed incomes, low crime, educational options, controlled development of low-income housing, and a range of financing to enable housing renovations and fix-ups. The downside of this attention to neighborhood market growth is that many urban neighborhoods are now gentrifying, limiting the access of new buyers.

Another factor encouraging market-based CED is the renewed attention to market-based revenue generation for CDCs and other CED organizations. For too long, CDCs have depended upon grants and subsidies as the mainstay of their financial models. This began to change in the 1980s as CDCs broke into affordable housing production and learned to take advantage of developer and partnership fees. The 1990s saw another wave of attention to revenue-generation and social enterprise models, particularly in the employment field. Advocates called this double-bottom line development, in which CDCs marry market and social benefits. What has distinguished this round of interest in nonprofit revenue-generation has been the investment in local and national infrastructures to provide technical assistance, management consulting and start-up, and long-term financing.

If Douglas Smith in *Values and Value* is correct that organizations are replacing geographic communities as the places for community building, then enterprises of all kinds need to be thought of in a new light. He further argues that the values of the market and values of ethics have many more points of convergence than we usually acknowledge, and these commonalities are growing. What this means is that all private firms, not only socially responsible exemplars, are becoming locations and actors on behalf of CED.

So what exactly is market-based CED? Bob Weissbourd and Riccardo Bodini, theorists of market-based CED, argue that "[I]t reconnects poorer communities to the mainstream economy rather than creating alternative programmatic 'solutions' that further isolate and stigmatize them." This implies, first of all, making durable connections to regional economies, economic transactions, firms, and private sector financing. Second, it means investing in mixed-income communities and neighborhood market development as well as linking neighborhoods to economic engines like university and hospital complexes. Third, market-based CED always seeks to build entrepreneurial organizations, generate private revenues, and join public/private partnerships. Finally, market-based CED uses market mechanisms to leverage private resources, change the behaviors of market institutions, and scale up CED innovations.

Market-based CED is on the upswing and offers a lot of corrective wisdom to a CED field that has grown too insular, disconnected from real economics, and fed on grants and unrealistic fantasies about social change. But there are also serious drawbacks with market-based CED that suggest caution in its wholesale adoption. Market-based CED is best thought of as using market mechanisms to produce additional marginal benefits rather than as a bold alternative that will open untapped economic opportunities. And market-based CED has some fundamental limitations: it says little about job quality and labor markets and is premised on the economic status quo; insufficient evidence has been gathered about the impacts of mixed-income housing or about those families relocated from public housing projects; revenue generation by CED nonprofits remains minimal; the fascination with social enterprises has led to numerous cases of nonprofit failure and overreaching; and market mechanisms are robbing working families through predatory practices. We need to separate the wisdom of market-based CED from the hype and another set of ill-placed high hopes.

Daydreaming a Different CED Future

With all this talk about market-based CED, I've been stimulated to begin some new daydreams about CED. I'm not sure what my role will be in acting upon these daydreams, but I'm reminded of the poet Delmore Schwartz's short story title, "in dreams begin responsibilities." Maybe our CED innovations—co-ops, greenhouses, self-help, and social enterprises—were just a few decades premature. I'm getting the sense that the next few decades will see a rebirth of CED, one comprised of a creative amalgam of market-based CED, the best practices of CDCs, and our own versions of Mondragon.

What's making me have such wild, and perhaps unrealistic, daydreams? One of the key conditions for making these daydreams seem more feasible is that we can actually see the end, or at least the faltering, of the American empire in the decades ahead. The twenty-first century is likely to be the Chinese or Indian century as the U.S. lives off its prosperity and takes on new and different roles as a world leader. There are many ramifications of this likely empire evolution, but at least two are important for our daydreams about CED. On the one hand, cheaper international labor costs will continue to erode U.S. wages and incomes and, in conjunction with higher energy costs, will create a lower or stagnant standard of living for our children and grandchildren. On the other hand, future U.S. skill shortages, combined with the U.S. competitive advantage in innovation and creativity, may create favorable political conditions for rethinking how we invest in education and training, particularly for the low-income, low-skilled, who will be a major source of untapped human capital. Competitiveness may become a unifying narrative for joining economic and workforce development, market-based growth, and social equity. Moreover, some economists believe that the age of neo-liberal globalization is about over, to be replaced by a variety of nationalisms that will protect and nurture local economies.

The United States is again becoming an immigrant nation—in cities, suburbs, or rural regions. This influx of diverse immigrants into the U.S. brings with it new entrepreneurial energies and social forms not eroded by the temptations and practices of consumer capitalism. Immigration is rejuvenating grassroots economies of self-employment, communal economics, extended household asset-building, and civic engagement. This energy and innovation is manifest in the labor movement, banking, community-building, and the informal sector. Immigrant practices merged with traditional and market-based CED are producing new variations that in turn are likely to create unforeseen CED opportunities.

We are also likely to see further growth of innovative labor organizing in the service sector by unions like the Service Employees International Union (SEIU). With its expanded commitment to organizing, willingness to partner with employers, provision of expanded member services, and openness to being a part of coalitions, SEIU is creating an exciting model for twenty-first-century unionism that is relevant for CED. Lifting up the service sector complements other efforts to invest in education and training to fill skill shortages.

Federal budget woes seem to be guaranteed for decades to come, given tax cuts and the costs of the war on terrorism. At the same time, local and state budgets are reviving and are becoming the arena for policy innovation and action, as has traditionally been the case at key junctures in U.S. history. This situation is likely to push the CED sector more toward revenue generation and market-based CED at the same time new civic partnerships address the issues of economic competitiveness and quality of life. Dramatic growth in philanthropy may provide a source of venture capital and glue money for these partnerships to start up and thrive in the areas of workforce development, energy generation, community-building, and social enterprises.

As all of this is unfolding, we have a CED infrastructure throughout the U.S. that consists of thousands of grassroots organizations, community-based financial institutions, nonprofits, technical assistance and financial intermediaries, unions, think tanks, and advocacy groups. What role might this CED infrastructure play as the incentives grow more favorable for developing and supporting localized cooperative production, innovation, buying, and services? What if new global and national conditions make it imperative that we tap all our human and financial resources to create new energy sources, support urban agriculture, band together in consumer and producer co-ops, live in denser communities, and collectively invest in our educational futures? Can this CED infrastructure rise to the occasion and reinvent itself?

I'm trying these new CED daydreams on for size, so I admit that the argument has a few holes. We still need federal action on health care and other social safety nets for the new economy. But trying on these daydreams has made me more curious about the variables at play and whether we are starting to see evidence of this new kind of CED. At this stage of my CED career, I think I can play an important role in paying attention to new and provocative daydreams like these and maybe even in figuring out how to help them become realities.

The Adventure Continues

And Now What? Contemplating the next steps in my CED career creates the usual anxiety. It seems as if even now, as I anticipate next steps, all options are open to me, or at least I think they are open to me. This open-endedness of options has happened at every stage of my career, and I suspect it is the fate of the generalist with lots of different interests to constantly question, in the words of poet Robert Frost, "paths not taken." I do know that I want to keep myself firmly planted in never straying too far from practice, but also having the time to reflect and digest what I've experienced. There is a tendency as one moves through a CED career to become more of a coach or consultant, leaving the heavy design, start-up implementation, and political lifting to others. That's already somewhat true for me, but I believe strongly that having a feel for what it takes to deliver the goods on the ground is essential if CED daydreams are to become realities.

This book began with an expression of concern for helping old and new nonprofit leaders to become more effective and fill new leadership roles. Leadership at all levels of CED is critical for promoting and achieving important results, building high-performing organizations, creating social innovations, and advocating for bold public policies. A focus on nonprofit leadership is important because of leadership transitions and the demands on the nonprofit sector to be more effective. The continuing CED adventure is one training ground for civic leadership because CED requires both action and learning. I hope that my CED experiences and reflections have provided perspective on how personal attributes, skills, and relationships can turn CED adventures into sustained and effective leadership as well as a life's work.

The core of my adventure in CED has been jumping in and trying things out and then spending the time along the way thinking about where I've been and where I'm going. As I've said, my overall batting average has been pretty good, but my game has been singles and doubles, not home runs. I've only scratched the surface of my reflections and learning, and I suspect I will spend more time in the future reflecting on mistakes and messiness and on how to be a more effective CED coach. But I'm itching to jump into a new CED adventure. I hope I have the good luck to find a few more during my CED career. I hope that you are also able to find CED adventures that test your skills, leadership, and imagination.

Appendix

My father started as an electrical engineer with Bell Laboratories (now Lucent), but over his career came to see himself primarily as a manager of large-scale technology applications. Along the way in this career he honed a score of commandments and cardinal sins that he hung on his office wall, communicated to staff, laughed about, and tried to follow. They have a certain Ben Franklin, common-sense appeal that mixes advice about how to behave with tried and true management maxims. I offer my commentary after each list, not as counterpoint or rebuttal, but as a part of my own musings about managing change.

The Twelve Commandments According to Paul K. Giloth

- Nobody Is Perfect
- Life Is Short
- There Is No Excuse for Failure
- If It Doesn't Work, It's Your Fault
- If You Don't Test It, It Won't Work
- If You Don't Schedule, It Won't Happen
- Tell It Like It Is
- A List of Priority Problems Is an Indication of Progress
- Don't Say It Can't Be Done, Say What It Takes to Do It
- You Can Make HERO on Any Job Assignment
- Don't Take Yourself Too Seriously—Smile Once in a While
- You Can't Fly with the Owls at Night if You Want to Keep Up with the Eagles in the Daytime

My father's commandments call for humor, honesty, taking action, and self-control. They also suggest that leaders should take steps to try things out before making huge investments, like in prototyping. I don't like the "There is no Excuse for Failure," although he may have been referring to non-constructive mistakes, or stupid mistakes that should have been avoided. This maxim does have an old-fashioned ring to it that defies complexity and uncertainty. And then there's the commandment, "If It Doesn't Work, It's Your Fault." I believe in personal responsibility, and the blame game gets you nowhere. But putting all responsibility on your own shoulders is going too far in an era of teams.

The 10 Cardinal Sins of Management According to Paul K. Giloth

- Don't listen to what your subordinates are telling you (the NASA Syndrome)
- Delegate and do not keep up with what is being implemented (Reagan Syndrome)
- Believe that only certain aspects of the development cycle are important
- Don't attend status reviews
- Don't believe in project status charts based on hundreds of benchmarks
- Make "hero" by accepting new jobs even if you know you can't meet cost and schedule objectives
- Be overly optimistic and believe in miracles
- Reward people immediately for good ideas rather than waiting for proof of usefulness
- Kill the messenger of bad news
- Don't pay attention to history—new methods are always better than proven methods

My father's cardinal sins of management resonate with me much more than his commandments. It's a matter of temperament and of avoiding pitfalls or correcting for past mistakes. I have noticed that some of the sins are the proverbial other side of the coin to the commandments, whether about making "hero" or the blinders of optimism. Frankly, I find it much easier to think about not doing some things than about remaking myself to be cheerful. But that's me. My father was obviously able to play it both ways.

Bibliography

Most of the following texts are quoted or referenced directly in the book. A handful of references, however, functioned solely as sources of inspiration and argument and are not cited in the book. Further information about the Casey Foundation's *Jobs Initiative* or *Making Connections* can be found at www.aecf.org.

Abrahamson, Eric and David H. Freedman. *A Perfect Mess: The Hidden Benefits of Disorder—How Crammed Closets, Cluttered offices, and On-the-Fly Planning Make the World a Better Place.* New York: Little Brown, 2006.

Annie E. Casey Foundation. *Earn It! Keep It! Save It!* Baltimore, MD: Annie E. Casey Foundation, 2003.

Annie E. Casey Foundation. *High Costs of Being Poor.* Baltimore, MD: Annie E. Casey Foundation, 2003.

Appiah, Kwame Anthony. *Cosmopolitanism: Ethics in a World of Strangers.* New York: Norton, 2006.

Arbinger Institute. *Leadership and Self Deception: Getting Out of the Box.* San Francisco, CA: Berrett-Koehler Publishers, 2000.

Arbinger Institute. *Anatomy of Peace: Resolving the Heart of Conflict.* San Francisco: CA: Berrett-Koehler Publishers, 2006.

Badaracco, Joseph L., Jr. *Defining Moments: When Managers Must Choose Between Right and Right.* Cambridge, MA: Harvard Business School Press, 1997.

Balzac, Honoré de. *The Wrong Side of Paris.* New York: Modern Library, 2003.

Bellamy, Edward. *Looking Backwards.* New York: Signet Classic, 2000.

Bennett, Michael I. J., and Robert P. Giloth, Eds. *Economic Development in American Cities: The Pursuit of an Equity Agenda.* Albany, NY: SUNY Press, 2007.

Bennis, Warren. *Leaders: The Strategies for Taking Charge.* New York: Harper & Row, 1985.

Berlin, Isaiah. *The Hedgehog and the Fox: An Essay on Tolstoy's View of History.* Chicago, IL: Ivan R. Dee Publishers, 1953.

Bingham, Richard D., and Robert Mier, Eds. *Theories of Local Economic Development.* Newberry Park, CA: Sage Publications, 1993.

Bornstein, David. *How to Change the World: Social Entrepreneurship and the Power of New Ideas.* New York: Oxford University Press, 2004.

Bourdain, Anthony. *Kitchen Confidential: Adventures in the Culinary Underbelly.* New York: HarperCollins, 2000.

Bourdain, Anthony. *A Cook's Tour: Global Adventures in Extreme Cuisine.* New York: HarperCollins, 2001.

Bowden, Charles, and Lew Kreinberg. *Street Signs Chicago: Neighborhoods and Other Illusions of Big-City Life.* Chicago, IL: Chicago Review Press, 1981.

Brophy, Paul, and Alice Shabecoff. *A Guide to Careers in Community Development.* Washington, DC: Island Press, 2001.

Buckingham, Marcus, and Donald Clifton. *Now, Discover Your Strengths.* New York: Free Press, 2001.

Buckingham, Marcus, and Curt Coffman. *First, Break All the Rules.* New York: Simon and Schuster, 1999.

Capraro, James, Andrew Ditton, and Robert Giloth. *Neighborhood Economic Development: Working Together for Chicago's Future.* Chicago, IL: City of Chicago, Department of Economic Development/Local Initiatives Support Corporation, 1986.

Cather, Willa. *O Pioneers!* New York: Vintage Classics, 1992.

Chase, Stuart. *Tyranny of Words.* New York: Harcourt Brace & World, 1938.

Cohen, Eliot, and John Gooch. *Military Misfortunes. The Anatomy of Failure in War.* New York: Vintage, 1991.

Cohen, Lisbeth. *Making a New Deal: Industrial Workers in Chicago: 1919-1939.* New York: Cambridge University Press, 1990.

Coleman, Daniel, Richard Boyatzis, and Annie McKee. *Primal Leadership: Learning to Lead with Emotional Intelligence.* Boston, MA: Harvard Business School Press, 2002.

Coles, Robert. *The Call of Stories: Teaching and the Moral Imagination.* Boston, MA: Houghton-Mifflin, 1989.

Collins, Jim. *Good to Great.* New York: HarperCollins, 2001.

Collins, Jim. *Good to Great and the Social Sectors.* Boulder, CO: Author, 2005.

Collins, Jim, and Jerry I. Porras. *Built to Last: Successful Habits of Visionary Companies*, New York: Harper, 1994.

Cromwell, Patrice, Robert P. Giloth, and Marsha R.B. Schachtel. East Baltimore Revitalization Project: Opportunities and challenges in transforming an urban neighborhood. *Journal of Higher Education Outreach and Engagement* 10(2). Spring/Summer 2005: 127-140.

D'Emilio, John. Cycles of Change, Questions of strategy: The gay and lesbian movement after fifty years. In Craig Rimmerman, Kenneth Wald, and Clyde Wilcox, Eds. *The Politics of Gay Rights.* Chicago, IL: University of Chicago Press, 2000: 31-53.

Dees, J. Gregory, Jed Emerson, and Peter Economy. *Enterprising Nonprofits.* New York: Wiley, 2001.

Dennis, Carl. *Practical Gods.* New York: Penguin Books, 2001.

DeParle, Jason. *The American Dream: Three Women, Ten Kids, and the Nation's Drive to End Welfare.* New York: Viking Press, 2004.

Dewey, John. *The Quest for Certainty.* New York: Capricorn Books, 1960.

Drucker, Peter. *Managing the Nonprofit Organization: Principles and Practices.* New York: HarperCollins, 1990.

Egger, Robert. *Begging for Change.* New York: Harper, 2004.

Erickson, Kai. *New Species of Trouble: Explorations in Disaster, Trauma, and Community.* New York: W.W. Norton, 1994.

Fisher, Jo, and Robert Giloth. Adapting rowhomes for aging in place: The story of Baltimore's "Our Idea House." *Journal of Housing for the Elderly* 13(1/2). 1999: 3-18.

Fisher, Roger, and Daniel Shapiro. *Beyond Reason: Using Emotions as You Negotiate.* New York: Viking, 2005.

Flanagan, Mike. *It's About Time: How Long History Took.* Kansas City, MO: Andrews McMeel Universal, 2004.

Florida, Richard. *Cities and the Creative Class.* New York: Routledge, 2005.

Ford, Richard. *The Lay of the Land.* New York: Alfred E. Knopf, 2006.

Forester, John. *The Deliberative Practitioner: Encouraging Participatory Planning Processes.* Cambridge, MA: MIT Press, 1999.

Frankfurt. Harry G. *On Bullshit.* Princeton, NJ: Princeton University Press, 2005.

Freeman, Jo. Tyranny of structurelessness. *Berkeley Journal of Sociology* 17, 1972-73: 151-165.

Frug, Gerald. *City Making: Building Communities without Walls.* Princeton, NJ: Princeton University Press, 1999.

Fukuyama, Francis. *The End of History and the Last Man.* New York: Avon Books, 1992.

Gandhi, M.K. *An Autobiography, Or the Story of My Experiments with Truth.* Ahmedabad, India: Navajivan Publishing House, 1927.

Gardner, John W. *Self-Renewal: The Individual and the Innovative Society.* New York: Norton, 1965.

Gardner, John W. *On Leadership.* New York: The Free Press, 1990.

Gardner, John W. *Living, Leading, and the American Dream.* San Francisco, CA: Jossey-Bass, 2003.

Gardner, John W., and Francesca Gardner Reese. *Quotations of Wit and Wisdom.* New York: Norton, 1975.

Giloth, Robert. The value of 'networking.' *Chicago Tribune,* February 11, 1981.

Giloth, Robert. A-visioning we will ago, a-visioning we will go. *Baltimore Evening Sun*, August 14, 1991: A13.

Giloth, Robert. Reclaiming the village: Central Europe rediscovers community after communism. *The Neighborhood Works.* February/March 1993: 12-13, 28.

Giloth, Robert. A decade (& more) of neighborhood books. *The Neighborhood Works,* December 1993/January 1994: 35.

Giloth, Robert. Working the planning field. *Planning Theory* 10/11, Winter 1993/Summer 1994: 141-154.

Giloth, Robert P., Ed. *Jobs and Economic Development: Strategies and Practices.* Newberry Park, CA: Sage Publications, 1998.

Giloth, Robert P. Jobs, wealth, or place: The faces of community economic development. In Margaret S. Sherraden and William A. Ninacs, Eds. *Community Economic Development and Social Work.* Binghamton, NY: Haworth Press, 1998: 11-27.

Giloth, Robert P. Community building on Chicago's West Side—North Lawndale, 1960-1997. In W. Dennis Keating and Norman Krumholz, Eds. *Rebuilding Urban Neighborhoods* Thousand Oaks, CA: Sage Publications, 1999: 67-86.

Giloth, Robert P. Learning from the field: economic and workforce development in the 1990s. *Economic Development Quarterly* 14(4), November 2000: 340-359.

Giloth, Robert P. *Mistakes, Learning and Adaptation: Philanthropy and the Jobs Initiative.* Baltimore, MD: Annie E. Casey Foundation, 2004.

Giloth, Robert P. Social enterprise and urban rebuilding in the United States. *Entrepreneurship: A Catalyst for Urban Regeneration.* Paris, France: Organization for Economic Co-Operation and Development (OECD), 2004: 135-175.

Giloth, Robert P., Ed. *Workforce Development Politics: Civic Capacity and Performance*. Philadelphia, PA: Temple University Press, 2004.

Giloth, Robert P., Ed. *Workforce Intermediaries for the 21st Century*. Philadelphia, PA: Temple University Press, 2004.

Giloth, Robert, and David Casey. *Reinventing CDCs: Twenty-five Years of Community Planning and Development in Baltimore*. Unpublished manuscript, April 1995.

Giloth, Robert, Theresa Fujiwara, and Gail Hayes. *Community Building in White Center: Making Connections for Families and Neighborhoods*. Baltimore, MD: Annie E. Casey Foundation, March 2004.

Giloth, Robert, and Jill Kinney. Making connections helps families create the new ties that bind. *Seattle Post-Intelligencer*, January 12, 2000: A13.

Giloth, Robert, Judy Meima, and Patricia A. Wright. *Tax, Title, and Housing Court Research: Property Research for Action—A Manual for Chicago*. Chicago, IL: Center for Urban Economic Development, University of Illinois at Chicago, 1985.

Giloth, Robert, Charles Orlebeke, James Tickell, and Patricia Wright. *Choices Ahead: CDCs and Real Estate Production in Chicago*. Chicago, IL: Nathalie P. Voorhees Center for Neighborhood and Community Improvement, University of Illinois at Chicago, May 1992.

Giloth, Robert P., and William Phillips. *Getting Results: Outcome Management and the Annie E. Casey Foundation's Jobs Initiative*. Rensselaerville, NY: Rensselaerville Institute, 2001.

Giloth, Robert, and Wim Wiewel. Jobs: Should Your Group Start a Business Venture? *The Neighborhood Toolbox 1*. Chicago, IL: The Center for Neighborhood Technology, Spring 1988: 22-23.

Giloth, Robert, and Wim Wiewel. Equity development: Robert Mier's ideas and practice. *Economic Development Quarterly* 10(3). August 1996: 204-216.

Ginzburg, Eugenia. *Journey into the Whirlwind.* New York: Harcourt Brace Jovanovich, 1967.

Ginzburg, Eugenia. *Within the Whirlwind.* New York: Harcourt Brace Jovanovich, 1979.

Gladwell, Malcolm. *The Tipping Point: How Little Things Can Make a Big Difference.* Boston, MA: Little Brown, 2000.

Gladwell, Malcolm. *Blink: The Power of Thinking Without Thinking.* Boston, MA: Little Brown, 2005.

Gorz, Andre. *The Traitor.* London, UK: Verso Press, 1989.

Grogan, Paul, and Tony Proscio. *Comeback Cities: A Blueprint for Urban Neighborhood Revitalization.* Boulder, CO: The Westview Press, 2000.

Grudin, Robert. *Time and the Art of Living.* New York: Houghton-Mifflin, 1982.

Gunn, Christopher. *Third-Sector Development: Making Up for the Market.* Ithaca, NY: Cornell University Press, 2004.

Hadot, Pierre. *What Is Ancient Philosophy?* Cambridge, MA: Harvard University Press, 2002.

Hall, Donald. *Life Work.* Boston, MA: Beacon Press, 1993.

Halpern, Robert. *Rebuilding the Inner City: A History of Neighborhood Investment to Address Poverty in the U.S.* New York: Columbia University Press, 1995.

Han, Peter. *Somebodies to Nobodies: How 100 Leaders in Business, Politics, Arts, Science, and Nonprofits Got Started.* New York: Penguin, 2005.

Handy, Charles. *The Age of Paradox.* Cambridge, MA: Harvard Business School Press, 1995.

Harrington, Michael. *The Other America: Poverty in the United States.* Baltimore, MD: Penguin Books, 1963.

Harvey, Jerry. *The Abeline Paradox and Other Meditations on Management.* San Francisco, CA: Jossey-Bass, 1998.

Henton, Douglas, John Melville, and Kimberly Walesh. *Grassroots Leaders for a New Economy: How Civic Entrepreneurs Are Building Prosperous Communities*. San Francisco: Jossey-Bass, 1997.

Henton, Douglas, John Melville, and Kim Walesh. *Civic Revolutionaries: Igniting the Passion for Change in America's Communities*. San Francisco, CA: Jossey-Bass, 2004.

Hesselbein, Frances, Marshall Goldsmith, and Richard Beckhard, Eds. *The Leader of the Future*. San Francisco, CA: Jossey-Bass, 1996.

Hinden, Denice Rothman, and Paige Hull. Executive leadership transition: What we know. *The Nonprofit Quarterly*, Winter 2002: 24-29.

Hiss, Tony. *The Experience of Place*. New York: Alfred A. Knopf, 1990.

Hock, Dee. *Birth of the Chaordic Age*. San Francisco, CA: Berrett-Koehler Publishers.

Honore, Carl. *In Praise of Slowness: How a Worldwide Movement Is Challenging the Cult of Speed*. New York: HarperCollins, 2005.

Horton, Myles. *The Long Haul: An Autobiography*. New York: Anchor Books, 1990.

Horwitt, Sanford D. *Let Them Call Me Rebel: Saul Alinsky*. New York: Alfred A. Knopf, 1989.

Iversen, Roberta Rehner, and Annie Laurie Armstrong. *Jobs Aren't Enough: Toward a New Economic Mobility for Low-Income Families*. Philadelphia, PA: Temple University Press, 2006.

Jacobs, Jane. *Death and Life of Great American Cities*. New York: Vintage Books, 1961.

Jacoby, Russell. *The Last Intellectuals: American Culture in the Age of Academe*. New York: Basic Books, 1987.

Jacoby, Russell. *Picture Imperfect: Utopian Thought for an Anti-Utopian Age*. New York: Columbia University Press, 2005.

James, William. *Essays in Radical Empiricism and a Pluralistic Universe.* New York: E.P. Dutton and Co., 1971.

Johansson, Frans. *The Medici Effect: Breakthrough Insights at the Intersection of Ideas, Concepts & Cultures.* Cambridge, MA: Harvard Business School Press, 2004.

Just, Ward. *The Translator.* New York: Ballantine Books, 1991

Kanter, Rosabeth Moss. *World-Class: Thriving Locally in the Global Economy.* New York: Simon and Schuster, 1995.

Kauffman, Arnold. *Radical Liberalism: New Man in American Politics.* New York: Atherton Press, 1968.

Kazin, Alfred. *Starting Out in the Thirties.* Boston, MA: Little Brown, 1962.

Kelling, George, and Catherine M. Coles. *Fixing Broken Windows: Restoring Order and Reducing Crime in Our Communities.* New York: Simon and Schuster, 1996.

Klein, Gary. *The Power of Intuition.* New York: Random House, 2003.

Kochman, Thomas. *Black and White Styles in Conflict.* Chicago, IL: University of Chicago Press, 1981.

Kretzmann, Jody P., and John L. McKnight. *Building Communities From the Inside Out: A Path Toward Finding and Mobilizing a Community's Assets.* Evanston, IL: Center for Urban Affairs and Policy Research, Northwestern University, 1993.

Kunreather, Frances. *UpNext: Generational Change and the Leadership of Nonprofits.* Baltimore, MD: Annie E. Casey Foundation, 2005.

Lady Allen of Hurtwood. *Planning for Play.* Cambridge, MA: MIT Press, 1968.

Lakoff, George. *Don't Think of an Elephant! Know Your Values and Frame the Debate.* White River Junction, VT: Chelsea Green Publishing, 2004.

Laney, Mary Olsen. *The Introvert Advantage: How to Thrive in an Extrovert World.* New York: Workman Press, 2002.

Lao-tzu. *Tao Te Ching: A New English Version*, translated by Stephen Mitchell. New York: Harper & Row, 1988.

Lemann, Nicholas. Myth of community development. *New York Times Magazine*, January 9: 28-31, 50, 54, 60.

Lewis, Michael. *Coach: Lessons on the Game of Life*. New York: Norton, 2005.

Light, Paul C. *Sustaining Nonprofit Performance: The Case for Capacity Building and the Evidence to Support It*. Washington, DC: The Brookings Institution.

Liu, Eric. *Guiding Lights: The People Who Lead Us Toward Purpose in Our Life*. New York: Random House, 2004.

Llosa, Mario Vargas. *Letters to a Young Novelist*. New York: Picador, 2002.

Louv, Richard. *The Last Child in the Woods: Saving Our Children from Nature-Deficit Disorder*. New York: Workman Publishing, 2005.

Lynch, Kevin. Ed. *Growing Up in Cities*. Cambridge, MA: MIT Press, 1977.

Margalit, Avishai. *The Ethics of Memory*. Cambridge, MA: Harvard University Press, 2002.

Medvedev, Roy. *Let History Judge*. New York: Oxford University Press, 1989.

Mier, Robert. *Social Justice and Local Economic Development*. Newberry Park, CA: Sage Publications, 1993.

Mier, Robert, and Richard D. Bingham. Metaphors and economic development. In Richard D. Bingham and Robert Mier, Eds. *Theories of Local Economic Development*. Newberry Park, CA: Sage Publications, 1993: 284-304.

Miles, Martha A. *Good Stories Aren't Enough: Becoming Outcomes-Driven in Workforce Development*. Philadelphia, PA: Public/Private Ventures.

Mishra, Pankaj. *An End to Suffering: The Buddha in the World*. New York: Farrar, Straus, and Giroux, 2004.

Montaigne, Michel de. *Montaigne: Essays*. New York: Penguin Classics, 1993.

More, Sir Thomas. *Utopia (Translator, Paul Turner)*. New York: Penguin Group, 2003.

Morgan, Edward S. *Ben Franklin*. New Haven, CT: Yale University Press, 2002.

Morgan, Gareth. *Images of Organization*. Newberry Park, CA: Sage Publications, 1986.

Mumford, Lewis. *Culture of Cities*. New York: Harcourt Brace Jovanovich, 1938.

Nicholson, Simon. The theory of loose parts. *Man—Society—Technology—A Journal of Industrial Arts Education* 32,4, January 1973:172-175.

O'Conner, Alice. *Poverty Knowledge: Social Science, Social Policy, and the Poor in Twentieth-Century U.S. History*. Princeton, NJ: Princeton University Press, 2001.

Oliver, Mary. *New and Selected Poems Volume 1*. Boston, MA: Beacon Press, 1992.

Osborne, David, and Peter Plastrik. *Banishing Bureaucracy: The Five Strategies for Reinventing Government*. Reading, PA: Addison-Wesley, 1997.

Osborne, David, and Peter Plastrik. *Reinventor's Fieldbook: Tools for Transforming Your Government*. San Francisco, CA: 2000.

Orwell, George. *Animal Farm*. New York: Harcourt Brace, 1946.

Orwell, George. *Nineteen Eighty-Four*. New York: Harcourt Brace, 1949.

Penna, Robert M., and William J. Phillips. *Outcome Frameworks: An Overview for Practitioners*. Rensselaerville, NY: The Rensselaerville Institute, 2004.

Peters, Thomas, and Robert Waterman. *In Search of Excellence: Lessons from America's Best Run Companies*. New York: Warner Books, 1982.

Philanthropic Initiative, Inc. *Lessons from Wingspread: The Ten Trillion Dollar Intergenerational Transfer of Wealth—A Philanthropic Game Plan*. Boston, MA: Author, 1994.

Pink, Daniel H. *The Whole New Mind*. New York: Berkley Publishing Group, 2005.

Plato. *The Republic*. New York: Norton, 1996.

Proscio, Tony. *Bad Words for Good: How Foundations Garble Their Message and Lose Their Audience*. New York: The Edna McConnell Clark Foundation, 2001.

Rand, Ayn. *Atlas Shrugged*. New York: The Penguin Group, 1999.

Redfield, Robert. *The Little Community: Peasant Society and Culture*. Chicago, IL: University of Chicago Press, 1960.

Rittel, Horst, and Melvin Webber. General dilemmas of planning. *Journal of Policy Sciences* 4, 1973: 155-169.

Robinson, Eugene. The catastrophe wasn't Katrina. *Washington Post*, May 30, 2006: A17.

Rogers, Mary Beth. *Cold Anger: A Story of Faith and Power in Organizing*. Austin, TX: University of Texas Press, 1990.

Rorty, Richard. *Contingency, Irony, and Solidarity*. New York: Cambridge University Press, 1989.

Rudolph, Nancy. *Workyards*. New York: Teachers College Press, Columbia University, 1974.

Russell, Bertrand. *Skeptical Essays*. London, UK: Routledge Classics, 2004.

Russert, Tim. *Wisdom of Our Fathers*. New York: Random House, 2006.

Ryan, William P. *Nonprofit Capital: A Review of Problems and Strategies*. New York: The Rockefeller Foundation, 2001.

Salamon, Lester M. The resilient sector: the state of nonprofit America. *The Nonprofit Quarterly*, Winter 2002: 32-38.

Santos, Bob. Hum Bows, *Not Hot Dogs!* Seattle, WA: International Examiner Press, 2002.

Schell, Jonathan. *The Unconquerable World: Power, Nonviolence, and the Will of the People*. New York: Henry Holt and Co., 2003.

Schön, Donald. *The Reflective Practitioner: How Professionals Think in Action.* New York: Basic Books, 1983.

Schwartz, Peter. *Inevitable Surprises: Thinking Ahead in a Time of Turbulence.* New York: Gotham Books, 2003.

Scott, James. *Seeing Like a State: How Certain Schemes to Improve the Human Condition Have Failed.* New Haven, CT: Yale University Press, 1998.

Seneca, *On the Shortness of Life.* London, UK: Penguin Books, 1997.

Senge, Peter M. *The Fifth Discipline: The Art and Practice of the Learning Organization.* New York: Doubleday, 1990.

Sennett, Richard. *Uses of Disorder: Personal Identity and City Life.* New York: Vintage Books, 1970.

Sennett, Richard. *Conscience of the Eye: The Design and Social Life of Cities.* New York: Alfred A. Knopf, 1990.

Shlay, Anne B., and Robert Giloth. The social organization of a land-based elite: the case of the failed Chicago 1992 World's Fair. *Journal of Urban Affairs* 9(4), Winter 1987: 205-224.

Shore, Bill. *Revolution of the Heart: A New Strategy for Creating Wealth and Meaningful Change.* New York: The Penguin Group, 1996.

Smith, Douglas K. *On Value and Values: Managing Ourselves in a Fragmented World.* Upper Saddle River, NJ: Prentice Hall.

Spitz, Ellen Handler. *The Brightening Glance: Imagination and Childhood.* New York: Pantheon, 2006.

Stern, Andy. *A Country That Works: Getting America Back on Track.* New York: Free Press, 2006.

Strom, Stephanie. Foundations find benefits in facing up to failures. *New York Times*, July 26, 2007.

Sviridoff, Mitchell. *Inventing Community Renewal: The Trials and Errors That Shaped the Modern Community Development Corporation*. New York: Community Development Research Center, New School University, 2004.

Thich Nhat Hanh. *The Miracle of Mindfulness*. Boston, MA: Beacon, 1975.

Thurman, Robert A.F. *Anger*. New York: Oxford University Press, 2005.

Titmuss, Christopher. *An Awakened Life: Uncommon Wisdom from Everyday Experience*. Boston, MA: Shambhala Publications, 2000.

Toulmin, Stephen. *Cosmopolis*. Chicago, IL: University of Chicago Press, 1990.

Waldron, Tom, Brandon Roberts, Andrew Reamer, with assistance from Sara Rab and Steve Ressler. *Working Hard, Falling Short: America's Working Families and the Pursuit of Economic Security*. Chevy Chase, MD: Working Poor Families Project, Brandon Roberts and Associates, 2004.

Ward, Colin. *Anarchy in Action*. New York: Harper, 1973.

Weiss, Carol. Nothing as practical as good theory: Exploring theory-based evaluation for comprehensive community initiatives for children and families. In J. Connell, A. Kubish, L. Schorr, and C. Weiss, Eds. *New Approaches to Evaluating Community Initiatives*. Washington, DC: Aspen Institute, 1995: 65-92.

Weissbourd, Robert, and Riccardo Bodini. *Market-Based Community Economic Development*. Washington, DC: The Brookings Institution, Metropolitan Policy Program, March, 2005.

Welch, Jack, with Suzy Welch. *Winning*. New York: Harper, 2005.

Wheatley, Margaret. *Leadership and the New Science: Learning About Organization from an Orderly Universe*. San Francisco, CA: Berrett-Kohler Publishers, 1992.

Whitehead, Alfred North. *Adventures in Ideas*. New York: The Free Press, 1933.

Whyte, William Foote, and Kathleen King Whyte. *Making Mondragon: The Growth and Dynamics of the Worker Cooperative Complex*. Ithaca, NY: ILR Press, Cornell University, 1988.

Wieck, Karl, and Kathleen Sutcliffe. *Managing the Unexpected.* San Francisco, CA: Jossey-Bass, 2001.

Wiewel, Wim, Michael Teitz, and Robert Giloth. The economic development of neighborhoods and localities. In Richard D. Bingham and Robert Mier, Eds. *Theories of Local Economic Development.* Newberry Park, CA: Sage Publications, 1993.

Wills, Garry. *A Necessary Evil: A History of American Distrust of Government.* New York: Simon and Schuster, 1999.

Wright, Patricia. *The Pilsen Community Plan—The Organizing Effort: A Case Study of Citizen Participation.* Master's thesis, University of Illinois at Chicago School of Urban Sciences, 1979.

Wright, Richard. *Black Boy.* New York: Literary Classics of the United States, 1991.

Wright, Richard. *Haiku: This Other World.* New York: Anchor Books, 1998.

Zamyatin, Yevgeny. *We.* New York: HarperCollins, 1972.

Index

ACORN, 126, 128, 129
Adaptation, 66, 68, 100,104, 114, 120
Adventure playgrounds, 99-101
Adventures, 1, 59
   in community economic development (CED), 2-3, 5, 7, 9, 11, 13, 15,101, 180
African Americans, 52, 176
Alinsky, Saul, 19, 31, 51, 126, 149, 158
Anger, 65, 70, 72-74
Annie E. Casey Foundation, xv, 31, 70, 79, 87, 111, 131, 135
Ashé, 18
Assets, 5-7, 11, 43, 55, 62-65, 67-75, 98, 141, 168-169, 174
Attention deficit hyperactivity disorder (ADHD), 63, 65, 70, 152
Autobiography, 88

Baltimore, 4, 13, 17, 72-73, 76, 85, 89, 103, 106, 110, 130, 134-137, 154, 165
   east, 86-87, 136-137
   southeast, 17, 51-52, 54-57, 73, 87-89, 155, 158
Bebelle, Carol, 18
Bell Laboratories, 9, 10, 181
Book reviews, 147-148
Books, 9, 20-22, 27, 36, 43, 52, 66, 118, 128, 144, 147-151, 154, 158, 168
Bradford, Calvin, 2
Buddhism, 91, 155

Capacity, 6, 13, 15, 20, 60, 71, 131, 150, 165
   building, 83, 111,165
   community, 136

government, 27, 52
Capitalism, 38, 88, 178
Casey, David, 18
Center for Employment Training (CET), 12, 112
Change, theory of, 31, 112, 115-116, 165
Chaos, 35, 42, 64, 98, 104-105
Chicago, 1-18, 24, 34-42, 48-52, 56-57, 69, 77-80, 85-103, 122-128, 139-168
   Chicago Rehab Network, 128
   Chicago Tribune, 128, 159
   Democratic National Convention, Chicago, 1968, 24
   Department of Economic Development (DED), 52, 56
Chinatown, 1
Cincotta, Gail, 2
City Limits, 9
Cities
   comeback, 19
   creativity and, 23
   Living Cities, 16, 31
   major, in the twenty-first century, 89
   mega, 100
   Model Cities agency, 37, 85-86, 136
   neighbors and,
   San Francisco, 110, 128
   shrinking, 8
City (Urban) planning, 28-29, 36-37, 106, 143
Civil rights, 35, 38, 45, 52, 163
   movement, 85,141
Coaching, 22, 24,144, 150-153
Community building, 9, 17, 38-41, 71, 92-95, 101, 130, 153, 156, 167-179

Community development, 5-6, 12, 16-19, 32-56, 67, 110-113, 136, 149, 155, 158, 174
Community development corporations (CDCs), xvi, 6 16, 77, 111, 158
Community development financial institutions (CDFIs), 5, 12, 16
Community economic development (CED),1-23, 29-33, 77-78, 85, 90, 92, 109, 121, 133, 168, 171-176
Community organizing, 13, 18, 56-58, 77, 126-130, 173-175
 blockbusting, 85
 development and, 6, 12, 141, 149
 for family issues, 160
 local group and, 48
 network and, 17
 public policy and, 8
Community Reinvestment Act (CRA), 2, 12, 173
Complexity, 1, 11, 45, 92, 107, 167, 182
 chaos and, 104-105
Comprehensive community initiatives (CCIs), 79,85, 87, 96
Comprehensive Employment and Training Act of 1973 (CETA), 49
Cooperatives (co-ops), 171-173, 177, 179
Cornell University, 56, 141, 143-144
Credit unions, 10, 149

Daley, Richard J., 34, 37, 56
Daley, Richard M., 103
Deficits, 43, 62-75, 168, 175
Deliberative practitioner, 28-29
Democratic participation, 35, 39-41
DePaul University, 89
 Egan Center, 89
Disasters, xiv, 48, 107, 173
Disinvestment, 2, 36, 85, 93, 143, 174
Disorder, 36, 63, 92, 100, 105
Drucker, Peter, xix, 20-21, 82

Earned Income Tax Credit (EITC), 5, 128-129
East Baltimore Revitalization Project (Initiative), 135-136
East-West Gateway, 115
Economic development, 1-24, 29, 40, 52-59, 89, 110-114, 133, 141-144, 156, 159, 172-175
 affordable housing and, 16
 job-centered, 9
 targeted, 9
Eighteenth Street Development Corporation (ESDC), 18, 48-51, 109, 127
Emotional intelligence, 22, 50, 70, 74
 on the job, 140
Employers, 5, 12, 111-118, 179
Enterprising practitioner, 18, 27-29
ESDC, 48-52
Evaluation, 53, 93, 111-121, 149, 167
Evidence, 28, 115, 126, 165-167, 177
Executive coach, 151-152

Failures, 7, 94, 109-112, 120-121, 173
 constructive, 109-110
Family Economic Success (FES), 9-10, 32
Federal, 38, 126
 Empowerment Zone, 85-86
 enterprise zone, 136, 174
 health care and budget, 179
 policy, 9
 Urban Development Action Grants (UDAGs), 124
 workforce, 162-167
Federal Housing Administration (FHA), 2, 157
 housing programs, 108
 low-income housing tax credit, 174
FOCUS HOPE, 113-115, 172
Foundations, 30-31, 44, 119-128, 159-165. *See also* Philanthropy

Garcia, Jesus, 19
Gaudette, Tom, 52

Gentrification, 2, 14-15, 135
Gilding the ghetto, 175
Giloth, Paul K., 181-182
  [Giloth,] Emma, 147-148
Globalization, 8, 21, 87, 141, 175, 178
Government, 7, 29, 33-59, 105, 149, 157, 168, 171. *See also* Federal
  bureaucrats, 119
  city, 82
  county, 131
  local, 1, 52
  projects, 84
  student loans, 158
Grameen Bank, 170
Great Society, 38

H&R Block, 128-129
Home Mortgage Disclosure Act (HMDA), 12
Homeownership, 5, 48, 72, 176
Horton, Myles, xx, 19, 149
Housing, 5, 8, 14-15, 45-48, 58, 80
  affordable, 4, 12-13, 16-17, 21, 54, 130, 137, 158, 173-176
  Department of Housing and Urban Development (HUD), 17
  Federal Housing Administration (FHA), 2
  low-income, 5, 17, 85, 102, 174, 176, 178
  mixed-income, 15, 174
  Pilsen, 123
  public, 102, 105, 131-132, 174, 177
  rehabilitation, 86, 128, 135, 176
  SDI programs, 53
Hudson, Lee, 154
Hungary, 3

Immigrants, 15, 36, 102, 176
Impatience, 65-67, 70, 81-82, 152
Individual Development Accounts (IDAs), 12, 16

Industrial Areas Foundation (IAF), 126, 158
Industry, 122, 124-125
Informal sector, 179
Initiative for a Competitive Inner City, 176
Internal Revenue Service, 129, 163
  VITA (volunteer tax campaigns), 129
Introversion, 64-71
Intuition, 71

Jewish Council on Urban Affairs (JCUA), 141
Jobs Initiative, xviii, 78-82, 94, 111-115, 159, 166
Johns Hopkins University, 3, 135
  medical center, 86
Jones, Barclay Gibbs, 141, 145

Katrina, 166
  gulf coast, 4
  hurricane, 17, 107
Kellogg, William, III, 122-124, 137
Kreinberg, Lew, 99, 141, 148

Lady Allen of Hurtwood, 99
Latinos, 52
Leadership, 2-38
  civic, 32, 92-93, 179
  literature, 18-25, 32, 53
  succession, 20, 50, 85
  transition, 50, 56, 60, 67, 72, 179
Linkage, 9-10, 114, 129-130
  Southeast Linkage Group, 54
Living Cities, 17, 32
Living wage ordinances, 7, 158, 175
Loans, rapid anticipation (RALs), 128
Local Initiatives Support Corporation (LISC), 17, 78, 111
Lynch, Kevin, 100

Making Connections, xviii, 79-80, 85, 93-97, 108, 110, 130-132

Management, 181-183
Manufacturing, 6, 7, 58, 103, 114-115, 125, 159, 170
Markets, 3, 7-17, 68, 87, 101-114, 172-177
   labor, 8, 79, 114, 117-118, 143, 166, 177
Maxwell Street, 103
Mega-projects, 134-135
Memoirs, 151
Memories, 52, 88, 90
Mentoring, 75, 120-131
Messes, 33, 92-107
Messiness, 83-96, 155, 180
Metaphors, 10-11, 15, 66, 98, 161, 166-167
Metis, 28-29
Mier, Robert (Rob), 11, 24, 40, 69, 141, 143-144
Milwaukee, 34, 111, 115, 157, 161
Mindfulness, 98
Mistakes, xvii-xviii, 97-106, 2, 24, 32, 37, 44, 60, 96, 137, 142, 167, 180, 182
Mixed-income development, 15, 175
Mondragon, 170-173, 177
Mondragon Cooperative Corporation, 171-173, 178
Mumford, Lewis, 4, 36, 102, 154

Naturally occurring retirement communities (NORCs), 89
Neighborhood development, 18, 85, 87, 89, 109
Nelson, 70
New Deal, 38, 151, 161
New Orleans, 4, 17, 106, 110-111, 168
Nicholson, Simon, 101
Nonprofits, 7,8, 10, 11, 17, 24, 60, 95, 110, 177-178
   non-governmental organizations (NGOs), 21
   organizations, 16, 20, 38, 41, 45, 59-60, 94

   sector, 110, 121, 140, 179
North Lawndale, 86-87, 141

Organizations, 4-13, 20-32, 42-69, 75, 85-120, 128, 134-146, 154, 179
   CED, 15, 172, 177
   grassroots, 3, 178
   NGOs, 21
   nonprofit, 16, 38-41, 45, 59-60, 94

Partners Group, 130-132
Partnerships, 5-6, 56, 101, 107-119, 150, 173-178
   business, 24, 113
   hospital, 86
People versus place, 7, 14
Peter Drucker Foundation, 20-21
PhAME, 114-115
Philadelphia Jobs Initiative, 113
Philanthropy, 111, 136, 163-164, 178. *See* Foundations
   engagement, 30-31, 120
Philosophy, 25-27
Pilsen, 18, 36-39, 48, 50, 52-56, 100, 122-124, 142
   Housing and Business Alliance, 123
   Neighborhood Plan, 48, 122
   Neighbors Community Council, 48
Plastrik, Peter, 96
Playskool, 58, 160
Porter, Michael, 175
Poverty, 4-8, 28, 36-38, 50, 86, 106, 151, 158, 174-175
   anti-poverty, 35, 128
   concentrated, 9, 12, 15, 131, 135, 174
   War on Poverty, 86, 156
Premortem, 71
Private Sector, xiii, 30, 45, 97, 115, 123, 131, 171
Problems, 2, 28, 42-54, 66, 74-75, 99-109, 116-124, 133-136, 181
   non-routine, 42
   routine, 42

social, 20, 96, 127, 132
  solving, 74-75, 92, 133, 171
  wicked, 42, 97
Project QUEST, 13, 128
Program-related investments (PRIs), 31
Public sector, 6, 7, 19-20, 96, 106, 113

Race, 24, 39-40, 90, 102, 112, 141, 144, 149
Rapid anticipation loans (RALs), 128
Rashomon, 161-162, 168
Recycling, 3, 72-73, 110
Reflective practitioner, 28-29
Regions, 6-8, 29, 101, 137, 145-146, 172-178
Religion, 45
Responsible relocation, 174
Results, 8, 12-41, 55, 60, 69-81, 112-118, 131-134, 137, 150, 164, 179
Results-based investing and accountability, 132
Romania, 3

Schoenhofen Brewery, 122
Self-employment, 170, 178
  microenterprise, 12
Self-evaluation, 116-120
Self-organizing systems, 96
Self-sufficiency standards, 175
Service Employees International Union (SEIU), 6, 178
Simplicity, 92, 104, 107
Sixties, the, 162
Skepticism, 27, 39, 43-44, 59, 66, 79, 103, 110, 117, 133, 157
Smith, Ralph, 70
Social enterprises, 5, 12, 20, 30, 32, 109, 178-179
Social entrepreneurs, xiv, 19-21, 29-30, 60, 168
Social investor, 18, 30-32, 39, 78, 163
Social safety nets, 179

South East Community Organization (SECO), 17, 51, 100, 130, 154, 158, 165
Southeast Community Plan, 1993, 54
Southeast Development Inc. (SDI), 51
Spiritual practice, 25, 32
Strengths, 42, 58-64, 68-75, 129, 146
Structurelessness, 106
Subsidiarity, 105
Suburbs, opening up, 174
Sustainability, 4, 12, 25, 46, 55, 59-60, 107, 172

The Neighborhood Works (TNW), 9, 28, 148
The Reinvestment Fund (TRF), 114
Third Sector, 10, 171. *See* Nonprofits, Nonprofit sector
Time, 71-82
  and Art of Living, 98
Tufts University, 77

Unions, 5, 10, 134, 161, 172, 179
  labor, 124, 126
  trades, 49, 130
University of Illinois at Chicago, 6, 14, 36, 103, 122, 143
Unlikely partners, 33, 123-126, 132-138
Urban planning, 6, 143
Utopia, 87-88, 90

Values, *Chapter 3*, 4, 84, 96, 136-137, 148, 155-163, 168
  common, 84, 123
  community, 52, 157
  fundamental, 93
  land, 1, 14
  market, 175-177
  organizational, 21
  personal, 27, 59, 67, 69, 155, 168
  social, 96
Venture capital, 30-31, 111, 178

Vietnam War, 34, 37-38, 143

Wall Street Journal, 159
Washington, Harold, 18, 38, 40, 56-59, 80, 89, 104, 139, 168
Wealth, 6, 8, 11, 72, 175
White Center, 130-132
Wisconsin Regional Training Partnership, 115
Workforce Development, 12, 16, 32, 40, 128, 134
   career advancement

and job retention, 79, 163
competitiveness and, 178
JI (jobs initiative) design and, 111-112
job readiness, 118
low-skilled/low-income and, 133
philanthropy, 179
Working Poor Families Project, 160

About the Author

Robert Giloth, Ph.D., has devoted thirty years to community economic development and the nonprofit sector, most recently leading workforce development and family economic success efforts for the Annie E. Casey Foundation. He has directed community development corporations in Baltimore and Chicago, worked in the administration of Chicago Mayor Harold Washington, and written widely about jobs and economic development.

978-0-595-45411-2
0-595-45411-9

Printed in the United States
200766BV00004B/1-78/A